留学生本科必修课系列教材

第二版

精读课本

Intensive Reading
TEXTBOOK

马燕华　编著
[英] Connor Walsh　江南　翻译

北京语言大学出版社
BEIJING LANGUAGE AND CULTURE
UNIVERSITY PRESS

图书在版编目(CIP)数据

汉语·纵横精读课本.0/马燕华编著;(英)沃尔什(Walsh, C.),江南译.—2版.—北京:北京语言大学出版社,2011.9
留学生本科必修课系列教材
ISBN 978-7-5619-3114-1

Ⅰ.①汉… Ⅱ.①马…②沃…③江… Ⅲ.①汉语—对外汉语教学—教材 Ⅳ.①H195.4

中国版本图书馆CIP数据核字(2011)第178417号

书　　名:	汉语·纵横　精读课本 0
责任印制:	汪学发

出版发行:	北京语言大学出版社
社　　址:	北京市海淀区学院路15号　邮政编码:100083
网　　址:	www.blcup.com
电　　话:	发行部　010-82303650 / 3591 / 3651
	编辑部　010-82303647 / 3592
	读者服务部　010-82303653 / 3908
	网上订购电话　010-82303668
	客户服务信箱　service@blcup.net
印　　刷:	北京画中画印刷有限公司
经　　销:	全国新华书店

版　　次:	2011年9月第1版　2011年9月第1次印刷
开　　本:	889毫米×1194毫米　1/16　印张:17.25
字　　数:	401千字
书　　号:	ISBN 978-7-5619-3114-1 / H·11156
定　　价:	65.00元

凡有印装质量问题,本社负责调换。电话:010-82303590

第二版前言

《汉语·纵横》是《外国学生汉语言专业本科系列教材》（中国社会科学出版社，2004年）的修订版，包括汉语精读、汉语会话、汉语听力/视听说、汉语写作、外汉翻译五大纵向技能，从预科到三年级下册七大横向层次，纵横匹配的留学生本科必修课系列教材，共计38册。

此次修订，主要体现在以下几方面。

 补齐初版空缺的部分教材

目前国内设置的留学生本科学制一般为四年。四年级大多开设专业课、撰写毕业论文，汉语技能训练课一般安排在从预科到三年级下学期共计7个学期内学习。此次修订我们补齐了三年级下册的精读课本、三年级上下册的会话课本、汉语写作（上、下）以及英汉、日汉、韩汉翻译教程。这样本套教材在横向的七个层次、纵向的听说读写译五大技能的匹配上更为完善。

 课本与练习各自独立成册

本系列教材练习题型多样，题量丰富，此次修订仍保留了这一特点。为便于学习和使用，将课本与相应练习各自独立成册。

 词语表增加了词语在《汉语国际教育用音节汉字词汇等级划分》中所属等级

初版教材每册课本"词语总表"标注了每个词语在《高等学校外国留学生汉语言专业教学大纲》、《汉语水平词汇与汉字等级大纲》中所属等级，此次修订增加了词语在2010年10月颁布的《汉语国际教育用音节汉字词汇等级划分》中所属等级，方便使用者参考。

 预科和一年级上册课本增加了英语注释

国内对外汉语教学模式一般都将汉语基础语法项目和语言点安排在初级阶段学习，而此时正是学习者汉语水平最低阶段，讲解语法点和语言点会遇到一些专业术语，将增加学习负担。此次修订，我们采纳了使用者的意见，增加了预科、一年级上册两个等级各类教材的英语注释。

 每册课本前增加了"使用说明"

每册课本前增加的"使用说明"详细说明了本册课本的适用对象、课时安排、讲解重点以及注意事项。

 版式设计更精美

北京语言大学出版社以出版对外汉语教材而享誉全球，此次修订在版式设计上更美观，图片精美，排版疏朗大方，更适合学习使用。

初版教材自出版以来受到广大使用者的普遍好评，2008年获得北京师范大学本科教育优秀奖。现在《汉语·纵横》出版在即，我们全体编写者衷心感谢几年来教材使用者向我们提供的宝贵修改意见；衷心感谢北京师范大学汉语文化学院对本教材修订给予的支持和资助；衷心感谢北京语言大学出版社为编辑、出版第二版付出的大量认真辛苦的工作。

原编写委员会主任之一陈绂教授已退休多年，此次修订出版工作由马燕华全面负责。在此，本人衷心感谢全体编写人员对我的充分信任和大力支持。

《汉语·纵横》编写委员会主任　马燕华

2011 年 8 月

使用说明

 适用对象

本册教材适用于对象为零起点或汉语学习时间在 20 小时以内的汉语学习者。

 课时安排

本册教材共有 30 课,可供每周 8 课时的教学单位使用一个学期。每课由课文、词语表、注释、练习(独立成册)四部分组成。建议每篇课文的学习时间为 4~6 小时。具体时间可分配如下:

理解课文、熟悉生词:1 个小时

讲解语法点:1~2 个小时

完成练习:1~2 个小时

复习、听写:1 个小时

 讲解重点

本教材为精读课本,以讲解语法点、常用句型为主。建议在理解和熟悉课文的基础上结合课文范句讲解语法点,边讲解边在课堂上做练习册中的相应练习。本册的常用句型均为汉语高频句型,结合句型讲解语法点学生更容易理解。

编者充分重视入门阶段的朗读训练,建议将"正确而大声地朗读课文"设计为一个教学环节,以培养学生良好的诵读习惯。

四 **其他**

1. 可用提问方式导入新课,边提问边板书本课关键词语。

2. 结合生词学习,用已学过的词语做搭配练习,如"数词 + 量词 + 名词"搭配、"动词 + 名词"搭配。

3. 结合课文讲解本课语法点、常用句型。讲解过程可先用本课包含这一语法点的句子作为例句,然后用已学过的词语编制 1~2 个精当例句补充讲解。

4. 本教材题型丰富、题量较大,建议一边讲解语法点一边做相应练习。

5. 一定要在课堂上完成阅读练习。每课的阅读短文虽然都有些未学过的词语,但关键词语都随文增加了汉语拼音和英语翻译,阅读练习也较为简单容易。入门阶段养成良好的汉语阅读习惯,对日后的汉语学习必将会起到事半功倍的作用。

6. 建议在课堂上完成单元测试卷和总测试卷,前者可用 60 分钟,后者可用 90 分钟。教师阅卷后要安排时间讲评试卷。

编者　马燕华

2011 年 8 月

词类简称表
Abbreviations of parts of speech

缩写 Abbreviations	英文全称 Parts of speech in English	词类名称及简称 Parts of speech and abbreviations in Chinese	拼音 Parts of speech in *pinyin*
Adj	Adjective	形容词（形）	xíngróngcí
Adv	Adverb	副词（副）	fùcí
AsPt	Aspect Particle	动态助词	dòngtài zhùcí
Conj	Conjunction	连词（连）	liáncí
Int	Interjection	叹词（叹）	tàncí
M	Measure Word	量词（量）	liàngcí
MdPt	Modal Particle	语气助词	yǔqì zhùcí
N	Noun	名词（名）	míngcí
Nu	Numeral	数词（数）	shùcí
Ono	Onomatopoeia	拟声词（拟声）	nǐshēngcí
OpV	Optative Verb	能愿动词（能愿）	néngyuàn dòngcí
PN	Proper Noun	专有名词（专名）	zhuānyǒu míngcí
Pr	Pronoun	代词（代）	dàicí
Pref	Prefix	词头（头）	cítóu
Prep	Preposition	介词（介）	jiècí
Pt	Particle	助词（助）	zhùcí
Q	Quantifier	数量词（数量）	shùliàngcí
StPt	Structural Particle	结构助词	jiégòu zhùcí
Suf	Suffix	词尾（尾）	cíwěi
V	Verb	动词（动）	dòngcí
V//O	Verb-object Compound	离合词（离）	líhécí

目 录

页码	题目	注释
1	1 nǐ shì liú xué shēng ma 你是留学生吗 Are you an international student	1. "是"字句（表判断） 2. 用"吗"提问的疑问句 3. 主语、谓语 4. 宾语 5. 标点符号的用法（1）： 　逗号（，）句号（。）问号（？）叹号（！）
9	2 nǐ jiā yǒu jǐ kǒu rén 你家有几口人 How many people are there in your family	1 "有"字句（表领有） 2. 用"几"提问的疑问句 3. 定语 4. 副词"也" 5. 状语 6. 标点符号的用法（2）：冒号（：）顿号（、）
19	3 nǐ qù nǎr 你去哪儿 Where are you going	1. 动词谓语句 2. 用"哪儿"提问的疑问句 3. "去"+地点+动词 4. 名量词 5. 100以下的称数法 6. 副词"都" 7. 用"几"、"多少"提问的疑问句
27	4 dì sì kè de shēng cí duō ma 第四课的生词多吗 Are there many new words in Lesson 4	1. 序数词 2. 结构助词"的" 3. 形容词谓语句 4. 用"请"的兼语句 5. 标点符号的用法（3）：引号（" "）
35	5 tā shì shéi 他是谁 Who is he	1. 用"谁"提问的疑问句 2. 指示代词"这"、"那" 3. 主谓谓语句 4. 辨析：教师、老师 5. 辨析：在、给 6. 介宾短语 7. "想"+人／动物

Contents

语音基础知识	汉字基础知识
1.《汉语拼音方案》 2. 声母 3. 韵母 4. 声调 5. 音节	汉字简介
1. 声调 2. 声母：b p m f d t n l 3. 韵母：a o e i u ü er 4. 拼写规则（1）：声调符号标写规则	汉字的笔画（1）
1. 声母：g k h 2. 韵母：ai ei ao ou ua uo uai uei (ui) 3. 拼写规则（2）：uei 的省略	汉字的笔画（2）
1. 声母：j q x 2. 韵母：ia ie iao iou (iu) üe 3. 拼写规则（3）：i、ü、üe、iou、uen 的省略	汉字的偏旁
1. 前鼻音韵尾韵母：an en in ian uan uen (un) ün üan 2. 后鼻音韵尾韵母：ang eng ing iang uang ueng iong ong 3. 拼写规则（4）： 　（1）隔音符号（'）的使用 　（2）y、w 的使用	汉字的笔顺

3

页码	题目	注释
43	**6** nǐ zhù nǎr 你 住 哪儿 Where do you live	1. 楼号的表示 2. 房间号的表示 3. 辨析：二、两 4. 副词"还"（表示数量增加、范围扩大） 　辨析：还、也 5. 电话号码的表示 6. 辨析：或者、还是 7. 用"谁的"提问的疑问句
51	**7** nǐ tóng wū shì nǎ guó rén 你 同 屋 是 哪 国 人 Which country does your roommate come from	1. 用"哪"提问的疑问句 2. 名词谓语句 3. 询问年龄 4. "会" + 动词 5. 辨析：经常、常常 6. "喜欢" + 动词 7. 数量词"俩"
58	**8** xiàn zài jǐ diǎn 现 在 几 点 What time is it	1. 钟点的读法 2. 时间状语 3. 名词"以后" 4. "有时候……有时候……" 5. "从……到……"（表时间） 6. 副词"比较" 7. 时间的顺序
66	**9** nǐ de ài hào shì shén me 你 的 爱 好 是 什 么 What are your hobbies	1. 用"什么"提问的疑问句 2. 名词"以前"、"以后" 3. 副词"特别" 4. 动词"觉得"
72	**10** zhōng guó yǒu duō shao rén 中 国 有 多 少 人 What is the population of China	1. 100 以上的称数法 2. 百分数的读法 3. 动词"像" 4. "挺……的" 5. 动词"比如" 6. 助词"等"
79	dān yuán xiǎo jié　yī shí kè 单 元 小 结（1~10课） Review (Lessons 1~10)	

语音基础知识	汉字基础知识
声母：zh ch sh r z c s	汉字的笔画搭配方式
第三声的变调	汉字的结构
1."一"的变调 2."不"的变调	常用形旁（部首）(1)
轻声和儿化	常用形旁（部首）(2)
声韵拼合规律	同音字、多音字、形近字

页码	题目	注释
80	**11** zhè shì kā fēi hái shi kě lè 这是咖啡还是可乐 Is this coffee or coke	1. 选择疑问句"(是)……还是……" 2. 副词"最" 3. "等+名词"表示列举 4. "又……又……" 5. 主谓短语做定语
85	**12** nǐ men yào le shén me yǐn liào 你们要了什么饮料 What would you like to drink	1. 动态助词"了₁" 2. "因为……所以……"
91	**13** píng guǒ zěn me mài 苹果怎么卖 How much is the apple	1. 用"怎么"提问的疑问句 2. 集合名词 3. 人民币的写法和读法 4. 副词"一共" 5. 离合词 6. "……, 好吗?" 7. "……, 对吗?"
96	**14** nǐ chuān duō dà hào de niú zǎi kù 你穿多大号的牛仔裤 What size are your jeans	1. 用"多+形容词"提问的疑问句 2. "的"字短语 3. 商品牌子的三种说法 4. "有点儿"+形容词
102	**15** wáng lǎo shī jiāo nǐ men shén me 王老师教你们什么 What does Mr. Wang teach you	1. 双宾语 2. 动宾短语做定语 3. 用"让"的兼语句 4. 结构助词"地" 5. 副词"别"
107	**16** jīn tiān lěng hái shi zuó tiān lěng 今天冷还是昨天冷 Which day is colder, today or yesterday	1. A 比 B+形容词 2. 温度的写法和读法 3. A 比 B+形容词+"一点儿"/"多了"/数量补语 4. 动词"忘" 5. A 没有 B+形容词 6. 副词"刚" 7. 句中语音停顿

页码	题目	注释
112	17 běi jīng de tiān qì gēn dōng jīng de yí yàng ma 北京的天气跟东京的一样吗 Is the weather in Beijing the same as that in Tokyo	1. A跟B+"一样/不一样" 2. 语气助词"了₂" 3. 辨析：不、没(有)、别 4. "一天比一天"
117	18 nǐ zuì jìn zěn me yàng 你最近怎么样 gěi péng you de yì fēng xìn ——给朋友的一封信 How are you doing these days — A letter to a friend	1. 用"怎么样"提问的疑问句 　辨析：什么、怎么、怎么样 2. "像……什么的" 3. 副词"还"(表示情况没有变化) 4. 用"吧"提问的疑问句 5. "要……了"表示动作即将发生 6. 能愿动词"得"(děi)
125	19 nǐ xué hàn yǔ duō cháng shí jiān le 你学汉语多长时间了 How long have you been studying Chinese	1. 时量补语 2. 形容词"一般" 3. 动词重叠 4. 时段短语 5. "有/没有时间"+动词
132	20 tiān ān mén guǎng chǎng dà bu dà 天安门广场大不大 Is Tian'anmen Square large	1. 正反疑问句 2. 方位词 3. 副词"一直" 4. 形容词重叠 5. 感叹句 6. "啊"的音变
139	dān yuán xiǎo jié shí yī èr shí kè 单元小结(11~20课) Review (Lessons 11~20)	
141	21 nín yào duì huàn shén me 您要兑换什么 What do you want to convert	1. 动词"听说" 2. 辨析：想、要 3. 介词"对" 4. 辨析：可以、能 5. 辨析：会、能 6. 能愿动词"应该"

页码	题目	注释
147	**22** qù zhōng guān cūn zěn me zuò chē **去中关村怎么坐车** How can I get to Zhongguancun by bus	1. 介词"往"、"向" 2. 副词"就"(加强肯定) 3. 地址的顺序 4. "一边……一边……" 5. 连词"如果"
153	**23** kè tīng hòu bian shì shén me **客厅后边是什么** What is behind the sitting room	1. 方位短语 2. 存在句("有"、"在"、"是") 3. 动词"离" 4. "虽然……但是……"
159	**24** zhè shì shéi sòng nǐ de shēng rì lǐ wù **这是谁送你的生日礼物** Who gave you this birthday gift	1. 状态补语(带宾语) 2. "除了……以外,还/也……" 3. 数量词"一些" 4. 辨析:的、地、得 5. 状态补语(不带宾语) 6. "只有……才……" 7. "……呢"表示确认
166	**25** shēng rì wǎn huì jǐ diǎn kāi shǐ **生日晚会几点开始** When will the birthday party begin	1. "像……一样"+形容词 2. "正在/正/在……呢" 3. 动态助词"着" 4. "除了……以外,都……" 5. 汉语的句调
172	**26** nǐ cān jiā guo hàn yǔ shuǐ píng kǎo shì **你参加过汉语水平考试** ma **(HSK)吗** Did you take HSK	1. 动态助词"过" 2. 概数的表示法 3. 连词"因此" 4. 动量词 5. 用"为什么"提问的疑问句 6. 汉语水平考试(HSK)
178	**27** nǐ zěn me yòu lái bàn yán cháng shǒu **你怎么又来办延长手** xù le **续了** Why do you come to extend your programme again	1. "通知上说" 2. "连……也……" 3. 辨析:刚才、刚 4. 辨析:再、又 5. 副词"只好" 6. 副词"其实"

页 码	题 目	注 释
184	**28** nǐ xǐ huan kàn nǎ ge pín dào de diàn shì jié mù 你喜欢看哪个频道的电视节目 Which TV channel do you like to watch	1. "不但……而且……" 2. 副词"就"（表示动作发生得早、快、顺利） 3. 副词"才" 4. 体育比赛比分的写法和读法 5. 连词"而" 6. 辨析：越来越、一天比一天
190	**29** nǐ shì yí ge rén qù lǚ yóu de ma 你是一个人去旅游的吗 Did you travel alone	1. "是……的"句式 2. 动词"提前" 3. "一……就……" 4. "对……感兴趣"
196	**30** xìng qián hé yǒu qián yǒu guān xi ma 姓钱和有钱有关系吗 Does the surname Qian have anything to do with money	1. "A和B有/没有关系" 2. 副词"仍然" 3. 名词"其中" 4. 介词"按照" 5. 副词"当然"
201	dān yuán xiǎo jié èr shí yī sān shí kè 单元小结（21～30课） Review (Lessons 21~30)	
203	fù lù yī hàn yǔ pīn yīn fāng àn 附录1　汉语拼音方案 Appendix 1　Scheme for the Chinese phonetic alphabets	
204	fù lù èr hàn yǔ yīn jié biǎo 附录2　汉语音节表 Appendix 2　List of Chinese syllables	
206	fù lù sān hàn yǔ jù zi chéng fèn 附录3　汉语句子成分 Appendix 3　Chinese sentence elements	
207	fù lù sì cháng yòng hàn zì bǐ huà míng chēng 附录4　常用汉字笔画名称 Appendix 4　Commonly used strokes of Chinese characters	
208	fù lù wǔ hàn zì bǐ shùn guī zé 附录5　汉字笔顺规则 Appendix 5　Rules of writing Chinese characters	

页码	题目
209	fù lù liù　cháng yòng hàn zì bù shǒu míng chēng 附录 6　常 用 汉 字 部 首 名 称 Appendix 6　Commonly used radicals of Chinese characters
210	fù lù qī　cháng yòng xíng jìn zì duì zhào 附录 7　常 用 形 近 字 对 照 Appendix 7　Comparison of commonly used characters similar in form
212	fù lù bā　cháng yòng tóng yīn zì 附录 8　常 用 同 音 字 Appendix 8　Commonly used homophones
215	fù lù jiǔ　cháng yòng duō yīn zì 附录 9　常 用 多 音 字 Appendix 9　Commonly used polyphones
216	fù lù shí　yǔ fǎ diǎn suǒ yǐn 附录 10　语 法 点 索 引 Appendix 10　Index of grammatical points
223	cí yǔ zǒng biǎo 词 语 总 表 Vocabulary

你是留学生吗
nǐ shì liú xué shēng ma

Are you an international student

课文 Text

你好！我姓山下，叫京美，我是日本人。我是留学生。再见！

(nǐ hǎo! wǒ xìng shān xià, jiào jīng měi, wǒ shì rì běn rén. wǒ shì liú xué shēng. zài jiàn!)

词语表 Vocabulary

1.	你	nǐ	Pr	you
2.	是	shì	V	to be
3.	留学生	liúxuéshēng	N	international student
4.	吗	ma	MdPt	*used at the end of a question*
5.	好	hǎo	Adj	good
6.	我	wǒ	Pr	I

1

7.	姓	xìng	V	to be surnamed
8.	叫	jiào	V	to be called or named
9.	人	rén	N	person, people
10.	再见	zàijiàn	V	to see you again

专有名词 Proper Nouns

| 1. | 山下京美 | Shānxià Jīngměi | | name of a person |
| 2. | 日本 | Rìběn | | Japan |

补充词语 Complementary Word

| | 不 | bù | Adv | no, not |

1 你是留学生吗？

"是"字句（表判断）：由动词"是"充当谓语中心词，表示判断的句子。例如：

The "是" sentence (indicating judgment) : In the "是" sentence, "是" is used as the main word in the part of predicate indicating judgment. For example,

① 我是留学生。　　I am an international student.
② 他是日本人。　　He is Japanese.
③ 我是美国人。　　I am American.
④ 她是老师。　　　She is a teacher.

"是"字句的疑问式是："是"字句 + "吗？"例如：

Its interrogative form is: the "是" sentence + "吗？" For example,

⑤ 你是留学生吗？　　Are you an international student?
⑥ 你是日本人吗？　　Are you Japanese?
⑦ 你是老师吗？　　　Are you a teacher?

否定式是："不 + 是"。例如：

2

Its negative form is "不 + 是". For example,

⑧ 我不是留学生。　　I am not an international student.
⑨ 我不是日本人。　　I am not Japanese.
⑩ 我不是老师。　　　I am not a teacher.

2 你是留学生吗?

用"吗"提问的疑问句：句子末尾用"吗"提问的疑问句叫"是非疑问句"。只要回答"是"或"不是"、"对"或"不对"、"有"或"没有"就可以。例如：

The question using "吗": A question using "吗" at the end of a sentence is known as a yes-no question. Such a question is answered by "是" or "不是", "对" or "不对", "有" or "没有". For example,

① A：你是日本人吗？　　Are you Japanese?
　 B：是。(不是。)　　　Yes, I am. (No, I am not.)
② A：你有哥哥吗？　　　Do you have an elder brother?
　 B：有。(没有。)　　　Yes, I do. (No, I don't.)
③ A：你是姓山下吗？　　Is your family name Yamashita?
　 B：对。(不对。)　　　Yes, it is. (No, it isn't.)

3 我姓山下。

主语、谓语：汉语句子一般由主语和谓语两大部分组成。主语是谓语陈述的对象，谓语是陈述主语的。主语在前，谓语在后。主语部分的中心词语是主语，谓语部分的中心词语是谓语。如"我姓山下"中，"我"是主语，"姓山下"是谓语部分，"姓"是谓语。主语部分的连带成分还有定语，谓语部分的连带成分还有状语、补语和宾语。例如：

The subject and predicate: In general, a Chinese sentence is composed of two parts: a subject and a predicate. The former is stated by the latter. The subject is used before the predicate. The main word in the part of subject is the subject, and the main word in the part of predicate is the predicate. For example, in "我姓山下", "我" is the subject, "姓山下" the part of predicate and "姓" the predicate. The related element of the part of subject is the attribute and the related elements of the part of predicate are the adverbial, complement and object. For example,

① 我是留学生。　　I am an international student.
② 我叫王小京。　　My name is Wang Xiaojing.
③ 我是中国人。　　I am Chinese.

4 我姓山下。

宾语：宾语是动词的连带成分，表示与动作行为有关联的事物。如"我姓山下"中，"山下"是动词"姓"的宾语。例如：

The object: The object is the related element of a verb, indicating something related to an action. For example, in "我姓山下", "山下" is the object of the verb "姓". For example,

① 是中国人　　　　　　is Chinese
② 叫小京　　　　　　　(sb.'s) given name is Xiaojing
③ 学习汉语　　　　　　study Chinese

5 标点符号的用法（1）
The usage of punctuation marks (1)

（1）逗号（dòuhào）：表示一句话中间的停顿。例如：
Comma: It denotes a pause in a sentence. For example,

① 我姓山下，叫京美。　　　　My family name is Yamashita, and given name is Kyomi.
② 我不是中国人，是日本人。　I am not Chinese, but Japanese.
③ 他姓王，叫小京。　　　　　His family name is Wang, and given name is Xiaojing.

（2）句号（jùhào）：表示一个陈述句完了的停顿，用在陈述句的末尾。例如：
Full stop: It denotes a pause after a declarative sentence and is used at the end of a declarative sentence. For example,

④ 我是留学生。　　　　I am an international student.
⑤ 他家在北京。　　　　His home is in Beijing.
⑥ 我学习汉语。　　　　I study Chinese.

（3）问号（wènhào）：表示一个疑问句完了的停顿，用在疑问句的末尾。例如：
Question mark: It denotes a pause after a question and is used at the end of a question. For example,

⑦ 你是日本人吗？　　　Are you Japanese?
⑧ 你是留学生吗？　　　Are you an international student?
⑨ 你是老师吗？　　　　Are you a teacher?

（4）叹号（tànhào）：表示感情强烈的句子完了的停顿，用在感叹句的末尾。例如：
Exclamation mark: It denotes a pause after a sentence expressing strong emotions and is used at the end of an exclamation sentence. For example,

⑩ 你好！　　　　　　　Hello!
⑪ 老师好！　　　　　　Hello, sir!
⑫ 北京真大啊！　　　　Beijing is so big!

课堂用语（1） Classroom expressions (1)

1. 同学们好。 Tóngxuémen hǎo. Hello, everyone!
2. 老师好。 Lǎoshī hǎo. Hello, sir!
3. 我是汉语老师。 Wǒ shì Hànyǔ lǎoshī. I am a Chinese teacher.
4. 现在上课。 Xiànzài shàng kè. Now class begins.
5. 下课了。 Xià kè le. Class is over.
6. 明天见。 Míngtiān jiàn. See you tomorrow.

语音基础知识（1）
Basics on Chinese phonetics (1)

 《汉语拼音方案》 *Scheme for the Chinese Phonetic Alphabets*

汉语拼音是给汉字注音的工具。《汉语拼音方案》由五个部分组成：字母表、声母表、韵母表、声调符号、隔音符号。

Chinese phonetic alphabets (*pinyin*) are used to indicate the pronunciation of characters. *Scheme for the Chinese Phonetic Alphabets* is composed of five parts: table of alphabets, table of initials, table of finals, tone marks and syllable-dividing mark.

字母表：汉语拼音使用国际通用的拉丁字母。

Table of Alphabets: Chinese *pinyin* uses Latin alphabets widely used arourd the world.

Aa	Bb	Cc	Dd	Ee	Ff	Gg	Hh	Ii	Jj
Kk	Ll	Mm	Nn	Oo	Pp	Qq	Rr	Ss	Tt
Uu	Vv	Ww	Xx	Yy	Zz				

声母表：汉语拼音有 22 个声母（含零声母）。

Table of Initials: There are 22 initials (including a zero initial) in Chinese *pinyin*.

b	p	m	f	d	t	n	l	g	k	h
j	q	x		zh	ch	sh	r	z	c	s

韵母表：汉语拼音有 36 个韵母。

Table of Finals: There are 36 finals in Chinese *pinyin*.

单韵母 Simple finals	a	o	e	i	u	ü	er			
复元音韵母 Compound finals	ai	ei	ao	ou	ia	ie	ua	uo	üe	iao	iou (iu)	uai	uei (ui)
前鼻音韵尾韵母 Anterior nasal finals	an	en	in	ian	uan	uen (un)	üan	ün			
后鼻音韵尾韵母 Posterior nasal finals	ang	eng	ing	iang	uang	ueng	ong	iong			

声调符号：共 4 个：第一声（ ˉ ） 第二声（ ˊ ） 第三声（ ˇ ） 第四声（ ˋ ）

Tone marks: There are four tone marks: the 1st tone (ˉ), the 2nd tone (ˊ), the 3rd tone (ˇ), and the 4th tone (ˋ).

声调符号写在韵母的主要元音上面。
The tone mark is placed above the main vowel of a final.

隔音符号：a、o、e 开头的音节连接在其他音节后面的时候，如果音节的界限发生混淆，用隔音符号(')隔开，如 Xī'ān（西安）。

Syllable-dividing mark: When a syllable beginning with a, o or e goes after a syllable, and if there is confusion about the division of the syllables, a syllable-dividing mark (') is used. For example, Xī'ān（西安）.

 声母　Initials

声母是音节开头的辅音。如"lán（蓝）、chē（车）"中的 l、ch。
An initial is the consonant at the beginning of a syllable. For example, l in lán（蓝）and ch in chē（车）.

 韵母　Finals

音节里声母后面的部分。如"lán（蓝）、chē（车）"中的 an、e。
A final is the part that follows an initial in a syllable. For example, an in lán（蓝）and e in chē（车）.

 声调　Tones

声调是音节的音高变化。汉语有四个声调，叫第一声、第二声、第三声、第四声，又叫阴平、阳平、上声、去声。有的汉字念轻声，如"你是留学生吗"中的"吗"。

Tones indicate the pitch change in a syllable. There are four tones in Chinese: the first tone, the second tone, the third tone and the fourth tone, which are also respectively known as high-and-level tone, rising tone, low-and-level tone and falling tone. Some characters are pronounced in the neutral tone, such as: "吗" in "你是留学生吗".

 音节　Syllables

音节是语音的基本结构单位，汉语的音节由声母、韵母、声调组成。即：
A syllable is the basic unit in phonetics. A Chinese syllable is composed of an initial, a final and the tone, i.e.:

$$\text{音节} = \overset{\ulcorner 声调 \urcorner}{\text{声母} + \text{韵母}}$$

$$\text{syllable} = \overset{\ulcorner \text{tone} \urcorner}{\text{initial} + \text{final}}$$

一般一个汉字一个音节。如"你好"有两个音节：nǐ、hǎo。
Generally speaking, a syllable is represented by a character. For example, there are two syllables in "你好": nǐ and hǎo.

汉字基础知识（1）
Basics on Chinese characters（1）

汉字简介
Brief introduction to Chinese characters

汉字是记录汉语的书写符号系统，是表意文字，已经有3000多年的历史了。一般来说，一个汉字代表一个音节，每个汉字都有独立的方块形体，都记录了汉语中的一个词或语素意义，因此，汉字的字音、字形、字义是可以分析的。

Chinese characters, the written form of the Chinese language, are ideograms with a history of more than 3,000 years. Generally speaking, a character represents a syllable. Each character has an independent square shape, which indicates the meaning of a word or a morpheme in Chinese. Therefore, the pronunciation, form and meaning of each character can be analyzed.

汉字由偏旁（部件）按一定的结构方式组成。
A character is formed by radicals (components) following certain structural rules.

笔画是汉字的书写单位。
Strokes are the written units of a character.

汉字是一种古老的文字。几千年来，汉字的字体发生了不少变化，使用过的汉字数量也很多。但是，常用汉字只有2500个，常用偏旁只有500多个。

Chinese characters are one of the oldest written languages. The form of the characters has changed a lot over thousands of years. A large number of characters have been used, but only 2,500 characters and 500 radicals are commonly used.

汉字的标准字体是楷书，不过中国人在日常生活中常常写手写体的汉字，我们经常能看到手写体的汉字。

The standard form of Chinese characters is the regular script. However, people often see its handwritten form since the Chinese people often use it in their daily life.

nǐ jiā yǒu jǐ kǒu rén
你家有几口人

How many people are there in your family

课文 Text

wǒ shì rì běn liú xué shēng　wǒ jiā zài
我是日本留学生。我家在
dōng jīng　wǒ jiā yǒu wǔ kǒu rén　bà ba　mā ma
东京。我家有五口人：爸爸、妈妈、
gē ge　dì di　hé wǒ　wǒ méi yǒu jiě jie　yě méi
哥哥、弟弟和我。我没有姐姐，也没
yǒu mèi mei
有妹妹。

词语表 Vocabulary

1.	家	jiā	N	home, family
2.	有	yǒu	V	to have
3.	几	jǐ	Nu	How many…?
4.	口	kǒu	M	*a measure word for family members*
5.	在	zài	V	to be in / at
6.	爸爸	bàba	N	dad
7.	妈妈	māma	N	mum
8.	哥哥	gēge	N	elder brother

9

9.	弟弟	dìdi	N	younger brother
10.	和	hé	Conj	and
11.	没有	méiyǒu	V	not to have
12.	姐姐	jiějie	N	elder sister
13.	也	yě	Adv	also, too
14.	妹妹	mèimei	N	younger sister

专有名词 Proper Noun

	东京	Dōngjīng	the capital of Japan

补充词语 Complementary Words

1.	〇/零	líng	Nu	zero
2.	一	yī	Nu	one
3.	二	èr	Nu	two
4.	三	sān	Nu	three
5.	四	sì	Nu	four
6.	五	wǔ	Nu	five
7.	六	liù	Nu	six
8.	七	qī	Nu	seven
9.	八	bā	Nu	eight
10.	九	jiǔ	Nu	nine
11.	十	shí	Nu	ten
12.	两	liǎng	Nu	two

注释 Notes

1 你家有几口人？

"有"字句（表领有）：动词"有"充当谓语中心词，表示领有、具有。例如：
The "有" sentence (indicating possession): The verb "有" is used as the main word of the predicate to indicate possession. For example,

① 我家有四口人。 There are four people in my family.
② 他有一个姐姐。 He has an elder sister.
③ 他有弟弟。 He has a younger brother.

"有"字句的疑问式是："有"字句 + "吗？"例如：
Its interrogative form is: the "有" sentence + "吗？" For example,

④ 你有哥哥吗？ Do you have an elder brother?
⑤ 山下有姐姐吗？ Does Yamashita have an elder sister?
⑥ 你有妹妹吗？ Do you have a younger sister?

否定式是："没 / 没有" + 名词。例如：
Its negative form is: "没 / 没有" + noun. For example,

⑦ 我没有弟弟。 I don't have a younger brother.
⑧ 她没有姐姐。 She doesn't have an elder sister.

2 你家有几口人？

用数词"几"提问的疑问句：用来询问 1~10 的数目。例如：
The question using the numeral "几": It is used to enquire a number from 1 to 10. For example,

① A：你有几个弟弟？ How many younger brothers do you have?
　B：我有一个弟弟。 I have one.
② A：你有几个姐姐？ How many elder sisters do you have?
　B：我有两个姐姐。 I have two.

3 我是日本留学生。

定语：句子里修饰、限制主语或宾语的词语是定语，定语在主语或宾语前面。由于名词常常充当主语或宾语，因此定语常常修饰、限制名词。例如：

The attribute: An attribute is used before the subject or object to modify or restrict the subject or object. Since a noun is often used as the subject or object, an attribute is often used to modify or restrict the noun. For example,

① （日本）留学生　　　　international student from Japan
② （中国）人　　　　　　Chinese people
③ （汉语）老师　　　　　Chinese teacher
④ （四口）人　　　　　　four persons
⑤ （我）家　　　　　　　my home
⑥ （你）家　　　　　　　your home

4　也没有妹妹。

也：副词，表示与前面的情况相同，充当状语，位于主语后面。例如：

也: It is an adverb used as an adverbial after the subject, indicating the same as what is mentioned above. For example,

① 他家在北京，我家也在北京。　　His home is in Beijing. So is mine.
② 他家有四口人，我家也有四口人。　His family has four people. So does mine.
③ 我没有姐姐，也没有妹妹。　　　I don't have an elder sister or a younger sister.

5　也没有妹妹。

状语：句子里修饰、限制谓语中心词的词语是状语，状语在谓语中心词前面。由于动词、形容词常常充当谓语中心词，因此状语常常修饰、限制动词或形容词。例如：

The adverbial: An adverbial is used before the main word in the predicate to modify or restrict it. An adverbial is often used to modify or restrict a verb or an adjective since a verb or an adjective is often used as the main word in the predicate. For example,

① ［不］是日本人　　　is not Japanese
② ［也］没有　　　　　don't have, either
③ ［也］是留学生　　　is also an international student
④ ［很］好　　　　　　very good

6　标点符号的用法（2）

The usage of punctuation marks (2)

（1）冒号（màohào）：表示提示下文。例如：
Colon: It denotes something is to be followed. For example,

① 我家有五口人：爸爸、妈妈、哥哥、弟弟和我。
There are five people in my family: my father, mother, elder brother, younger brother and I.

② 我家有三口人：爸爸、妈妈和我。
There are three people in my family: my father, mother and I.

（2）顿号（dùnhào）：表示句中较短的并列词语之间的停顿。例如：

Slight-pause mark: It denotes a pause among short coordinate words in a sentence. For example,

③ 我家有五口人：爸爸、妈妈、哥哥、弟弟和我。
There are five people in my family: my father, mother, elder brother, younger brother and I.

④ 我们班有美国人、日本人、韩国人。
There are Americans, Japanese and Koreans studying in our class.

课堂用语（2） Classroom expressions (2)

1. 今天我们学习第二课。
   Jīntiān wǒmen xuéxí dì èr kè.
   Let's study Lesson 2 today.

2. 请大家打开书，翻到第9页。
   Qǐng dàjiā dǎkāi shū, fāndào dì jiǔ yè.
   Please open your book to page 9.

语音基础知识（2）
Basics on Chinese Phonetics（2）

1 声调 Tones

汉语声调有区别意义的作用，出现频率比声母、韵母高得多，是语音学习的重点。首先要学好第四声，因为37%的汉字读第四声。学习汉语声调，掌握每个声调的调型特征很重要。

Tones in Chinese language are used to differentiate meanings and are much more frequently used than initials and finals. Therefore, they are the focus of our phonetic study. The fourth tone needs to be learned first since 37% Chinese characters are pronounced in the fourth tone. When we study the tones of Chinese language, it is very important to know their characteristics.

第一声：高平调型。例如：
The first tone: high-and-level tone. For example,
　　yī（一）　　bā（八）　　pīnyīn（拼音）　　jīntiān（今天）

第二声：上升调型。例如：
The second tone: rising tone. For example,
　　shí（十）　　lái（来）　　xuéxí（学习）　　Chángchéng（长城）

第三声：低平调型。第三声本调是降升调型，但是说汉语的时候，84%的第三声念低平调，调值大约是211。低平调型是第三声的常见调型。例如：

The third tone: low-and-level tone. The original third tone is a falling-and-rising tone, but when speaking Chinese, 84% third tone is pronounced low and level, whose tone pitch is about 211. The low-and-level tone is the most commonly used. For example,
　　Běijīng（北京）　　Měiguó（美国）　　méiyǒu（没有）　　hǎokàn（好看）

第四声：下降调型。例如：
The fourth tone: falling tone. For example,
　　liù（六）　　sì（四）　　Hànzì（汉字）　　jiàoshì（教室）

声调调型图

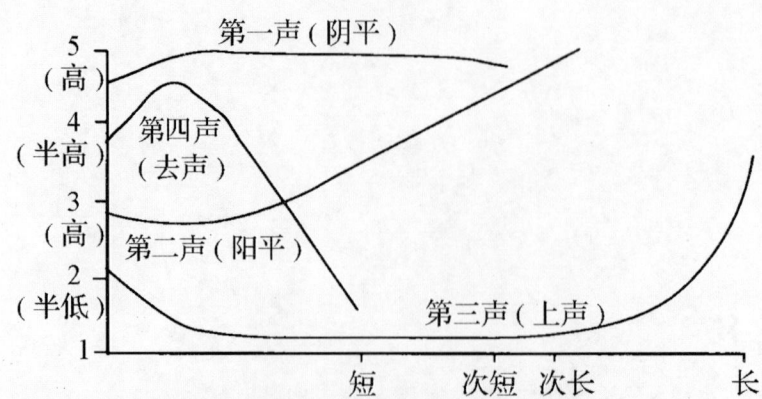

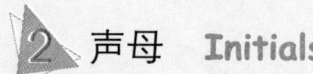

2 声母 Initials

b p m f d t n l

b [p] 双唇闭合，气流冲破双唇形成的阻碍，爆发成声。例如：
Keep your lips closed. Force the air out of the blockage and pronounce a plosive. For example,
bā（八）　bǐ（笔）　bàba（爸爸）　búcuò（不错）

p [p'] 发音方法和 b 相同，只是气流比较强。例如：
It is pronounced in the same way as b, but the air released is stronger than that for b. For example,
pǎo（跑）　píng（瓶）　péngyou（朋友）　píjiǔ（啤酒）

m [m] 双唇紧闭，声带颤动，气流从鼻腔出来。例如：
Keep your lips closed, then vibrate the vocal cords and let the air out of the nasal cavity. For example,
máng（忙）　mǎi（买）　māma（妈妈）　míngzi（名字）

f [f] 上齿接触下唇，气流从上齿与下唇之间的窄缝中摩擦出来。例如：
Your upper teeth touch your lower lips to let the air squeeze out of the narrow passage. For example,
fàn（饭）　fèi（费）　fángjiān（房间）　fēijī（飞机）

d [t] 舌尖抵住上齿龈，气流冲破舌尖与上齿龈形成的阻碍，爆发成声。例如：
Press the tip of the tongue against the alveolar ridge to let the air out of the blockage and pronounce a plosive. For example,
dà（大）　dōu（都）　diànhuà（电话）　dìdi（弟弟）

t [t'] 发音方法与 d 相同，只是气流比较强。例如：
It is pronounced in the same way as d, but the air released is stronger than that for d. For example,
tā（他）　tāng（汤）　tóngxué（同学）　tiānqì（天气）

n [n] 舌尖抵住上齿龈，气流振动声带，从鼻腔通过，同时冲开舌尖与上齿龈形成的阻碍。例如：
Press the tip of the tongue against the upper gum to let the air vibrate the vocal cords through the nasal cavity. Meanwhile, force the air out of the blockage between the tip of the tongue and the alveolar ridge. For example,
nǐ（你）　nǎ（哪）　niúnǎi（牛奶）　nǚ'ér（女儿）

l [l] 舌尖抵住上齿龈，气流振动声带，从舌头两边通过。例如：
Press the tip of the tongue against the upper gum to let the air vibrate the vocal cords and release from both sides of the tongue. For example,
lái（来）　liù（六）　lǎoshī（老师）　liànxí（练习）

15

3 韵母 Finals

a o e i u ü er

a [A] 舌头前伸，嘴张得最大。例如：
Protrude your tongue and open your mouth to the widest. For example,
mǎ（马）　dǎ（打）　bàba（爸爸）　dàxué（大学）

o [o] 舌头后缩，舌位半高，唇形略圆。例如：
Draw back your tongue and keep it to the semi-high position. Slightly round your lips. For example,
pò（破）　mò（末）　bōli（玻璃）　zhōumò（周末）

e [ɤ] 发音情况和 o 基本相同，但是唇形不圆。例如：
It is pronounced in the same way as o except that the mouth is not rounded. For example,
gè（个）　chē（车）　gēge（哥哥）　kělè（可乐）

i [i] 舌尖靠近或抵住下齿背，嘴张得很小，唇形不圆。例如：
Let the tip of the tongue touch the back of the lower teeth ridge. Open your mouth silghtly, but don't round your lips. For example,
yī（一）　qī（七）　dìdi（弟弟）　dōngxi（东西）

u [u] 舌头后缩，嘴张得很小，唇形圆。例如：
Draw back your tongue. Open your mouth a little bit and round your lips. For example,
wǔ（五）　bù（不）　mǎlù（马路）　bāngzhù（帮助）

ü [y] 发音和 i 相同，但是唇形圆。例如：
It is pronounced in the same way as i except that the mouth is rounded. For example,
yǔ（雨）　qù（去）　Hànyǔ（汉语）　lǔxíng（旅行）

er [ɚ] 发 e 的同时舌头往上翘。例如：
Pronounce e while holding up your tongue. For example,
èr（二）　ěrduo（耳朵）　értóng（儿童）

声母和韵母拼合表
Table of Combinations of Initials and Finals

声母＼韵母	a	o	e	i	u	ü
b	ba	bo		bi	bu	
p	pa	po		pi	pu	
m	ma	mo	me	mi	mu	
f	fa	fo			fu	

续表

声母＼韵母	a	o	e	i	u	ü
d	da		de	di	du	
t	ta		te	ti	tu	
n	na		ne	ni	nu	nü
l	la		le	li	lu	lü

4 拼写规则（1）：声调符号标写规则
Spelling rules (1): Rules of placing a tone mark

声调符号写在韵母的主要元音上面，有四条规则：
A tone mark is placed above the main vowel of a final. There are four rules:

（1）首先写在韵母中的 a 上面。例如：
Firstly the tone mark is placed above a of a final. For example,

    hǎo（好）   zài（在）   jiào（叫）   jiàn（见）   jiāng（江）

（2）韵母中没有 a，就写在 o 上面；没有 o，就写在 e 上面。例如：
If there is no a in the final, the tone mark is placed above o; if there is no o, it is placed above e. For example,

    duō（多）   kǒu（口）   qióng（穷）   xiè（谢）   méi（没）   xué（学）

（3）韵母 iou、uei 前面有声母时，写成 iu、ui，声调写在后一个元音上。例如：
If the finals iou and uei are preceded by an initial, they are written as iu and ui respectively. The tone mark is placed above the last vowel. For example,

    duì（对）   tuì（退）   liù（六）   jiǔ（九）

（4）韵母中只有一个元音时，声调写在这个元音上面。例如：
If there is only one vowel in the final, the tone mark is placed above it. For example,

    mā（妈）   gē（哥）   yīn（音）   bìng（病）   bù（不）   gāng（刚）

汉字基础知识（2）
Basics on Chinese characters（2）

汉字的笔画（1）
Strokes of Chinese character (1)

笔画是汉字的书写单位。从落笔到起笔是一个笔画，写汉字要一个笔画一个笔画地写。汉字的基本笔画有 8 种：

Strokes are the written units of a Chinese character. One stroke refers to the segment that is formed between setting the brush/pen down on paper and lifting it up again. A character must be written one stroke at a time in an orderly sequence. The basic strokes of Chinese characters fall into eight categories, namely:

笔画名称　Strokes	例　字　Examples
点（diǎn）　the dot	六　头
横（héng）　the horizontal stroke	一　三
竖（shù）　the vertical stroke	十　本
撇（piě）　the left-falling stroke	八　牛
捺（nà）　the right-falling stroke	及　来
提（tí）　the diagonal stroke, rising from left to right	把　我
折（zhé）　the turning stroke	四　口
钩（gōu）　the hook	同　买

3 你去哪儿
Where are you going

课文 Text

我是北京师范大学留学生。现在我去教室上课。我在一班。我们班有三位汉语老师，他们都是中国人。我们班有十四个学生，十个女同学，四个男同学，有英国人、韩国人、美国人和日本人。我们都学习汉语。

词语表 Vocabulary

1.	去	qù	V	to go
2.	哪儿	nǎr	Pr	where
3.	现在	xiànzài	N	now

19

4.	教室	jiàoshì	N	classroom
5.	上课	shàng kè	V//O	to attend class
6.	班	bān	N	class
7.	位	wèi	M	used in deferential reference to people
8.	汉语（中文）	Hànyǔ（Zhōngwén）	N	Chinese (language)
9.	老师	lǎoshī	N	teacher
10.	他们	tāmen	Pr	referring to the third person plural, usually of male or indefinite gender
	们	men	Suf	used after a personal pronoun or a noun to show plural number
11.	都	dōu	Adv	all
12.	个	gè	M	used before a noun having no particular classifier of its own
13.	学生	xuésheng	N	student
14.	女	nǚ	Adj	female
15.	同学	tóngxué	N	classmate
16.	男	nán	Adj	male
17.	学习	xuéxí	V	to learn, to study

专有名词　Proper Nouns

1.	北京师范大学	Běijīng Shīfàn Dàxué	Beijing Normal University
2.	中国	Zhōngguó	China
3.	英国	Yīngguó	UK
4.	韩国	Hánguó	Korea
5.	美国	Měiguó	USA

补充词语　Complementary Word

	多少	duōshao	Pr	How many…?

注释 Notes

1 你**去**哪儿?

动词谓语句:动词充当谓语中心词的句子叫动词谓语句。例如:

The sentence with a verbal predicate: A sentence in which the main word in the predicate is a verb is known as the sentence with a verbal predicate. For example,

① 我有一个哥哥。　　　　I have an elder brother.
② 我学习汉语。　　　　　I study Chinese.
③ 她家在北京。　　　　　Her home is in Beijing.

2 你去**哪儿**?

用"哪儿"提问的疑问句:用来询问地址。例如:

The question using "哪儿": It is used to ask the address. For example,

① 你去哪儿?　　　　　　Where are you going?
② 你家在哪儿?　　　　　Where is your home?
③ 你们班教室在哪儿?　　Where is your classroom?

3 现在我**去教室上课**。

"去"+地点+动词:表示去某地做某事,有时也可说成:"去"+动词。例如:

"去"+place+verb: It is used to express "going to some place to do something". Sometimes it is also referred to as "去"+verb. For example,

① 我去教室上课。　　　　I am going to the classroom for a class.
② 他去餐厅吃饭。　　　　He is going to the dining room for his meal.
③ 我去上课。　　　　　　I am going to class.
④ 他去吃饭。　　　　　　He is going for dinner.
⑤ 我去买东西。　　　　　I am going shopping.

4 我们班有三**位**汉语老师。/我们班有十四**个**学生。

名量词:汉语的数词和名词之间必须用量词,形成一种固定短语:数词+量词+名词。这种表示事物(名词)数量的量词叫名量词。例如:

The nominal measure word: In Chinese, a measure word must be used between a numeral and a noun, forming a set phrase: numeral + measure word + noun. A measure word indicating the number of

21

something (noun) is known as a nominal measure word. For example,

① 四口人　　　　　four people
② 三位老师　　　　three teachers
③ 一个学生　　　　one student
④ 六本书　　　　　six books

5 我们班有十四个学生，十个女同学，四个男同学。

100 以下的称数法：
Numerals less than 100:

（1）1~10 的读法：读数字。例如：
For numbers 1~10, you just need to read the number. For example,

　　1 → yī　　　　　2 → èr　　　　　3 → sān

（2）11~99 的读法：数字 + 单位。汉语 100 以下的基数单位只有"十"，读法是：~shí~。例如：
For numbers 11~99, you need to read the number and then the unit. In Chinese, for a cardinal number less than 100, "十" is the only unit. It is pronounced: ~shí~. For example,

　　21 → èrshíyī　　　　36 → sānshíliù　　　　43 → sìshísān
　　56 → wǔshíliù　　　 78 → qīshíbā　　　　 99 → jiǔshíjiǔ
　　20 → èrshí　　　　　40 → sìshí　　　　　 80 → bāshí

注意：Note：

　　10 → yīshí / shí　　　　17 → yīshíqī / shíqī

6 我们都学习汉语。

都：副词，表示总括，充当句子状语，放在谓语中心词前面。例如：
都：It is an adverb, meaning "all". It is used as an adverbial in a sentence before the main word in the predicate. For example,

① 他们都是留学生。　　　　They are all international students.
② 我们都学习汉语。　　　　We all study Chinese.
③ 我和他都没有姐姐。　　　Neither he nor I have an elder sister.

"都不 + 谓语"和"不都 + 谓语"意思不一样。例如：
"都不 + predicate" and "不都 + predicate" have different meanings. For example,

④ 我们都不是日本人。
　　（意思是："我们"中没有日本人　It means none of "us" is Japanese.）

22

⑤ 我们不都是日本人。
　　（意思是："我们"中有日本人，也有韩国人、美国人、英国人等　It means some of "us" are Japanese, while others are Koreans, Americans and British, etc.）

⑥ 我们都不学习汉语。
　　（意思是："我们"中没有人学习汉语　It means none of "us" learns Chinese.）

⑦ 我们不都学习汉语。
　　（意思是："我们"中有人学习汉语，也有人学习英语、学习教育等　It means some of "us" study Chinese, while others study English, pedagogy and so on.）

7 用"几"、"多少"提问的疑问句

用"几"提问的句子： 询问 10 以下的数目。我们在第二课已经学过。例如：

The question using "几": It is used to enquire a number less than 10. We have learned it in Lesson 2. For example,

① 你家有几口人？　　　　　　How many people are there in your family?
② 你有几个弟弟？　　　　　　How many younger brothers do you have?
③ 你们班有几位汉语老师？　　How many Chinese language teachers do you have in your class?

用"多少"提问的句子： 询问 10 以上的数目。例如：

The question using "多少": It is used to enquire a number more than 10. For example,

④ 你们班有多少同学？　　　　How many students are there in your class?
⑤ 中国有多少人？　　　　　　What is the population of China?
⑥ 这所大学有多少留学生？　　How many international students are there in this university?

课堂用语（3）　Classroom expressions (3)

1. 听懂了吗？	Tīngdǒng le ma?	Do you understand what I said?
2. 听懂了。	Tīngdǒng le.	Yes, I do.
3. 老师，我没听懂。	Lǎoshī, wǒ méi tīngdǒng.	Sorry, I don't.
4. 请再说一遍。	Qǐng zài shuō yí biàn.	I beg your pardon.

语音基础知识（3）
Basics on Chinese phonetics（3）

 声母 Initials

g k h

g [k] 舌根抵住软腭，气流冲破舌根与软腭形成的阻碍，爆发成声。例如：
Raise the base of the tongue against the soft palate. Force the air out of the blockage and pronounce a plosive. For example,
    gè（个）   gāo（高）   gōngzuò（工作）   gèzi（个子）

k [k'] 发音方法与 g 相同，只是气流比较强。例如：
It is pronounced in the same way as g, but the air is comparatively stronger. For example,
    kè（课）   kuài（快）   kǒu（口）   kèqi（客气）

h [x] 舌根接近软腭，气流从舌根与软腭之间的窄缝中摩擦出来。例如：
Raise the base of the tongue close to the soft palate to let the air out of the narrow passage. For example,
    hǎo（好）   hē（喝）   hé（和）   hǎochī（好吃）

 韵母 Finals

ai ei ao ou ua uo uai uei (ui)

ai、ei、ao、ou 前面的元音要念得长而响亮、清晰。例如：
For ai, ei, ao and ou, the former vowel of the two is pronounced long, loud and clear. For example,

ai [ai]	ài（爱）	mǎi（买）	báitiān（白天）	kāi mén（开门）
ei [ei]	gěi（给）	děi（得）	hěn lèi（很累）	hēisè（黑色）
ao [au]	lǎo（老）	māo（猫）	gāoxìng（高兴）	zǎoshang（早上）
ou [ou]	tóu（头）	shǒu（手）	Ōuzhōu（欧洲）	lóu shang（楼上）

ua、uo 后面的元音要念得长而响亮、清晰。例如：
For ua and uo, the latter vowel of the two is pronounced long, loud and clear. For example,

ua [uA]	shuā（刷）	huà（画）	xīguā（西瓜）	xiānhuā（鲜花）
uo [uo]	wǒ（我）	duō（多）	shēnghuó（生活）	guójiā（国家）

uai、uei（ui）中间的元音要念得长而响亮、清晰。例如：
For uai and uei (ui), the vowel in the middle is pronounced long, loud and clear. For example,

| uai [uai] | kuài（快） | huài（坏） | wàiyǔ（外语） | qíguài（奇怪） |
| uei (ui) [uei] | guì（贵） | shuǐ（水） | wèishēng（卫生） | shuì jiào（睡觉） |

声母和韵母拼配合表
Table of Combinations of Initials and Finals

韵母 声母	ai	ei	ao	ou	ua	uo	uai	uei (ui)
g	gai	gei	gao	gou	gua	guo	guai	gui
k	kai	kei	kao	kou	kua	kuo	kuai	kui
h	hai	hei	hao	hou	hua	huo	huai	hui

 拼写规则（2）：uei 的省略 Spelling rules (2): the omission of uei

韵母 uei 与声母相拼时，写成 ui，声调符号写在 i 上面。例如：

When the final uei is preceded by an initial, it is written as ui and the tone mark is placed above i. For example,

huì（会）   duì（对）

汉字基础知识（3）
Basics on Chinese characters (3)

汉字的笔画（2）
Strokes of Chinese characters (2)

汉字的基本笔画有 8 种，但是还有一些常用笔画是在这 8 种基本笔画的基础上变化而成的。主要有：

Although the basic strokes of characters fall into eight categories, there are some commonly used strokes derived from the basic ones. They mainly include:

笔画名称 Strokes			例字 Examples	
斜钩	（xiégōu）	the slanting hook stroke	我	或
撇折	（piězhé）	the left-falling turning stroke	红	级
横折	（héngzhé）	the horizontal turning stroke	口	四
撇点	（piědiǎn）	the left-falling dot stroke	女	好
竖提	（shùtí）	the vertical rising stroke	很	饭
横折提	（héngzhétí）	the horizontal turning-and-rising stroke	语	话
横折钩	（héngzhégōu）	the horizontal turning hook	同	月
横折折撇	（héngzhézhépiě）	the horizontal turning-and-turning left-falling stroke	建	廷

dì sì kè de shēng cí duō ma
第四课的生词多吗

Are there many new words in Lesson 4

课文 Text

wǒ men bān de jīng dú kè lǎo shī xìng
我们班的精读课老师姓
lǐ   shì yí wèi nǚ lǎo shī   wǒ men jīn tiān xué
李，是一位女老师。我们今天学
xí dì sì kè   dì sì kè zài jīng dú shū de
习第四课。第四课在精读书的
dì èr shí yè   wǒ men gēn lǐ lǎo shī dú shēng
第20页。我们跟李老师读生
cí   dú kè wén   zuò liàn xí   dì sì kè de
词、读课文、做练习。第四课的
shēng cí bù duō   hàn zì yě bù nán
生词不多，汉字也不难。

lǐ lǎo shī qǐng zhēn ni yòng   yě   zào
李老师请珍妮用"也"造
jù   zhēn ni de jù zi hěn hǎo
句。珍妮的句子很好。

lǐ lǎo shī qǐng qiáo zhì zuò pīn yīn liàn xí   qiáo zhì de fā yīn bú cuò
李老师请乔治做拼音练习。乔治的发音不错。

zuó tiān wǒ men méi yǒu zuò yè   jīn tiān de zuò yè shì liàn xí   de fā
昨天我们没有作业。今天的作业是练习 j、q、x 的发
yīn   chāo xiě dì sì kè de shēng cí   zhǔn bèi míng tiān tīng xiě shēng cí hé jù zi
音，抄写第四课的生词，准备明天听写生词和句子。

27

词语表 Vocabulary

1.	第	dì	Pref	*indicating ordinal numerals*
2.	课	kè	N	*lesson*
3.	的	de	StPt	*used after an attribute*
4.	生词	shēngcí	N	*new word*
5.	多	duō	Adj	*many*
6.	精读	jīngdú	V	*to read intensively*
7.	今天	jīntiān	N	*today*
8.	书	shū	N	*book*
9.	页	yè	M	*page*
10.	跟	gēn	Prep	*used to introduce the recipient of an action*
11.	读	dú	V	*to read*
12.	课文	kèwén	N	*text*
13.	做	zuò	V	*to do*
14.	练习	liànxí	N/V	*exercise; to do an exercise, to practice*
15.	汉字	Hànzì	N	*Chinese character*
16.	难	nán	Adj	*difficult*
17.	请	qǐng	V	*to ask*
18.	用	yòng	V	*to use*
19.	造句	zào jù	V//O	*to make a sentence*
20.	句子	jùzi	N	*sentence*
21.	很	hěn	Adv	*very*
22.	拼音	pīnyīn	N	*pinyin, Chinese phonetic alphabets*
23.	发音	fāyīn	N	*pronunciation*
24.	不错	búcuò	Adj	*good, not bad*
25.	昨天	zuótiān	N	*yesterday*

26.	作业	zuòyè	N	homework
27.	抄写	chāoxiě	V	to copy by hand
28.	准备	zhǔnbèi	V	to prepare
29.	明天	míngtiān	N	tomorrow
30.	听写	tīngxiě	V	to dictate

专有名词 Proper Nouns

1.	李	Lǐ	a family name
2.	珍妮	Zhēnni	name of a person
3.	乔治	Qiáozhì	name of a person

1 第四课的生词多吗?

序数词：汉语一般在基数前加词头"第"表示序数，即："第" + 基数。例如：

Ordinal numeral: In Chinese, an ordinal numeral is formed by adding the prefix "第" in front of a cardinal numeral, i.e., "第" + cardinal numeral. For example,

① 第一　　　　the first
② 第三　　　　the third
③ 第三页　　　Page 3
④ 第四课　　　Lesson 4

2 第四课的生词多吗?

结构助词"的"：放在定语后面，是定语的标志。但是有些定语后面也可以不用"的"。例如：

The structural particle "的": It is used after an attribute as the marker of an attribute. However, for some attributes, "的" may be omitted. For example,

① 珍妮的句子　　　Jenny's sentence
② 乔治的发音　　　George's pronunciation
③ 我们班的老师　　the teacher of our class

④ 很好的书　　　　　very good book
⑤ 他家　　　　　　　his home
⑥ 我爸爸　　　　　　my father
⑦ 好朋友　　　　　　good friend
⑧ 女老师　　　　　　female teacher
⑨ 听力课　　　　　　listening course

3 第四课的生词多吗？

形容词谓语句：由形容词充当谓语中心词的句子是形容词谓语句。只有一个形容词谓语时，要在形容词前面加副词修饰。例如：

The sentence with an adjectival predicate: A sentence in which the main word in the predicate is an adjective is known as a sentence with an adjectival predicate. When there is only one adjectival predicate, the adjective is preceded and modified by an adverb. For example,

① 珍妮的句子很好。　　　Jenny's sentence is very good.
② 他很忙。　　　　　　　He is very busy.
③ 我不累。　　　　　　　I am not tired.

4 李老师请珍妮用"也"造句。

兼语句：句子的谓语部分是一个动宾短语与一个主谓短语套在一起的短语，使这个动宾短语的宾语同时兼做主谓短语的主语，动宾短语的动词有使令意义。如"我请你喝茶"、"爸爸让我学习汉语"。第一个动词是"请"时，也可以省略句子的主语。例如：

The pivotal sentence: In the predicate of a pivotal sentence, a verb-object phrase combines with a subject-predicate phrase, making the object of the verb-predicate phrase also the subject of the subject-predicate phrase, and the verb of the verb-object phrase causative. For example, "我请你喝茶", "爸爸让我学习汉语". When the first verb is "请", the subject of the sentence may be omitted. For example,

① 老师请珍妮造句。　　　The teacher asked Jenny to make a sentence.
② 我请他喝咖啡。　　　　I invited him to coffee.
③ 朋友请我吃饭。　　　　My friend invited me to dinner.
④ 请你再说一遍。　　　　Please say it again.
⑤ 今天朋友请吃饭。　　　Today my friend will invite me to dinner.
⑥ 请再说一遍。　　　　　Please say it again.

5 标点符号的用法（3）
Usage of punctuation marks (3)

引号（""）（yǐnhào）：表示文中引用的部分。例如：

Quotation mark（""）: It denotes the part of the text is quoted from another text or speech. For example,

① 李老师请珍妮用"也"造句。　　Mr. Li asked Jenny to make a sentence using "也".
② 请用"都"完成句子。　　　　　Please complete the sentences using "都".
③ 选择"几"、"多少"填空。　　　Fill in the blanks with "几" or "多少".

课堂用语（4）　Classroom expressions (4)

1. 老师，这个汉字怎么写？
   Lǎoshī, zhège Hànzì zěnme xiě?
   Sir, would you please tell me how to write this Chinese character?

2. 这个词是什么意思？
   Zhège cí shì shénme yìsi?
   What does this word mean?

语音基础知识（4）
Basics on Chinese phonetics（4）

1 声母 Initials

j q x

j ［tɕ］舌尖下垂，舌面抬起，接触上颚，然后稍微放松，气流从舌面与上颚之间的窄缝中摩擦出来。例如：

Lower the tip of the tongue and raise the blade of the tongue. Touch the upper jaw, then release slightly to let the air out of the narrow passage between the blade of the tongue and upper jaw and pronounce a fricative. For example,

  jǐ（几） jiào（叫） juéde（觉得） jùzi（句子）

q ［tɕ'］发音方法和 j 相同，只是气流比较强。例如：

It is pronounced in the same way as j, but the air is comparatively stronger. For example,

  qī（七） qiáng（墙） qúnzi（裙子） pínqióng（贫穷）

x ［ɕ］舌尖下垂，舌面抬起，气流从舌面与上颚之间的窄缝中摩擦出来。例如：

Lower the tip of the tongue and raise the blade of the tongue to let the air out of the narrow passage between the blade of the tongue and upper jaw. For example,

  xiǎo（小） xiě（写） xuéxí（学习） xiūxi（休息）

2 韵母 Finals

ia ie iao iou（iu） üe

ia、ie、üe 后面的元音要念得长而响亮、清晰。例如：

For ia, ie, and üe, the latter vowel of the two is pronounced long, loud and clear. For example,

ia［iA］	yá（牙）	jiā（家）	jiàqī（假期）	xià kè（下课）
ie［iɛ］	yě（也）	bié（别）	xièxie（谢谢）	yùndòngxié（运动鞋）
üe［yɛ］	yuè（月）	xuě（雪）	yuèdú（阅读）	juédìng（决定）

iao、iou（iu）中间的元音要念得长而响亮、清晰。例如：

For iao and iou (iu), the vowel in the middle is pronounced long, loud and clear. For example,

iao［iau］	yào（要）	xiào（笑）	xiǎo niǎo（小鸟）	shǒubiǎo（手表）
iou（iu）［iou］	yǒu（有）	jiǔ（九）	qiūtiān（秋天）	liúxuéshēng（留学生）

声母和韵母拼合表
Table of Combinations of Initials and Finals

韵母 声母	ia	ie	iao	iou (iu)	üe
j	jia	jie	jiao	jiu	jue
q	qia	qie	qiao	qiu	que
x	xia	xie	xiao	xiu	xue

 拼写规则（3）：i、ü、üe、iou、uen 的省略

Spelling rules (3): The omission of i, ü, üe, iou and uen

（1）i 上标写声调符号时，写成 ī、í、ǐ、ì。例如：

When a tone mark is placed above i, it is written as ī, í, ǐ, ì. For example,

　　chī（吃）　　dì（弟）

（2）ü、üe 和声母 j、q、x 相拼时，写成 u。例如：

When ü or üe occurs with the initials j, q or x, it is written as u. For example,

　　qù（去）　　xué（学）

（3）iou 和声母相拼时，写成 iu，声调符号写在 u 上。例如：

When iou occurs with an initial, it is written as iu and the tone mark is placed above u. For example,

　　jiǔ（九）　　qiú（球）

（4）uen 和声母相拼时，写成 un，声调符号写在 u 上。例如：

When uen occurs with an initial, it is written as un and the tone mark is placed above u. For example,

　　chūn（春）　　hūn（婚）

汉字基础知识（4）
Basics on Chinese characters (4)

汉字的偏旁
Radicals of Chinese characters

偏旁是汉字的基本结构单位。例如："好"可以分出"女"和"子"两个偏旁，"明"可以分出"日"和"月"两个偏旁。

Radicals are the basic structural units of characters. For example, "好" is made up of two radicals: "女" and "子"; "明" is made up of "日" and "月".

和汉字的意义有关系的偏旁叫"形旁"。例如：口（口字旁）、讠（言字旁）、氵（三点水旁）。形旁在汉字中的位置比较固定。掌握常用形旁的意义类别对学习汉字很有帮助。

The radical that denotes the meaning of a character is known as the "semantic radical", such as the radical "口", radical "讠" or radical "氵". The position of a semantic radical in a character is comparatively fixed. Mastering the meanings and categories of the commonly used semantic radicals is very helpful for us to learn Chinese characters.

和汉字的读音有关系的偏旁叫"声旁"。例如："钟"的读音 zhōng 和它的声旁"中（zhōng）"的一样，"座"的读音 zuò 和它的声旁"坐（zuò）"的一样。

The radical that denotes the pronunciation of a character is known as the "phonetic radical". For example, the character "钟（zhōng）" has the same pronunciation as that of its phonetic radical "中（zhōng）". And the character "座（zuò）" has the same pronunciation as that of its phonetic radical "坐（zuò）".

汉字已经有几千年的历史了，几千年来，汉语语音的变化比汉字字形的变化快得多，因此，现在很多汉字的声旁已经不能准确地表示这个汉字的读音了。例如："请"的声旁"青"读音是 qīng，但是"请"的读音是 qǐng。

Chinese characters have a history of thousands of years. During these years, the pronunciation of characters has undergone much greater change than that of the form of the characters. Therefore, many phonetic radicals of Chinese characters cannot accurately indicate the pronunciations of the characters any more. For example, the phonetic radical "青" is pronounced qīng, while "请" is pronounced as qǐng.

由两个或两个以上的偏旁组成的汉字叫合体字。例如："好"、"谢"、"多"。

Characters made up of two or more radicals are known as compound characters. For example, "好","谢" and "多".

由一个偏旁组成的汉字叫独体字。例如："日"、"女"、"生"。

Characters made up of only one radical are known as independent characters. For example, "日", "女" and "生".

tā shì shéi
他是谁
Who is he

课文 Text

zhè shì wǒ men quán jiā rén de zhào piàn
这是我们全家人的照片。
zhè shì wǒ bà ba， tā shì yì jiā jì suàn
这是我爸爸，他是一家计算
jī gōng sī de zhí yuán， tā gōng zuò hěn máng。 zhè
机公司的职员，他工作很忙。这
shì wǒ mā ma， tā shì jiào shī， tā zài zhōng xué
是我妈妈，她是教师，她在中学
jiāo yīn yuè， tā gōng zuò yě hěn máng。 nà shì wǒ gē
教音乐，她工作也很忙。那是我哥
ge， tā shì dà xué shēng， tā xué xí jīng jì。 nà
哥，他是大学生，他学习经济。那
shì wǒ dì di， tā shì xiǎo xué shēng， tā gè zi hěn
是我弟弟，他是小学生，他个子很
gāo。 wǒ men quán jiā rén shēn tǐ dōu hěn hǎo。
高。我们全家人身体都很好。
xiàn zài wǒ zài běi jīng xué xí hàn yǔ， wǒ hěn xiǎng tā men， wǒ yě hěn ài tā
现在我在北京学习汉语，我很想他们，我也很爱他
men。 wǒ cháng cháng gěi tā men dǎ diàn huà。
们。我常常给他们打电话。

35

词语表 Vocabulary

1.	他	tā	Pr	he, him
2.	谁	shéi / shuí	Pr	who, whom
3.	这	zhè	Pr	this
4.	全	quán	Adj	whole, all, entire
5.	家	jiā	M	a measure word for families or enterprises
6.	照片	zhàopiàn	N	photograph, picture
7.	计算机	jìsuànjī	N	computer
8.	公司	gōngsī	N	company
9.	职员	zhíyuán	N	employee
10.	工作	gōngzuò	N	work
11.	忙	máng	Adj	busy
12.	她	tā	Pr	she, her
13.	教师	jiàoshī	N	teacher
14.	中学	zhōngxué	N	secondary school
15.	教	jiāo	V	to teach
16.	音乐	yīnyuè	N	music
17.	那	nà	Pr	that
18.	大学生	dàxuéshēng	N	college student
19.	经济	jīngjì	N	economics
20.	小学生	xiǎoxuéshēng	N	elementary school student
21.	个子	gèzi	N	height, stature
22.	高	gāo	Adj	tall
23.	身体	shēntǐ	N	health
24.	想	xiǎng	V	to miss
25.	爱	ài	V	to love
26.	常常	chángcháng	Adv	often

27.	给	**gěi**	Prep	to
28.	打	**dǎ**	V	to make a phone call
29.	电话	**diànhuà**	N	phone call

专有名词 **Proper Noun**

| | 北京 | **Běijīng** | | the capital of China |

注释 Notes

1 他是**谁**?

用"谁"提问的疑问句：用来询问人。这种有疑问词的句子是特指疑问句。"谁"可以是主语，可以是宾语，也可以是定语。例如：

The question using "谁": It is used to enquire somebody. A sentence with an interrogative pronoun is known as a special interrogative sentence. "谁" can be used as a subject, an object, or an attribute. For example,

① 他是谁？ Who is he?
② 谁是我们班的老师？ Who is the teacher of our class?
③ 谁是中国人？ Who is Chinese?
④ 他是谁的同学？ Whose classmate is he?

2 **这**是我们全家人的照片。/ **那**是我哥哥。

这、那：指示代词，可以询问人，也可以询问物。"这"指离说话人比较近的人或物，"那"指离说话人比较远的人或物。例如：

"这" and "那": They are demonstrative pronouns used to enquire somebody or something. "这" indicates somebody or something near the speaker, "那" indicates somebody or something far away from the speaker. For example,

① A：这是谁？ Who is this?
　 B：这是我爸爸。 This is my father.
② A：那是谁？ Who is that?
　 B：那是我妈妈。 That is my mother.

③ A：这是什么？ What is this?
　B：这是汉语精读课本。 This is the textbook of Chinese intensive reading.
④ A：那是什么？ What is that?
　B：那是我们全家的照片。 That is a photo of my whole family.

3 他**工作很忙**。

主谓谓语句：由主谓短语充当谓语中心语的句子叫主谓谓语句。例如：

The S-P predicate sentence：A sentence in which a subject-predicate phrase is used as the main word in the predicate is known as the S-P predicate sentence. For example,

① 他身体很好。 He is in good health.
② 妈妈工作很忙。 My mother is busy with her work.
③ 弟弟个子很高。 My younger brother is tall.
④ 北京自行车很多。 There are many bicycles in Beijing.

4 她是**教师**。

辨析 Discrimination：教师、老师

"教师"指职业，"老师"是对教师的一种称呼。例如：
"教师" refers to one's occupation, while "老师" is an appellation of teacher. For example,

① 李老师，请再说一遍。
② 王老师，明天见。
③ 李教师，早上好。（×）
④ 王教师，再见。　（×）

5 她**在**中学教音乐。/ 我常常**给**他们打电话。

辨析 Discrimination：在、给

介词"在"常与处所词语组成介宾短语，充当句子的状语，说明动作发生的处所。例如：
The preposition "在" and the noun indicating place often form a prepositional phrase. This phrase is used as the adverbial of a sentence, indicating where an action takes place. For example,

① 现在我［在图书馆］看书。 I am reading a book in the library now.
② 妹妹［在上海］工作。 My younger sister works in Shanghai.
③ 她妈妈［在中学］工作。 Her mother works in a middle school.

介词"给"常与表示人的名词组成介宾短语，充当句子的状语，说明动作或状态关联的对象。例如：

The preposition "给" and the noun indicating somebody often form a prepositional phrase. This phrase is used as the adverbial of a sentence, indicating the receiver of an action or the person related to a state. For example,

④ 我［给他］打电话。　　　　I gave him a call.
⑤ 他［给我］发email。　　　　He sent me an email.
⑥ 姐姐［给我］买书。　　　　My elder sister bought me a book.

6 她在中学教音乐。

介宾短语：由介词和名词组成的短语叫介宾短语。介宾短语常常做状语。例如：

The preposition-object phrase: A phrase made up of a preposition and a noun is known as the preposition-object phrase. It is often used as an adverbial. For example,

① ［在商店］买东西　　　　　　buy something in the shop
② ［给朋友］写信　　　　　　　write a letter to one's friend
③ ［往前］走　　　　　　　　　go forward
④ 我［在北京］学习汉语。　　　I study Chinese in Beijing.
⑤ 他爸爸［在计算机公司］工作。His father works in a computer company.
⑥ 她［在教室］上课。　　　　　She is having a class in the classroom.
⑦ 他姐姐［在房间］听音乐。　　His elder sister is listening to the music in the room.

7 我很想他们。

"想" + 人 / 动物：动词"想"的宾语是表示人或动物的名词时，"想"的意思是"思念"。例如：

"想" + somebody/some animal: When the object of "想" is a noun indicating somebody or some animal, "想" means "to miss". For example,

① 想朋友　　　　　miss my friends
② 想妈妈　　　　　miss my mother
③ 想我的小狗　　　miss my little dog

语音基础知识（5）
Basics on Chinese phonetics（5）

1. 前鼻音韵尾韵母 Anterior nasal finals

an [an]	nán（男）	bān（班）	chī fàn（吃饭）	kànjiàn（看见）
en [ən]	běn（本）	rén（人）	shēntǐ（身体）	hěn hǎo（很好）
in [in]	xìn（信）	jīn（金）	pīnyīn（拼音）	jīntiān（今天）
ian [iɛn]	yān（烟）	biān（边）	zàijiàn（再见）	niánlíng（年龄）
uan [uan]	chuān（穿）	wǎn（碗）	guānxi（关系）	huàn qián（换钱）
uen [uən]	wèn（问）	chūn（春）	kùnnan（困难）	jié hūn（结婚）
ün [yn]	yún（云）	jūn（军）	qúnzi（裙子）	yùndòng（运动）
üan [yɛn]	yuǎn（远）	yuán（元）	quán jiā（全家）	gōngyuán（公园）

2. 后鼻音韵尾韵母 Posterior nasal finals

ang [aŋ]	máng（忙）	zhāng（张）	Chángchéng（长城）	shàng kè（上课）
eng [əŋ]	děng（等）	lěng（冷）	shēnghuó（生活）	péngyou（朋友）
ing [iŋ]	líng（零）	qǐng（请）	míngzi（名字）	Běijīng（北京）
iang [iaŋ]	yáng（羊）	xiǎng（想）	Cháng Jiāng（长江）	tàiyáng（太阳）
uang [uaŋ]	wàng（忘）	huáng（黄）	guǎngchǎng（广场）	wǎngbā（网吧）
ueng [uəŋ]	wēng（翁）	wèng（瓮）		
iong [yŋ]	yòng（用）	qióng（穷）	xióngmāo（熊猫）	yóuyǒng（游泳）
ong [uŋ]	hóng（红）	kōng（空）	dōngtiān（冬天）	gōngsī（公司）

前鼻音韵尾韵母音节表
Table of Anterior Nasal Finals

声母＼韵母	an	en	in	ian	uan	uen	ün	üan
0	an	en	yin	yan	wan	wen	yun	yuan

后鼻音韵尾韵母音节表
Table of Posterior Nasal Finals

声母＼韵母	ang	eng	ing	iang	uang	ueng	iong	ong
0	ang	eng	ying	yang	wang	weng	yong	/

拼写规则（4） Spelling rules (4)

（1）隔音符号（'）的使用　The use of syllable-dividing mark（'）

以 a、o、e 开头的音节，连接在其他音节后面的时候，要用隔音符号（'）与前面的音节隔开。例如：

When a syllable beginning with a, o or e connects with another syllable, the syllable-dividing mark（'）is used to separate the syllable from the preceding one. For example,

Xī'ān（西安）　　nǚ'ér（女儿）

（2）y、w 的使用　The use of y and w

以 ü 开头的音节，一律改写成 yu。例如：

For a syllable beginning with ü, ü is written as yu. For example,

yǔ（雨）　　yuè（月）　　Hànyǔ（汉语）

以 i 开头的音节，除了 i、in、ing 以外，一律将 i 改写成 y。例如：

For a syllable beginning with i, i is written as y, except i, in and ing. For example,

ie — yě（也）　　iao — yào（要）　　iou — péngyou（朋友）　　iang — yàngzi（样子）

i、in、ing 独立成音节时，在 i 前面加写 y，写成 yi、yin、ying。例如：

When i, in or ing forms a syllable on its own, i is preceded by y and is written as yi, yin, ying respectively. For example,

i — yī（一）　　in — yīnyuè（音乐）　　ing — Yīngyǔ（英语）

以 u 开头的音节，除了 u 以外，一律将 u 改写成 w。例如：

For a syllable beginning with u, u is written as w, except u. For example,

uo —— wǒ（我）　　　　　　　uen —— wèn（问）
uai —— wàiguó（外国）　　　　uang —— wǎngbā（网吧）

u 独立成音节时，在 u 前面加 w，写成 wu。例如：

When u forms a syllable on its own, u is preceded by w and is written as wu. For example,

u —— wǔ（五）　　　　　　　u —— xiàwǔ（下午）

汉字基础知识（5）
Basics on Chinese characters（5）

汉字的笔顺
Stroke order

笔顺是书写汉字的笔画顺序。汉字笔顺的一般规则是：
Stroke order refers to the order in which a character is written. The general rules of writing Chinese characters are:

笔顺规则　Rules of stroke order	例字 Examples	笔顺演示　Stroke order demonstration
先横后竖（xiān héng hòu shù） the horizontal stroke before the vertical stroke	十 干	一 十 一 二 干
先撇后捺（xiān piě hòu nà） the left-falling stroke before the right-falling stroke	八 人	丿 八 丿 人
从上到下（cóng shàng dào xià） the upper stroke before the lower stroke	三 李	一 二 三 一 十 才 木 本 李 李
从左到右（cóng zuǒ dào yòu） from left to right	汉 说	丶 丶 氵 氵 汉 丶 讠 讠 讠 证 诮 诮 说
从外到内（cóng wài dào nèi） the outer strokes before the inner strokes	同 月	丨 冂 冂 同 同 同 丿 冂 月 月
先中间后两边（xiān zhōngjiān hòu liǎngbiān） the strokes in the middle before the strokes on both sides	小 水	亅 小 小 亅 刁 水 水
先进"人"后关"门"（xiān jìn "rén" hòu guān "mén"） the enclosing strokes before the enclosed strokes	回 国	丨 冂 冂 回 回 回 丨 冂 冂 冃 囯 国 国
主笔最后出（zhǔ bǐ zuìhòu chū） the main stroke written at last	中 书 事	丶 口 口 中 乛 弓 书 书 一 亠 크 写 写 写 事

你住哪儿
Where do you live

 课文 Text

我是美国人。我的英语名字是Younger，汉语名字是杨歌。

我住留学生宿舍，我的房间在一号楼二层，房间号码是1234。我有一个同屋。他是泰国人。他在历史系学习中国历史。他的汉语很好。

我们房间有两张床、两张桌子、两台电脑、两把椅子、两个衣柜，还有一台彩色电视、一部电话，电话号码是76543210。

我和同屋每天都上网看新闻或者发电子邮件。我们欢迎大家来我们宿舍玩儿。

43

词语表 Vocabulary

1.	住	zhù	V	to live
2.	英语（英文）	Yīngyǔ (Yīngwén)	N	English (language)
3.	名字	míngzi	N	name
4.	宿舍	sùshè	N	dormitory
5.	房间	fángjiān	N	room
6.	号	hào	M	number
7.	楼	lóu	N	building
8.	层	céng	M	floor, storey
9.	号码	hàomǎ	N	number
10.	同屋	tóngwū	N	roommate
11.	历史	lìshǐ	N	history
12.	系	xì	N	department
13.	两	liǎng	Nu	two
14.	张	zhāng	M	a measure word for beds, tables, etc.
15.	床	chuáng	N	bed
16.	桌子	zhuōzi	N	table, desk
17.	台	tái	M	a measure word for mechanical devices or machines
18.	电脑	diànnǎo	N	computer
19.	把	bǎ	M	a measure word for objects with handles
20.	椅子	yǐzi	N	chair
21.	衣柜	yīguì	N	wardrobe
22.	还	hái	Adv	also
23.	彩色电视	cǎisè diànshì		colour TV
24.	部	bù	M	a measure word for equipments
25.	每	měi	Pr	every

26.	天	tiān	N	day
27.	上网	shàng wǎng	V//O	to surf the Internet
28.	看	kàn	V	to watch
29.	新闻	xīnwén	N	news
30.	或者	huòzhě	Conj	or
31.	发	fā	V	to send
32.	电子邮件	diànzǐ yóujiàn		email
33.	欢迎	huānyíng	V	to welcome
34.	大家	dàjiā	Pr	everybody
35.	来	lái	V	to come
36.	玩儿	wánr	V	to enjoy oneself

专有名词 Proper Nouns

1.	杨歌	Yáng Gē		name of a person
2.	泰国	Tàiguó		Thailand

补充词语 Complementary Word

	还是	háishi	Conj	or

1 我的房间在一号楼二层。

楼号的表示：~号楼。读的时候，要读出每个数字。例如：

The expression of a building number: ~号楼. The number on each digit must be read. For example,

5 号楼 → wǔ hào lóu   16 号楼 → shíliù hào lóu

2 房间号码是 1234。

房间号的表示：~号房间。房间号的读法和楼号的读法一样。例如：

The expression of a room number: ~号房间. The expression of a room number is the same as that of a building number. For example,

1234号房间 → yāo èr sān sì hào fángjiān　　　3445号房间 → sān sì sì wǔ hào fángjiān

3 我们房间有两张床。

🖊 **辨析 Discrimination：二、两**

"二"与"两"都表示数字"2"，但是在个体名量词和动量词前面一般用"两"，不用"二"。在中国传统度量衡单位前，用"二"或者用"两"都可以。例如：
Both "二" and "两" mean "two". However, "两" instead of "二" is generally used before an individual nominal measure word or a verbal measure word. Both can be used before traditional Chinese weight and measure units. For example,

① 两台电脑　　　　　　　　two computers
② 两本书　　　　　　　　　two books
③ 两杯咖啡　　　　　　　　two cups of coffee
④ 两张照片　　　　　　　　two photos
⑤ 二斤苹果 / 两斤苹果　　　two *jin* of apples

4 还有一台彩色电视。

还：副词，表示数量的增加、范围的扩大，在句中充当状语。例如：
还：It is an adverb used as the adverbial in a sentence to indicate the growth of number or the widening of scope. For example,

① 我们房间有电视，还有空调。　　　There is a TV set and an air conditioner in our room.
② 他有一个哥哥、一个姐姐，还有三个妹妹。
　　He has an elder brother, an elder sister, and three younger sisters.
③ 我们班有日本人、韩国人，还有英国人、西班牙人。
　　There are Japanese, Koreans, Englishmen and Spaniards in our class.

🖊 **辨析 Discrimination：还、也**

副词"还"表示数量、范围、语气等更进一步。例如：
The adverb "还" indicates the growth in number, widening in scope or further emphasis in tone. For example,

④ 我有一个哥哥、一个弟弟，还有三个妹妹。
　　I have an elder brother, a younger brother and three younger sisters.
⑤ 他会说英语、法语，还会说日语、汉语。
　　He can speak English, French, Japanese and Chinese.

⑥ 我的房间有电话、电视，还有电脑。
There is a telephone, a TV set and a computer in my room.

副词 "也" 表示和前面的句子并列。例如：
The clause with the adverb "也" coordinates with the previous clause. For example,

⑦ 我有哥哥，也有弟弟。 I have an elder brother and a younger brother.
⑧ 他住留学生宿舍，我也住留学生宿舍。
He lives in international student dormitory. So do I.
⑨ 他会说英语，也会说法语。 He can speak English and French.
⑩ 我的房间有电视，也有电话。 There is a TV set and a telephone in my room.

5 电话号码是 76543210。

电话号码的表示：读的时候，要读出每位数字。例如：
The expression of a telephone number: The number on each digit must be read. For example,
0086-10-58808101 → líng líng bā liù yāo líng wǔ bā bā líng bā yāo líng yāo

注意：为了避免 "1（yī）" 和 "7（qī）" 的误听，在读房间号码、电话号码时，常常将 "1" 读做 "yāo"。例如：

Note: To avoid arousing confusion between the pronunciation of "1（yī）" and "7（qī）", "1" is often read yāo when people pronounce a room number or telephone number. For example，

1234 号房间 → yāo èr sān sì hào fángjiān

6 我和同屋每天都上网看新闻或者发电子邮件。

辨析 Discrimination：或者、还是

连词 "或者" 表示选择，用在陈述句里。例如：
The conjunction "或者" is used to indicate an alternative in a declarative sentence. For example,

① 我和同屋每天都上网看新闻或者发电子邮件。
My roommate and I surf the Internet to read news or send emails every day.
② 我下午或者晚上去买东西。 I will go shopping in the afternoon or in the evening.
③ 他的房间是 1234 号或者 1235 号。 His room number is either 1234 or 1235.

连词 "还是" 表示选择，用在疑问句里。例如：
The conjunction "还是" is used to indicate an alternative in a question. For example,

④ 今天有听力课还是明天有听力课？ Will you have a listening class today or tomorrow?

⑤ 你在一班还是在二班？ Are you in Class One or Class Two?
⑥ 你住一号楼二层还是一号楼三层？
Do you live on the second floor or the third floor of Building One?

7 用"谁的"提问的疑问句

The question using "谁的"

询问某物归谁所有。如"这是谁的电脑"，意思是问这台电脑归谁所有。"谁"一般读 shéi，有时也读 shuí。例如：

It is used to enquire the owner. For example, "这是谁的电脑" is used to ask whom this computer belongs to. "谁" is usually read shéi and sometimes read shuí. For example,

① 这是谁的宿舍？   Whose dormitory is this?
② 那是谁的椅子？   Whose chair is that?
③ 他是谁的同屋？   Whose roommate is he?

语音基础知识（6）
Basics on Chinese phonetics（6）

声母 Initials

zh　ch　sh　r　z　c　s

zh ［tʂ］舌尖翘起，接触上颚前端，然后稍微放松，留出一条窄缝，气流从窄缝中摩擦出来。
例如：
Hold up the tip of the tongue against the front part of the upper jaw, then release slightly to let the air out of the narrow passage and pronounce a fricative. For example,
　　zhǐ（纸）　　zhāng（张）　　zhīdao（知道）　　zhēnzhèng（真正）

ch ［tʂ'］发音方法和 zh 相同，只是气流较强。例如：
ch has the same pronunciation as that of zh except the air released is relatively stronger. For example,
　　chī（吃）　　cháng（长）　　zìxíngchē（自行车）　　chuānghu（窗户）

sh ［ʂ］舌尖翘起，接近上颚前端，留一条窄缝，气流从窄缝中摩擦出来。例如：
Hold up the tip of the tongue toward the front part of the upper jaw, then let the air out of the narrow passage and pronounce a fricative. For example,
　　shì（是）　　shǎo（少）　　lǎoshī（老师）　　shàng kè（上课）

r ［ʐ］发音方法与 sh 相同，但是发音时声带颤动。例如：
r has the same pronunciation as that of sh except the vocal cords vibrate when you pronounce r. For example,
　　rè（热）　　ràng（让）　　Rìběn（日本）　　rúguǒ（如果）

z ［ts］舌尖接触下齿背，然后稍微放松，留出一条窄缝，气流摩擦出来。例如：
Press the tip of the tongue against the back of the lower teeth, then release slightly to let the air out of the narrow passage and pronounce a fricative. For example,
　　zuò（坐）　　zuì（最）　　zǎoshang（早上）　　zuótiān（昨天）

c ［ts'］发音方法与 z 相同，只是气流比较强。例如：
c has the same pronunciation as that of z except the air released is relatively stronger. For example,
　　cí（词）　　cǎo（草）　　cāntīng（餐厅）　　yí cì（一次）

s ［s］舌尖接近下门齿背，气流从中间的窄缝摩擦出来。例如：
Draw the tip of the tongue toward the back of the lower teeth, then squeeze the air through the narrow passage. For example,
　　sì（四）　　sǎn（伞）　　sàn bù（散步）　　yánsè（颜色）

汉字基础知识（6）
Basics on Chinese characters(6)

汉字的笔画搭配方式
Modes of stroke collocation

汉字的笔画搭配方式有三种，见下表：
There are three modes of stroke collocation as follows:

笔画搭配方式 Modes of stroke collocation	例 字 Examples
相交 （xiāng jiāo） Crossing	十
相接 （xiāng jiē） Connecting	工
相离 （xiāng lí） Separating	八

50

7 你同屋是哪国人
Which country does your roommate come from

课文 Text

山下的同屋是法国人，叫南希。南希二十一岁，她爸爸是法国人，妈妈是德国人。南希会说法语、德语，也会说英语、西班牙语，还会说汉语。

南希是教育学院教育技术专业的研究生。她的汉语很好，她经常帮助山下学习汉语。南希不会说日语，她和山下在房间说汉语或者英语。

南希喜欢听音乐，山下喜欢看电影。周末她们常常一起去游览北京的名胜古迹。她们俩是好朋友。

她们住留学生第三公寓。她们房间有电话、电视，

51

hái yǒu kōng tiáo　 dōng tiān bù lěng　 xià tiān bú rè　 fáng zū yě bú guì　 měi rén měi tiān bā
还有空调。冬天不冷，夏天不热，房租也不贵，每人每天八
měi yuán　 tā men hěn mǎn yì
美元。她们很满意。

词语表 Vocabulary

1.	哪	nǎ/něi	Pr	which
2.	岁	suì	M	year (of age)
3.	会	huì	OpV	can, to be able to
4.	说	shuō	V	to speak
5.	法语（法文）	Fǎyǔ (Fǎwén)	N	French (language)
6.	德语（德文）	Déyǔ (Déwén)	N	German (language)
7.	西班牙语（西班牙文）	Xībānyáyǔ (Xībānyáwén)	N	Spanish (language)
8.	教育	jiàoyù	N	education
9.	学院	xuéyuàn	N	college, institute, academy
10.	技术	jìshù	N	technology
11.	专业	zhuānyè	N	major, speciality
12.	研究生	yánjiūshēng	N	postgraduate
13.	经常	jīngcháng	Adv	often
14.	帮助	bāngzhù	V	to help
15.	日语（日文）	Rìyǔ (Rìwén)	N	Japanese (language)
16.	喜欢	xǐhuan	V	to like
17.	听	tīng	V	to listen to
18.	电影	diànyǐng	N	movie, film
19.	周末	zhōumò	N	weekend
20.	一起	yìqǐ	Adv	together

21.	游览	yóulǎn	V	to visit, to go sightseeing
22.	名胜古迹	míngshèng gǔjì		place of historic interest and scenic beauty
23.	俩	liǎ	Q	two
24.	朋友	péngyou	N	friend
25.	公寓	gōngyù	N	apartment
26.	空调	kōngtiáo	N	air conditioner
27.	冬天	dōngtiān	N	winter
28.	冷	lěng	Adj	cold
29.	夏天	xiàtiān	N	summer
30.	热	rè	Adj	hot
31.	房租	fángzū	N	house rent
32.	贵	guì	Adj	expensive
33.	美元	měiyuán	N	US dollar
34.	满意	mǎnyì	Adj	satisfied

专有名词　Proper Nouns

1.	法国	Fǎguó	France
2.	南希	Nánxī	name of a person
3.	德国	Déguó	Germany

1 你同屋是哪国人？

用"哪"提问的疑问句：要求在几个同类事物或人中确定一个，格式是："哪" + 量词、"哪" + 数词 + 量词。"哪"口语常常读 něi。例如：

The question using "哪": It is used to specify one thing (or one person) of the same category. The pattern is: "哪" + measure word / "哪" + numeral + measure word. It is often read něi in spoken Chinese. For example,

① 你是哪国人？　　　　　　　Which country do you come from?
② 你在哪个班？　　　　　　　Which class are you in?
③ 你们班教室在哪个楼？　　　Which building is your classroom in?
④ 哪位老师是精读课老师？　　Who teaches you intensive reading course?

2 南希二十一岁。

名词谓语句：由名词或者名词性短语充当谓语中心词的句子是名词谓语句。名词谓语句一般用来表示时间、年龄等。例如：

The sentence with a nominal predicate: A sentence in which the main word in the predicate is a noun or a noun phrase is known as a sentence with a nominal predicate. It is usually used to indicate time or age, etc. For example,

① 南希今年21岁。　　　　　Nancy is 21 years old this year.
② 我弟弟18岁。　　　　　　My younger brother is 18 years old.
③ 今天星期五。　　　　　　　Today is Friday.

3 南希二十一岁。

询问年龄：用"你几岁了"或者"你多大了"问小孩或者年龄比较小的人的年龄。用"您多大年纪了"或者"您多大岁数了"问老人或年纪比较大的人的年龄。

To enquire one's age: "你几岁了" or "你多大了" is used to enquire the age of a child or a young person. While "您多大年纪了" or "您多大岁数了" is used to enquire the age of an old person.

4 南希会说法语、德语。

"会"+动词：表示经过学习掌握了一门技术。例如：

"会"+verb: It indicates having mastered a skill through learning. For example,

① 南希会说汉语。　　　　　Nancy can speak Chinese.
② 他会开车。　　　　　　　He can drive.
③ 我会发电子邮件。　　　　I can send an email.

5 她经常帮助山下学习汉语。/周末她们常常一起去游览北京的名胜古迹。

辨析 Discrimination：经常、常常

"经常"和"常常"都表示动作的频率，但是"经常"比"常常"的频率高。例如：
Both "经常" and "常常" indicate the frequency of action, but "经常" is more commonly used than "常常". For example,

① 她经常帮助山下学习汉语。　　She often helps Yamashita to study Chinese.
② 她经常给妈妈打电话。　　　　She often calls her mother.
③ 他经常迟到。　　　　　　　　He is often late.
④ 她常常去上海。　　　　　　　She often goes to Shanghai.
⑤ 我常常感冒。　　　　　　　　I often catch a cold.
⑥ 他常常去中国朋友家。　　　　He often goes to the home of his Chinese friend.

6 南希喜欢听音乐，山下喜欢看电影。

"喜欢" + 动词：表示一种爱好或喜爱。例如：

"喜欢" +verb: It is used to express one's hobby or fondness. For example,

① 山下喜欢游览名胜古迹。　　Yamashita likes visiting places of historical interests.
② 乔治喜欢踢足球。　　　　　George likes playing football.
③ 她喜欢唱歌。　　　　　　　She likes singing.

7 她们俩是好朋友。

俩：数量词，表示两个，用在表示人的名词、代词后。例如：

俩：The quantifier "俩" means "two", which is used after a noun or pronoun indicating somebody. For example,

① 姐妹俩　　elder sister and younger sister
② 夫妇俩　　husband and wife
③ 我们俩　　we two
④ 他们俩　　they two

语音基础知识（7）
Basics on Chinese phonetics（7）

第三声的变调
The third tone sandhi

第三声的本调是降升调型，先降后升（调值为214）。但实际说汉语时，第三声念降升调的时候很少，常常念它的变调。第三声的变调规律是：

The original third tone is a falling-and-rising tone（the tone pitch is 214）, but in spoken Chinese the falling-and-rising tone is seldom used. In most cases, it is read in its variant tone. The rules of the changes of the third tone are as follows:

（1）第三声 + 第三声 ——→ 第二声 + 第三声

the 3rd tone + the 3rd tone ——→ the 2nd tone + the 3rd tone

yǒngyuǎn（永远）　　hěn hǎo（很好）　　hǎojiǔ（好久）　　wǒ jiějie（我姐姐）

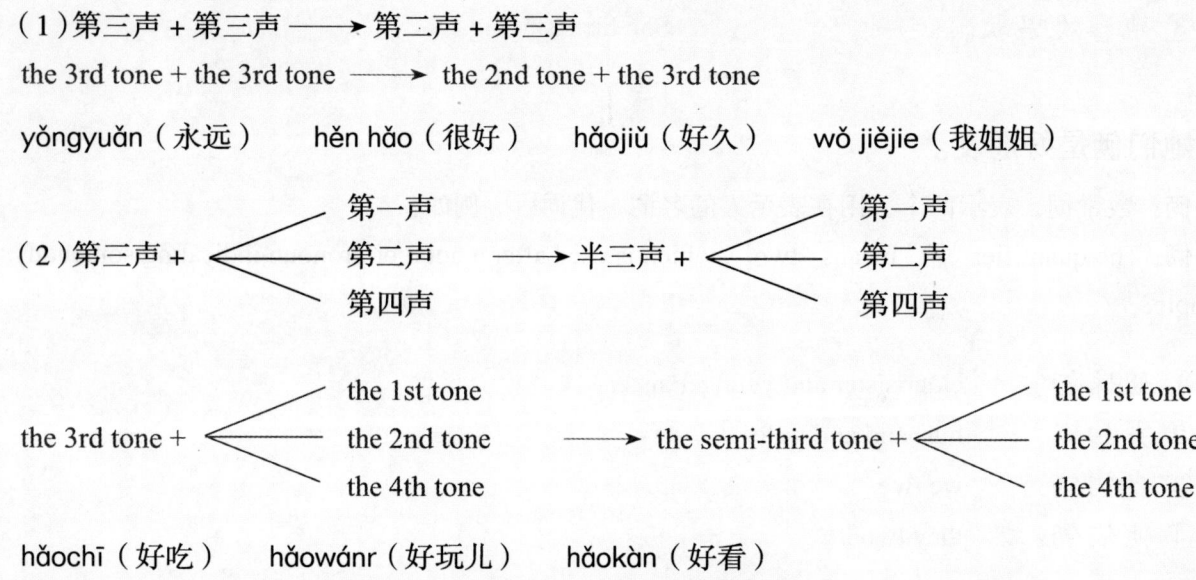

hǎochī（好吃）　　hǎowánr（好玩儿）　　hǎokàn（好看）

在写拼音时，仍然写第三声的声调符号，如上面例子中的拼音。

When writing *pinyin*, the tone mark of the third tone is still used. Refer to the *pinyin* above.

汉字基础知识（7）
Basics on Chinese characters (7)

汉字的结构
The structures of Chinese characters

汉字是由偏旁（部件）按一定的方式组成的。汉字的构成方式就是汉字的结构。汉字主要有三种结构方式：

Chinese characters are made up of radicals (components) following certain rules. The ways in which they are constructed are the structures of characters. Chinese characters are mainly constructed in the following three ways:

笔画名称 Strokes	例 字 Examples
左右结构（zuǒ yòu jiégòu） left-right structure	明　语　谢　树
上下结构（shàng xià jiégòu） top-bottom structure	学　字　意　些
内外结构（nèi wài jiégòu） inside-outside structure	国　这　问　句

左右结构的汉字最多，大约有 68% 的汉字是左右结构，而且形旁常常在左边。例如："河"、"请"、"忙"、"狗"。上下结构的汉字有 20%，形旁常常在上边。

The majority of Chinese characters are of the left-right structure. They make up about 68% of all the characters, in which the semantic radicals are often on the left, such as "河", "请", "忙" and "狗". Characters of the top-bottom structure make up about 20% of all the characters, in which the semantic radicals are often on the top.

8 现在几点
What time is it

课文 Text

我现在是留学生。我的一天从早上 7:00 开始。我每天 7:00 起床，7:25 吃早饭，7:45 去教室

上课。我们 8:00 上课，11:30 下课。下课以后，我常去留学生食堂吃午饭。下午我有时候在宿舍做作业，复习、预习课文，有时候去商店买东西。晚上 7:00

吃晚饭。晚饭以后我在房间看电视，或者去图

书馆看报纸。10:00 我去操场跑步，11:30 洗澡，12:00 睡觉。

我从星期一到星期五每天上午都有四节课,下午没有课,星期六、星期天我也没有课。我们一个星期有六节精读课,六节会话课,六节听力课。我们的课比较多,但是很有意思。我喜欢上汉语课,我喜欢学习汉语。

词语表 Vocabulary

1.	点	diǎn	M	o'clock, hour
2.	早上	zǎoshang	N	morning
3.	开始	kāishǐ	V	to start, to begin
4.	起床	qǐ chuáng	V//O	to get up
5.	吃	chī	V	to eat
6.	早饭	zǎofàn	N	breakfast
7.	下课	xià kè	V//O	to dismiss class
8.	以后	yǐhòu	N	after
9.	常	cháng	Adv	often
10.	食堂	shítáng	N	canteen
11.	午饭	wǔfàn	N	lunch
12.	下午	xiàwǔ	N	afternoon
13.	有时候	yǒushíhou	Adv	sometimes
14.	复习	fùxí	V	to review, to go over
15.	预习	yùxí	V	to preview
16.	商店	shāngdiàn	N	shop, store
17.	买	mǎi	V	to buy
18.	东西	dōngxi	N	thing, stuff

19.	晚饭	wǎnfàn	N	supper, dinner
20.	图书馆	túshūguǎn	N	library
21.	报纸	bàozhǐ	N	newspaper
22.	操场	cāochǎng	N	sports ground
23.	跑步	pǎo bù	V//O	to run, to jog
24.	洗澡	xǐ zǎo	V//O	to have a shower, to take a bath
25.	睡觉	shuì jiào	V//O	to go to bed
26.	从……到……	cóng……dào……		from…to…
27.	星期	xīngqī	N	week, day of the week
28.	节	jié	M	*a measure word for classes*
29.	会话	huìhuà	N	conversation
30.	听力	tīnglì	N	listening comprehension (in language acquisition)
31.	比较	bǐjiào	Adv	relatively, comparatively
32.	但是	dànshì	Conj	but, however
33.	有意思	yǒu yìsi		interesting

补充词语 **Complementary Words**

1.	上午	shàngwǔ	N	morning
2.	分	fēn	M	minute
3.	半	bàn	Nu	half
4.	月	yuè	N	month
5.	日	rì	N	day

注释 Notes

1 我的一天从早上 7:00 开始。

钟点的读法：

Reading a specified time:

（1）整点：~点/点钟。例如：

Hour: "~点/点钟". For example,

8:00 → 八点 / 八点钟

12:00 → 十二点

14:00 → 十四点 / 下午两点

20:00 → 二十点 / 晚上八点

（2）非整点：~点~分。例如：

Hour and minute: "~点~分". For example,

8:10 → 八点十分 / 八点过十分

8:15 → 八点十五分 / 八点一刻

8:30 → 八点三十分 / 八点半

8:55 → 八点五十五分 / 九点差五分

注意：十分钟以上的钟点，还可以读做：~点~。例如：

Note: When the minute is more than 10, it can also be read "~点~". For example,

8:20 → 八点二十 / 八点二十分

8:40 → 八点四十 / 八点四十分

2 我每天 7:00 起床。

时间状语：由表示时间的词语充当的状语叫时间状语。时间状语可以放在主语后，也可以放在主语前。例如：

The adverbial of time: An adverbial formed by a time word is known as the adverbial of time. It can be placed before or after the subject. For example,

① 我们［8:00］上课。　　　　Our lecture will begin at 8 o'clock.

②［今天下午］我有课。　　　　I will have classes this afternoon.

③ 爸爸［星期六］来北京。　　　My father will come to Beijing on Saturday.

3 下课以后，我常去留学生食堂吃午饭。

以后：名词，常常出现在名词或动词性词语后面，表示时间。例如：

以后：It is a noun and often appears after a noun or a verbal phrase to indicate time. For example,

① 午饭以后　　　　　after lunch
② 起床以后　　　　　after getting up
③ 来中国以后　　　　after coming to China

4 下午我有时候在宿舍做作业，复习、预习课文，有时候去商店买东西。

有时候……有时候……：两个"有时候"常常连用，放在动词前面，表示两种情况。如果两个动作是一个主语发出的，主语在"有时候"前面，只用一个主语；如果两个动作不是一个主语发出的，两个主语分别放在"有时候"后面。例如：

有时候……有时候……：Sometimes "有时候" is used one after another, preceding a verb to indicate two situations. If the two actions are performed by the same subject which is used before "有时候", only one subject is used; if the two actions are not performed by the same subject, then the two subjects are used after "有时候" respectively. For example,

① 晚上**我**有时候去饭馆吃晚饭，有时候在留学生食堂吃晚饭。
Sometimes **I** have supper at the restaurant in the evening, and sometimes at the international students' canteen.

② 他有时候说英语，有时候说德语。
He sometimes speaks English, and sometimes speaks German.

③ 有时候**我**请他吃饭，有时候**他**请我吃饭。
Sometimes **I** invite him to dinner; sometimes **he** invites me.

④ 有时候**我**给朋友打电话，有时候**朋友**给我打电话。
Sometimes **I** call my friend; sometimes **my friend** calls me.

5 我从星期一到星期五每天上午都有四节课。

从……到……（表时间）：介词短语，表示一段时间的起点和终点。例如：

从……到……（indicating time）：It is a prepositional phrase, indicating the length of a period of time from the beginning to the end. For example,

① 今天我们从 8：00 到 9：30 上会话课。
Today we have the speaking course from 8: 00 to 9: 30.

② 妹妹从 6 岁到 12 岁在美国生活。
My younger sister lived in the U.S. from the age of 6 to 12.

6 我们的课比较多。

比较：副词，常用在形容词前面，可以表示程度高于一般水平。例如：

比较: It is an adverb often used before an adjective to indicate a degree higher than normal. For example,

① 爸爸比较忙。　　　　My father is rather busy.
② 他的房间比较大。　　His room is quite big.

7 时间的顺序
Time sequence

汉语表示时间的顺序是从大到小：～年～月～日（号）～时。例如：

Time is expressed in descending order in Chinese, i.e., "～年～月～日（号）～时". For example,

① 2010 年 9 月 8 日 10 点 / 2010 年 9 月 8 日上午 10 点
10 o'clock September 8, 2010 / 10 a.m. September 8, 2010

② 2011 年 12 月 15 日 20 点 / 2011 年 12 月 15 日晚上 8 点
20 o'clock December 15, 2011 / 8 p.m. December 15, 2011

语音基础知识（8）
Basics on Chinese phonetics（8）

 "一"的变调 The tone sandhi of "一"

"一"的本调是第一声，读数字的时候，念本调，例如：21 → èrshíyī；读年代也念本调，例如：1998 年 → yī jiǔ jiǔ bā nián。

The original tone of "一" is the first tone. It is pronounced in its original tone in a number. For example, "21" is pronounced èrshíyī; and the year "1998 年" is pronounced yī jiǔ jiǔ bā nián.

"一"的变调有两种：
The pronunciation of "一" has two variants：

（1）"一"在第一声、第二声、第三声的汉字前面读第四声。例如：
"一" is pronounced in the fourth tone before a character with a first-tone, second-tone or third-tone syllable. For example,

  yì bēi kāfēi（一杯咖啡） yì píng píjiǔ（一瓶啤酒） yì bǎ yǐzi（一把椅子）

（2）"一"在第四声的汉字前面读第二声。例如：
"一" is pronounced in the second tone before a character with a fourth-tone syllable. For example,

  yí liàng qìchē（一辆汽车） yí wèi lǎoshī（一位老师）

另外，"一"在两个相同的单音节动词中间读轻声。例如：
"一" is pronounced in the neutral tone when it is used between two identical monosyllabic verb. For example,

  kàn yi kàn（看一看） dú yi dú（读一读） tīng yi tīng（听一听）

 "不"的变调 The tone sandhi of "不"

"不"的本调是第四声，"不"在第四声的汉字前面要读第二声。例如：
The original tone of "不" is the fourth tone, but it is pronounced in the second tone when used before a character with a fourth-tone syllable. For example,

  bú qù（不去） búyào（不要） búcuò（不错）

"不"在两个相同的词中间时，读轻声。例如：
"不" is pronounced in the neutral tone when it is used between two identical words. For example,

  hǎo bu hǎo（好不好） qù bu qù（去不去）

汉字基础知识（8）
Basics on Chinese characters（8）

常用形旁（部首）（1）
Commonly used semantic radicals (components) (1)

形旁表示汉字的意义类别。了解汉字的形旁意义类别，对学习汉字很有帮助。常用汉字的常用形旁有21个，我们先学习10个。

The semantic radical denotes the category of a character's meaning; therefore, understanding the category of the semantic radical will help us to learn Chinese characters. There are 21 commonly used semantic radicals, 10 of which will be introduced first.

序号 No.	形 旁 Semantic radicals	名 称 Names	例 字 Examples	意 义 Meanings
1	扌	提手旁（tíshǒupáng）	打 抄 找	跟手有关 Related to one's hand
2	亻	单人旁（dānrénpáng）	你 他 们	跟人有关 Related to a person
3	氵	三点水（sāndiǎnshuǐ）	江 河 汤	跟水有关 Related to water
4	木	木字旁（mùzìpáng）	椅 树 桌	跟树有关 Related to a tree
5	忄、心	心字旁（xīnzìpáng）	忙 快 想	跟心理活动有关 Related to one's psychological activities
6	口	口字旁（kǒuzìpáng）	吃 喝 唱	跟嘴巴有关 Related to one's mouth
7	艹	草字头（cǎozìtóu）	草 茶 花	跟草有关 Related to grass
8	纟	绞丝旁（jiǎosīpáng）	红 绿 纸	跟丝有关 Related to silk
9	讠	言字旁（yánzìpáng）	说 话 语	跟说话有关 Related to speech
10	月	月字旁（yuèzìpáng）	期 肚 胖	"月"在右边跟月亮（时间）有关；"月"在左边跟身体有关 Related to the moon when used on the right side and related to body when used on the left side

65

你的爱好是什么
What are your hobbies

我叫珍妮，是美国留学生。山下和乔治是我的同班同学。我的爱好是听音乐和弹钢琴。我喜欢听欧洲古典音乐，也喜欢听现代流行音乐。来中国以后，我特别喜欢听中国民族音乐。我有不少音乐光盘，欢迎来我的房间听音乐。

山下的爱好是看电影和游泳。她特别喜欢看美国电影，她知道不少美国电影演员的名字和故事。

乔治的爱好是打篮球和上网。来中国以前，他是大学篮球队队

员。乔治的电子邮件地址是duibudui@hanyu.cn，很容易记住。

我们都很喜欢山下的同屋南希。南希很聪明，也很漂亮。她懂很多种外语，和她聊天儿很有意思。我觉得在北京的留学生活很愉快。

词语表 Vocabulary

1.	爱好	àihào	N	hobby
2.	什么	shénme	Pr	what
3.	同班	tóng bān	V//O	to be in the same class
	同	tóng	Adj	same
4.	弹	tán	V	to play (a musical instrument)
5.	钢琴	gāngqín	N	piano
6.	古典	gǔdiǎn	Adj	classical
7.	现代	xiàndài	N	modern times
8.	流行	liúxíng	V	to be popular
9.	特别	tèbié	Adv	especially
10.	民族	mínzú	N	folk
11.	光盘	guāngpán	N	CD
12.	游泳	yóuyǒng	V	to swim
13.	知道	zhīdao	V	to know
14.	演员	yǎnyuán	N	actor or actress
15.	故事	gùshi	N	story
16.	篮球	lánqiú	N	basketball
17.	以前	yǐqián	N	before
18.	队	duì	N	team

67

19.	队员	duìyuán	N	team member
	员	yuán	Suf	member
20.	地址	dìzhǐ	N	address
21.	容易	róngyì	Adj	easy
22.	记住	jìzhù	V	to remember
23.	聪明	cōngming	Adj	intelligent, clever
24.	漂亮	piàoliang	Adj	beautiful
25.	懂	dǒng	V	to know
26.	种	zhǒng	M	kind, type
27.	外语	wàiyǔ	N	foreign language
28.	和	hé	Prep	with
29.	聊天儿	liáo tiānr	V//O	to chat
30.	觉得	juéde	V	to think, to feel
31.	留学	liú xué	V//O	to study abroad
32.	生活	shēnghuó	N	life
33.	愉快	yúkuài	Adj	happy

专有名词　Proper Noun

欧洲	Ōuzhōu		Europe

1 你的爱好是**什么**?

用"什么"提问的疑问句：常常用来询问事物。例如：

The question using "什么": It is often used to enquire things. For example,

① 这是什么?　　What is this?
② 那是什么?　　What is that?

"什么+名词"可以用来询问事物的种类。例如：
"什么+ noun" is used to enquire which category something belongs to. For example,

③ 你有什么爱好？　　　　　What are your hobbies?
④ 明天我们有什么课？　　　What lessons will we have tomorrow?
⑤ 你买什么菜？　　　　　　What vegetable will you buy?

2　来中国**以后**，我特别喜欢听中国民族音乐。/ 来中国**以前**，他是大学篮球队队员。

以前、以后：名词，可以单独使用，也可以受定语修饰，表示一段具体时间。例如：

"以前" and "以后"：They are nouns used on their own or be modified by an attribute, indicating a specific duration. For example,

① 妈妈以前很忙。　　　　　My mother was very busy.
② 现在他学习汉语，以后他要在中国工作。
　　　He is studying Chinese now, and he will go to work in China in the future.
③ 下课以后　　　　　　　　after class
④ 晚饭以后　　　　　　　　after supper
⑤ 睡觉以前　　　　　　　　before going to bed

3　我**特别**喜欢听中国民族音乐。

特别：副词，表示不一般，常常用在表示心理活动的动词前面，充当状语。例如：

特别：It is an adverb meaning "especially". It is often used as an adverbial before the verb expressing psychological activities. For example,

① 她特别喜欢看美国电影。　　She likes seeing American films very much.
② 他的房间特别干净。　　　　His room is extremely clean.
③ 她同屋的汉语特别好。　　　Her roommate speaks Chinese very well.

4　我**觉得**在北京的留学生活很愉快。

觉得：动词，表示自己的一种感觉、感受或者想法。它的宾语可以是一个主谓短语。例如：

觉得：It is a verb used to express one's feeling or idea. A subject-predicate phrase can be used as its object. For example,

① 我觉得很累。　　　　　　　I feel very tired.
② 我觉得在北京生活很有意思。　I feel living in Beijing is very interesting.
③ 我觉得他不是留学生。　　　I don't think he is an international student.

69

语音基础知识（9）
Basics on Chinese phonetics (9)

轻声和儿化
The neutral tone and retroflex ending

轻声和儿化都是一种变调现象。
The neutral tone and retroflex ending are regarded as tone sandhi.

（1）轻声就是汉字失去原有的声调，读得又短又轻。第一声、第二声、第四声后面的轻声调值很低，第三声后面的调值高一点。写拼音时不标声调。例如：
The neutral tone is pronounced short and light if a Chinese character loses its original tone. The pitch of the neutral tone used after the first, second and fourth tone is very low, while the pitch after the third tone is a little bit higher. No tone mark is used in *pinyin* for the neutral tone. For example,

māma（妈妈）　　zhuōzi（桌子）　　yéye（爷爷）　　xiézi（鞋子）
nǎinai（奶奶）　　yǐzi（椅子）　　bàba（爸爸）　　kùzi（裤子）

（2）儿化就是后缀"儿"与前面一个音节的韵母融合在一起，使这个韵母带有卷舌色彩。写拼音时，在前一个音节后面加 r。例如：
If the suffix "儿" combines with the final of the preceding syllable and makes the final retroflexed, it is known as the retroflex ending. r is added after the *pinyin* of the preceding syllable. For example,

huār（花儿）　　cǎor（草儿）　　pír（皮儿）　　huàr（画儿）

汉字基础知识（9）
Basics on Chinese characters（9）

常用形旁（部首）（2）
Commonly used semantic radicals (components) (2)

序号 No.	形 旁 Semantic radicals	名 称 Names	例 字 Examples	意 义 Meanings
11	扌	提土旁（títǔpáng）	地 城 场	跟土有关　Related to soil
12	辶	走之儿（zǒuzhīr）	迎 进 远	跟走路有关　Related to walking
13	日	日字旁（rìzìpáng）	时 昨 早	跟太阳、时间有关 Related to the sun or time
14	宀	宝盖头（bǎogàitóu）	家 室 安	跟房屋有关　Related to a house
15	衤	衣字旁（yīzìpáng）	裤 衫 袜	跟衣服有关　Related to clothes
16	刂	立刀旁（lìdāopáng）	刻 别 列	跟刀有关　Related to a knife
17	火	火字旁（huǒzìpáng）	灯 炒 烟	跟火有关　Related to fire
18	钅	金字旁（jīnzìpáng）	钱 银 钟	跟金属有关　Related to metal
19	女	女字旁（nǚzìpáng）	妈 她 妻	跟女性有关　Related to female
20	贝	贝字旁（bèizìpáng）	贵 贫 费	跟钱有关　Related to money
21	目	目字旁（mùzìpáng）	看 睡 眼	跟眼睛有关　Related to one's eyes

10

zhōng guó yǒu duō shao rén
中国有多少人
What is the population of China

课文 Text

中国有五千年历史，是一个文明古国。中国在亚洲东部，有960万平方公里土地。北京是中国的首都。中国有13亿人，56个民族，92%的中国人是汉族。汉族人黑头发，黄皮肤，说汉语。

汉语用汉字记录。汉语有四个声调。许多外国朋友觉得说汉语像唱歌，写汉字像画画儿。学习汉语挺有意思的。

标准汉语是普通话，中国的广播、电视都用普通话。大多数中国人都会说普通话，很多中国人还会

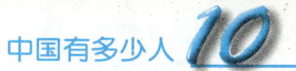

shuō fāng yán　　bǐ rú guǎng dōng huà　shàng hǎi huà děng
说方言，比如广东话、上海话等。

wài guó rén xué xí hàn yǔ　　shì xué xí pǔ tōng huà
外国人学习汉语，是学习普通话。

词语表 Vocabulary

1.	千	qiān	Nu	thousand
2.	文明	wénmíng	Adj	civilization
3.	古国	gǔ guó		country with a long history
4.	东部	dōngbù	N	east
5.	万	wàn	Nu	ten thousand
6.	平方	píngfāng	M	square
7.	公里	gōnglǐ	M	kilometer
8.	土地	tǔdì	N	land
9.	首都	shǒudū	N	capital
10.	亿	yì	Nu	100 million
11.	汉族	Hànzú	N	Han ethnic group
12.	黑	hēi	Adj	black
13.	头发	tóufa	N	hair
14.	黄	huáng	Adj	yellow
15.	皮肤	pífū	N	skin
16.	记录	jìlù	V	to record
17.	声调	shēngdiào	N	the pitch of a syllable in speaking
18.	许多	xǔduō	Nu	many
19.	像	xiàng	V	to be like
20.	唱	chàng	V	to sing
21.	歌	gē	N	song
22.	写	xiě	V	to write

73

23.	画	huà	V	to paint, to draw
24.	画儿	huàr	N	painting
25.	挺	tǐng	Adv	very, quite
26.	标准	biāozhǔn	Adj	standard
27.	普通话	pǔtōnghuà	N	Mandarin Chinese, standard Chinese pronunciation
28.	广播	guǎngbō	N	broadcast
29.	多数	duōshù	N	majority
30.	方言	fāngyán	N	dialect
31.	比如	bǐrú	V	to give an example
32.	话	huà	N	language
33.	等	děng	Pt	etc., and so on

专有名词 Proper Nouns

1.	亚洲	Yàzhōu	Asia
2.	广东	Guǎngdōng	a province in South China
3.	上海	Shànghǎi	the most populous city of China

注释 Notes

1 有960万平方公里土地。

100 以上的称数法：汉语基数是十进制，单位有"个"、"十"、"百"、"千"、"万"、"亿"。称说100以上数字的方法是：

A number more than 100: Chinese uses the decimal system in its numeration; the units including "个"、"十"、"百"、"千"、"万" and "亿". The ways to refer to a number more than 100 are as follows:

（1）"万"以下的数字以"百"、"千"、"万"为单位，读法是：数字＋单位。例如：

For a number less than "万", the units of "百"、"千" and "万" are pronounced, i.e., number + unit. For example,

562 → 五百六十二

74

5642 → 五千六百四十二

56789 → 五万六千七百八十九

（2）最后一个单位可以省略不读（数字中间没有0）。例如：

The last unit can be omitted when reading a number (when without a zero in the middle of the number). For example,

350 → 三百五十 / 三百五

3500 → 三千五百 / 三千五

35000 → 三万五千 / 三万五

（3）"万"以上的数字，以"万"为单位。例如：

For a number more than "万", the unit of "万" is used. For example,

350000 → 三十五万

9600000 → 九百六十万

12000000 → 一千二百万

（4）数字中间无论有几个0，都只读一个0。例如：

No matter how many zeroes used in the middle of a number, only one of them is pronounced. For example,

3050 → 三千零五十   30050 → 三万零五十

3005 → 三千零五   30005 → 三万零五

30500 → 三万零五百

2 92％的中国人是汉族。

百分数的读法："～%"读做"百分之～"（bǎi fēnzhī ～）。例如：

Reading a percentage: "～%" is read "百分之～". For example,

80％ → 百分之八十   98％ → 百分之九十八

3 写汉字像画画儿。

像：动词，表示两个事物相似。例如：

像：It is a verb meaning two things are similar. For example,

① 说汉语像唱歌。   Speaking Chinese is like singing a song.

② 他像他爸爸。   He resembles his father.

③ 他的书包像我的书包。   His schoolbag looks like mine.

4 学习汉语挺有意思的。

挺……的：表示程度较高。"挺"和"的"中间常常用形容词。例如：

挺……的：It indicates a relatively high degree. An adjective is often used between "挺" and "的". For example,

① 今天的作业挺容易的。　　My homework for today is quite easy.
② 他的发音挺好的。　　　　He pronounces it very well.
③ 妈妈工作挺忙的。　　　　My mother is very busy with her work.

5 很多中国人还会说方言，比如广东话、上海话等。

比如：动词，用在举例的词语前面。例如：

比如：It is a verb used before listing examples. For example,

① 他的宿舍有不少电器，比如电视、电脑等。
　　There are many electrical equipments in his dormitory, such as a TV set, a computer and so on.
② 她的爱好很多，比如看电影、听音乐、唱歌等。
　　She has many hobbies, such as seeing movies, listening to music, singing and so on.

6 比如广东话、上海话等。

等：助词，表示列举未尽，用在列举的事物后面。例如：

等：It is a particle meaning "and so on", used after the things or people listed. For example,

① 他买了词典、本子、笔等。　　He bought an dictionary, notebooks, pens and so on.
② 我们班有韩国人、美国人、法国人等。
　　There are Koreans, Americans, Frenchmen and people from other countries in our class.
③ 我们有精读课、会话课、听力课等。
　　We have intensive reading, speaking, listening and other courses.

语音基础知识（10）
Basics on Chinese phonetics (10)

声韵拼合规律
The rules of combining initials and finals

　　声韵拼合规律指哪类声母可以和哪类韵母相拼为一个音节，哪类声母不可以和哪类韵母相拼为一个音节。附录2的《汉语音节表》清楚地表明了汉语（普通话）的声韵拼合规律。

The rules of combining initials and finals indicate that certain initials can combine with certain finals, but cannot combine with others. *List of Chinese Syllables*, Appendix 2, explicitly demonstrates the rules of combining initials and finals in Mandarin Chinese (*Putonghua*).

汉字基础知识（10）
Basics on Chinese characters (10)

同音字、多音字、形近字
Homophones, polyphones and characters similar in form

 同音字　Homophones

指读音相同，字形、字义不同的汉字。例如：

Homophones refer to characters with the same pronunciation, but different forms and meanings. For example,

shí　十——十个　　　　　gōng　工——工作
　　　石——石头　　　　　　　　公——公司

zài　在——在中国　　　　míng　名——名字
　　　再——再见　　　　　　　　明——明天

 多音字　Polyphones

指一个汉字有两个或两个以上的读音。多音字不同的读音表示不同的意思。多音字在不同的词语中，读音只有一个。例如：

A polyphone refers to a character having two or more pronunciations. The different pronunciations of a polyphone indicate different meanings. However, a polyphone has only one pronunciation in a character. For example,

好　hǎo —— hěn hǎo（很好）　　　觉　jué —— juéde（觉得）
　　hào —— àihào（爱好）　　　　　jiào —— shuì jiào（睡觉）

 形近字　Characters similar in form

指字形相近的汉字。形近字常常是笔画的搭配方式不同。学习的时候要特别注意形近字的笔画。例如：

They refer to characters similar in form. For them, strokes are often written in different ways. Therefore, you need to pay much attention to the strokes of characters similar in form when studying them. For example,

休——体　　　　住——往　　　　几——九
天——夫　　　　午——牛　　　　公——么

单元小结（1~10 课）
Review (Lessons 1~10)

语法项目		例 句
是非疑问句	用"吗"提问	你是留学生吗？
特指疑问句	1. 用"几"提问	你家有几口人？
	2. 用"多少"提问	你们班有多少人？
	3. 用"谁"提问	他是谁？
	4. 用"谁的"提问	这是谁的电脑？
	5. 用"哪儿"提问	你家在哪儿？
	6. 用"哪"提问	你同屋是哪国人？
	7. 用"什么"提问	你的爱好是什么？
常用句型	1. "是"字句（表判断）	我是日本人。
	2. "有"字句（表领有）	我有一个弟弟。
	3. 动词谓语句	我学习汉语。
	4. 形容词谓语句	他很高。
	5. 名词谓语句	今天星期一。
	6. 主谓谓语句	他工作很忙。
	7. 兼语句	朋友请我喝咖啡。
	8. 连动句："去"（＋地点）＋动词	我去商店买东西。

语音知识	22 个声母、36 个韵母、4 个声调、拼写规则、第三声变调、"一、不"的变调、轻声、儿化
汉字知识	笔画名称、笔顺规则、笔画搭配方式、三种结构方式、常用形旁的意义、同音字、多音字、形近字

11 这是咖啡还是可乐
Is this coffee or coke

课文 Text

现在我离开家,一个人在中国留学。每天三顿饭是我生活的重要内容。

我的早饭常常是一杯牛奶、两片面包,或者是面包夹奶酪。但是我常常不吃早饭。

中午我喜欢在留学生餐厅吃午饭。留学生餐厅有很多我喜欢吃的中国菜,也有米饭、面条、包子、饺子,还有蔬菜沙拉、汉堡包、咖喱牛肉饭等。我最爱吃包子和饺子。餐厅还卖茶、可乐、咖啡等饮料。我觉得在这儿吃饭又方便又便宜。晚上我有时候和朋友们一起去小饭馆吃晚饭,有时候自己做晚饭。我做的晚饭很简单,比如面包夹火腿、方便面等。

这是咖啡还是可乐 11

词语表 Vocabulary

1.	咖啡	kāfēi	N	coffee
2.	还是	háishi	Conj	or
3.	可乐	kělè	N	coke
4.	离开	líkāi	V	to leave
5.	顿	dùn	M	*a measure word for meals*
6.	重要	zhòngyào	Adj	important
7.	内容	nèiróng	N	content
8.	杯	bēi	N	cup, glass
9.	牛奶	niúnǎi	N	milk
10.	片	piàn	M	slice
11.	面包	miànbāo	N	bread
12.	夹	jiā	V	to place in between
13.	奶酪	nǎilào	N	cheese
14.	餐厅	cāntīng	N	canteen
15.	菜	cài	N	dish
16.	米饭	mǐfàn	N	rice
17.	面条	miàntiáo	N	noodle
18.	包子	bāozi	N	steamed stuffed bun
19.	饺子	jiǎozi	N	dumpling
20.	蔬菜	shūcài	N	vegetable
21.	沙拉	shālā	N	salad
22.	汉堡包	hànbǎobāo	N	hamburger
23.	咖喱	gālí	N	curry
24.	牛	niú	N	cow
25.	肉	ròu	N	meat
26.	最	zuì	Adv	most
27.	爱	ài	V	to like

81

28.	卖	mài	V	to sell
29.	茶	chá	N	tea
30.	饮料	yǐnliào	N	drink
31.	这儿	zhèr	Pr	here
32.	又……又……	yòu……yòu……		both...and...
33.	方便	fāngbiàn	Adj	convenient
34.	便宜	piányi	Adj	inexpensive
35.	饭馆	fànguǎn	N	restaurant
36.	自己	zìjǐ	Pr	oneself
37.	简单	jiǎndān	Adj	simple
38.	火腿	huǒtuǐ	N	ham
39.	方便面	fāngbiànmiàn	N	fast noodle

注 释 Notes

1 这**是**咖啡**还是**可乐？

（是）……还是……：用于选择疑问句，选择的内容分别放在"是"与"还是"后面。连词"还是"只用在选择疑问句中。例如：

The structure "（是）……还是……": It is used in an alternative question. The alternatives are put after "是" and "还是" respectively. The conjunction "还是" is used only in an alternative question. For example,

① 这是包子还是饺子？　　　　　Is this a steamed stuffed bun or a dumpling?
② 你在一班还是在二班？　　　　Are you in Class One or Class Two?
③ 你喜欢看电影还是喜欢听音乐？　Do you like seeing a movie or listening to music?

2 我**最**爱吃包子和饺子。

最：副词，表示最高程度，用在形容词或者表示心理感受的动词前面。例如：

最：It is an adverb used before an adjective or a verb expressing feeling to indicate the superlative

82

degree. For example,

① 最便宜的菜　　　　　the most inexpensive dish
② 最小的妹妹　　　　　the youngest sister
③ 最好的大学　　　　　the best university
④ 最有意思的事　　　　the most interesting thing
⑤ 最爱吃的菜　　　　　favorite dish
⑥ 最喜欢的歌　　　　　favorite song
⑦ 最喜欢的颜色　　　　favorite color
⑧ 最想的人　　　　　　the person (one) misses the most

3 餐厅还卖茶、可乐、咖啡等饮料。

"等" + 名词：表示列举。"等"前面是列举的事物，后面是表示这一类事物的名词。例如：

"等" + noun: It is used to enumerate things or people. "等" is preceded by the enumerated things and followed by the noun indicating the category. For example,

① 我买了面包、牛奶、火腿等吃的东西。
　　I bought bread, milk, ham and other foods.
② 她会说英语、法语、汉语等外语。
　　She can speak English, French, Chinese and other languages.
③ 我们班有精读、会话、听力等汉语课。
　　We study intensive reading, speaking, listening and other Chinese courses.

4 我觉得在这儿吃饭又方便又便宜。

又……又……：表示几种动作、性质、状况同时存在，"又"后面要用动词、动词性短语或形容词、形容词性短语。例如：

又……又……: It indicates the co-existence of several kinds of actions, qualities or states. "又" can be followed by verbs, verbal phrases, adjectives or adjectival phrases. For example,

① 又说又唱　　　　　　speak and sing
② 又跑步又游泳　　　　jog and swim
③ 又说汉语又说英语　　speak Chinese and English
④ 又好又快　　　　　　well and fast
⑤ 又聪明又漂亮　　　　smart and beautiful

5 我做的晚饭很简单。

主谓短语做定语：定语是一个主谓短语。例如：

The subject-predicate phrase used as an attribute: The attribute is a subject-predicate phrase. For example,

① 这是我爱吃的中国菜。　　　This is my favorite Chinese dish.
② 他写的汉字很好看。　　　　He writes Chinese characters very well.

12 你们要了什么饮料

What would you like to drink

课文 Text

今天是星期五，晚上我和三个朋友一起去学校附近的一家四川饭馆吃饭。这家饭馆比较小，但是菜的味道很好，价格也不贵，所以我们老去那儿吃饭。

我们点了两个凉菜：小葱拌豆腐、糖醋黄瓜，四个热菜：青椒肉丝、炒土豆丝、麻婆豆腐、西红柿炒鸡蛋，要了两瓶啤酒、两瓶果汁、四听可乐，还要了一盘面粉做的点心，没有要汤。我们的主食是饺子，因为大家都爱吃饺子。

今天的饭菜都很好吃，啤酒也很好喝。我们结了账以后还唱了卡拉OK，大家都很高兴，因为明天没有课。

我想明天吃了早饭以后去买音乐光盘。

词语表 Vocabulary

1.	要	yào	V	to order
2.	了	le	AsPt	used after a verb to indicate the completion of an action
3.	附近	fùjìn	N	nearby
4.	味道	wèidao	N	flavor, taste
5.	价格	jiàgé	N	price
6.	所以	suǒyǐ	Conj	so
7.	老	lǎo	Adv	often
8.	那儿	nàr	Pr	there
9.	点	diǎn	V	to order
10.	凉菜	liángcài	N	cold dish
11.	葱	cōng	N	green onion
12.	拌	bàn	V	to mix
13.	豆腐	dòufu	N	bean curd, *tofu*
14.	糖	táng	N	sweet
15.	醋	cù	N	vinegar
16.	黄瓜	huánggua	N	cucumber
17.	热菜	rècài	N	hot dish
18.	青椒	qīngjiāo	N	green pepper
19.	丝	sī	N	shred
20.	炒	chǎo	V	to stir-fry
21.	土豆	tǔdòu	N	potato
22.	麻婆豆腐	mápó dòufu		Mapo Tofu (sauteed *tofu* in hot and spicy sauce)
23.	西红柿	xīhóngshì	N	tomato
24.	鸡蛋	jīdàn	N	egg
25.	瓶	píng	M	bottle

26.	啤酒	píjiǔ	N	beer
27.	果汁	guǒzhī	N	fruit juice
28.	听	tīng	M	can
29.	盘	pán	M	plate
30.	面粉	miànfěn	N	flour
31.	点心	diǎnxin	N	pastry
32.	汤	tāng	N	soup
33.	主食	zhǔshí	N	staple food
34.	因为	yīnwèi	Conj	because
35.	好吃	hǎochī	Adj	(of food) delicious
36.	好喝	hǎohē	Adj	(of drink) tasty
37.	结账	jié zhàng	V//O	to pay the bill
38.	卡拉OK	kǎlā-OK		karaoke
39.	高兴	gāoxìng	Adj	happy
40.	想	xiǎng	OpV	to think, to want

专有名词 Proper Noun

| | 四川 | Sìchuān | | a province in Southwest China |

注释 Notes

1 你们要了什么饮料?

动态助词"了₁":

The aspect particle "了₁":

（1）用在动词后面，表示动作的完成。比较下面的对话：
It is used after a verb to indicate the completion of an action. Compare the following dialogues:

A. 用"了₁"的：

With "了₁":

① A：你们点了什么菜？　　　　What did you order?
　　B：我们点了西红柿炒鸡蛋。　We ordered stir-fried eggs with tomatoes.
　　（动作"点"已经完成　The action "点" was completed.）

② A：你们晚饭吃了什么？　　　What did you eat for supper?
　　B：我们吃了饺子。　　　　We ate dumplings.
　　（动作"吃"已经完成　The action "吃" was completed.）

B. 不用"了₁"的：

Without "了₁":

③ A：你们点什么菜？　　　　　What would you like to order?
　　B：西红柿炒鸡蛋和土豆丝。　Stir-fried eggs with tomatoes and shredded potatoes.
　　（动作"点"还没完成　The action "点" was not completed.）

④ A：你们晚饭吃什么？　　　　What would you like to eat for supper?
　　B：我们想吃饺子。　　　　We'd like dumplings.
　　（动作"吃"还没完成　The action "吃" was not completed）

（2）用动态助词"了₁"的句子，否定形式是："没/没有+动词"。例如：
The negative form of a sentence using the aspect particle "了₁" is "没/没有+verb". For example,

⑤ 我们没买词典。　　　　　　We didn't buy a dictionary.
⑥ 我们没要果汁。　　　　　　We didn't order juice.
⑦ 昨天晚上我们没有喝啤酒。　We didn't drink beer last night.

（3）动态助词"了₁"只表示动作的完成，这个动作可以在说话以前完成，也可以在说话以后完成。例如：
The aspect particle "了₁" only indicates the completion of an action. The action can be done before or after speaking. For example,

⑧ 昨天我们上了听力课。（动作"上"在说话以前完成）
　　Yesterday we had the listening course. (The action "上" was completed before speaking.)

⑨ 昨天晚上我给家里打了电话。（动作"打"在说话以前完成）
　　Last night I called my family. (The action "打" was completed before speaking.)

⑩ 下了课以后我想回房间休息。（动作"下"在说话以后完成）
　　I want to go back to my room to have a rest after class. (The action "下" will be completed after speaking.)

⑪ 我明天晚上吃了晚饭以后去看朋友。（动作"吃"在说话以后完成）
　　I am going to visit my friend after supper tomorrow night. (The action "吃" will be completed after speaking.)

（4）在"去 + 地点 + 动词"的句子中，动态助词"了₁"放在第二个动词后面。例如：

In a sentence with the structure "去 + place + verb", the aspect particle "了₁" is used after the second verb. For example,

⑫ 昨天他去商店买了一台电视。

Yesterday he went to the store and bought a TV set.

⑬ 下午我去银行取了钱。

I went to withdraw some money from the bank in the afternoon.

2 这家饭馆比较小，但是菜的味道很好，价格也不贵，所以我们老去那儿吃饭。／我们的主食是饺子，因为大家都爱吃饺子。

因为……所以……：表示因果关系。"因为"用在因果复句中表示原因的分句前面，"所以"用在因果复句中表示结果的分句前面。例如：

因为……所以……：It is used to show a cause-and-effect relationship. "因为" is used before the clause indicating cause or reason, and "所以" is used before the clause indicating effect or result. For example,

① 因为大家都爱吃饺子，所以我们点了三斤饺子。

We ordered three *jin* of dumplings because everyone likes them.

② 因为他明天有课，所以今天晚上没去唱卡拉 OK。

He didn't go to karaoke tonight because he will have classes tomorrow.

③ 因为那家饭馆的菜又便宜又好吃，所以我们常去那儿吃饭。

We often go to have dinner at that restaurant because the dishes there are inexpensive and tasty.

也可以只用一个关联词。例如：

It is OK that only one conjunction is used in the sentence. For example,

④ 他妈妈是中国人，所以他会说一点儿汉语。

He can speak a little Chinese because his mother is Chinese.

⑤ 今天我们没有课，所以我 10 点才起床。

I didn't get up until 10 o'clock because we don't have classes today.

⑥ 因为下雨了，我们没去看电影。

We didn't see the movie because of rain.

⑦ 因为大家都爱吃饺子，我们点了两盘饺子。

We ordered two plates of dumplings because everyone likes them.

注意：表示原因的分句在后面的时候，一定要用"因为"。例如：

Note: "因为" must be used if the clause indicating reason is used after the clause indicating effect. For example,

⑧ 大家都很高兴，因为明天没有课。

We are all very happy, because we won't have a class tomorrow.

⑨ 他今天没来上课，因为他病了。

He didn't come to class, because he is sick today.

⑩ 今天他喝了很多酒，因为他很高兴。

He drank a lot, because he is very happy today.

13 苹果怎么卖 píng guǒ zěn me mài

How much is the apple

课文 Text

今天下午没有课，我和朋友骑自行车去市场买了很多水果。那个市场水果很新鲜，价格也很便宜，苹果五块五一斤，梨十块钱三斤。我买了四斤苹果、六斤梨，还买了一把香蕉。西瓜太大，我没买。我一共花了四十八块六毛钱。我朋友买了两斤半葡萄、一斤草莓，花了二十块五毛钱。

那个市场也有许多热带水果，如芒果、椰子等，还有不少进口的水果，如美国的橙子、新西兰的猕猴桃等。

我们从市场出来的时候，在市场大门口碰到了乔

zhì hé zhēn ni　　tā men yě lái mǎi shuǐ guǒ　　wǒ men sì ge rén zài shì chǎng dà mén kǒu
治和珍妮，他们也来买水果。我们四个人在市场大门口
zhào le　yì zhāng xiàng
照了一张相。

zhè zhāng zhào piàn shì wǒ men zài zhōng guó mǎi shuǐ guǒ de　jì niàn
这张照片是我们在中国买水果的纪念。

词语表 Vocabulary

1.	苹果	píngguǒ	N	apple
2.	怎么	zěnme	Pr	how
3.	骑	qí	V	to ride
4.	自行车	zìxíngchē	N	bicycle
5.	市场	shìchǎng	N	market
6.	水果	shuǐguǒ	N	fruit
7.	新鲜	xīnxiān	Adj	fresh
8.	斤	jīn	M	*jin*, unit of weight (=1/2 kilogram)
9.	梨	lí	N	pear
10.	香蕉	xiāngjiāo	N	banana
11.	西瓜	xīguā	N	watermelon
12.	太	tài	Adv	(*used to express admiration or exclamation*) excessively, too
13.	一共	yígòng	Adv	altogether, in total
14.	花	huā	V	to spend
15.	块（元）	kuài（yuán）	M	*used as a unit of money* (=1 yuan)
16.	毛（角）	máo（jiǎo）	M	*used as a unit of money* (0.1 yuan)
17.	钱	qián	N	money
18.	半	bàn	Nu	half
19.	葡萄	pútao	N	grape

20.	草莓	cǎoméi	N	strawberry
21.	热带	rèdài	N	tropics
22.	如	rú	V	to give an example
23.	芒果	mángguǒ	N	mango
24.	椰子	yēzi	N	coconut
25.	进口	jìn kǒu	V//O	to import
26.	橙子	chéngzi	N	orange
27.	猕猴桃	míhóutáo	N	kiwi fruit
28.	出来	chūlai	V	to come out
29.	时候	shíhou	N	(a point in) time, moment
30.	门口	ménkǒu	N	entrance
31.	碰到	pèngdào	V	to run into, to come across
32.	照相	zhào xiàng	V//O	to take a photo
33.	纪念	jìniàn	N	souvenir

专有名词　Proper Noun

| | 新西兰 | Xīnxīlán | | New Zealand |

注　释　Notes

1 苹果怎么卖?

用"怎么"提问的疑问句:用来询问动作的方式。后面一般是动词或动词性短语。例如:

The question using "怎么": It is used to ask about the manner of an action. It is often followed by a verb or verbal phrase. For example,

① 去他家怎么走?　　　　　　　How do I get to his home?
② 你的汉语名字怎么写?　　　　How do I write your Chinese name?

93

2 我和朋友骑自行车去市场买了很多水果。

集合名词：指一类事物。这里的"水果"就是集合名词。集合名词前面都不能用个体量词。例如：

Collective noun: It indicates a kind of things. In this case, "水果" is a collective noun. Before a collective noun, a measure word indicating an individual piece or individual pieces of something cannot be used. For example,

① 水果　　　fruits　　　　　一个水果（×）　　　a fruits（×）
② 书本　　　books　　　　　三个书本（×）　　　a books（×）
③ 人口　　　population　　　一个人口（×）　　　a population（×）
④ 饮料　　　beverages　　　 两个饮料（×）　　　a beverages（×）

3 苹果五块五一斤。

人民币的写法和读法：人民币的单位有三个：元（块）、角（毛）、分。三个单位实行十进制。

Reading and writing RMB: RMB has three basic units: *yuan (kuai)*, *jiao (mao)*, and *fen*, all of which follow the decimal system.

人民币的写法是：~．~~元。例如：

RMB is written as: ~．~~元. For example,

0.01 元　　　　0.15 元　　　　0.50 元　　　　1.00 元
36.00 元　　　 98.90 元　　　 180.00 元　　　 505.50 元

人民币的读法是：数字 + 单位。例如：

RMB is read as: number + unit. For example,

3.00 元 → 三元 / 三块
3.20 元 → 三元两角 / 三块两毛 / 三块二
3.02 元 → 三元零两分 / 三块零两分 / 三块零二
15.00 元 → 十五元 / 十五块
35.98 元 → 三十五元九角八分 / 三十五块九毛八
35.90 元 → 三十五元九角 / 三十五块九毛 / 三十五块九

4 我一共花了四十八块六毛钱。

一共：副词，后面一般是动词和数量短语。例如：

一共: It is an adverb generally followed by a verb and a quantifier phrase. For example,

① 我们班一共有 12 个学生。　　　There are 12 students altogether in our class.
② 我一共学了 400 个汉字。　　　 I have learned 400 characters altogether.
③ 我们昨天一共喝了 5 瓶啤酒。　 We drank 5 bottles of beer altogether yesterday.

5 我们四个人在市场大门口照了一张相。

离合词："照相"是离合词，中间加进了动态助词"了₁"、数量短语"一张"。离合词是动词的一类，它们的用法和一般的动词不太一样，如中间可以加进别的词语，后面不可以有宾语，重叠形式是AAB。例如：

Verb-object compound: "照相" is a verb-object compound in which the aspect particle "了₁" and the quantifier phrase "一张" are used between "照" and "相". Verb-object compounds are a kind of verbs with usages different from common verbs, i.e., other verbs can be used in between, cannot be followed by an object and has the reduplicative form of AAB. For example,

① 见了面．	见面一个朋友（×）	和一个朋友见面	见见面
② 聊了天儿	聊天儿中国朋友（×）	和中国朋友聊天儿	聊聊天儿
③ 照了相	照相老师（×）	和老师照相	照照相
④ 结了账	结账他们（×）	给他们结账	
⑤ 散了步	散步我们（×）		散散步
⑥ 睡了一会儿觉			睡睡觉

6 ……，好吗？

这种疑问句常常是先提出一种建议，希望得到对方的同意，比较客气。例如：

This kind of questions is often used to put forward a suggestion at first, indicating the speaker hopes the other party will agree with him. It is a polite expression. For example,

① A：下午我们去买水果，好吗？　　Shall we buy some fruit in the afternoon?
　 B：好的。　　　　　　　　　　　Sure.
② A：我们中午吃面条，好吗？　　　Shall we eat noodles for lunch?
　 B：好的。　　　　　　　　　　　OK.

7 ……，对吗？

这种疑问句常常是先说出自己的一种想法或推测，希望得到对方的证实。例如：

This kind of questions is often used to give an opinion or speculation at first, indicating the speaker hopes the other party will confirm his opinion or speculation. For example,

① A：你同屋是韩国人，对吗？　　　Is your roommate a Korean?
　 B：是的（对）。　　　　　　　　Yes.
② A：你住2号楼，对吗？　　　　　Do you live in Building 2?
　 B：是的（对）。　　　　　　　　Yes.

14 你穿多大号的牛仔裤

What size are your jeans

课文 Text

星期天我和同屋一起去买衣服。

我们先买牛仔裤。我穿28号的牛仔裤,她穿24号的。我喜欢黑色的,她喜欢蓝色的。我们逛了很多家商店,都没有看见合适的牛仔裤。最后我们在一家"李维斯"牌牛仔裤专卖店买到了自己喜欢的牛仔裤。我们试了新买的牛仔裤,非常合适。

那个市场的服装有很多是世界有名的牌子。我们每人还买了一件"阿迪达斯"的T恤衫。我的是红的,她的是白的。我还买了一顶"耐克"牌帽子、两双"耐克"牌袜子、一双"锐步"运动鞋。同屋买了两件衬衣、一件毛衣、一件帽衫和一条裙子。我们买的东西都很漂亮,也很合适,不过有点儿贵。

结账的时候,老板说他卖的服装都是真名牌,不是假名牌,所以比较贵。他欢迎我们以后还来他的商店买东西。

词语表 Vocabulary

1.	穿	chuān	V	to wear
2.	号	hào	N	size
3.	牛仔裤	niúzǎikù	N	jeans
4.	衣服	yīfu	N	clothes
5.	黑色	hēisè	N	black
6.	蓝色	lánsè	N	blue
7.	逛	guàng	V	to stroll
8.	看见	kànjiàn	V	to see
9.	最后	zuìhòu	N	at last
10.	专卖店	zhuānmàidiàn	N	exclusive shop
11.	试	shì	V	to try on
12.	新	xīn	Adj	new
13.	非常	fēicháng	Adv	very

14.	合适	héshì	Adj	suitable, appropriate
15.	那个	nàge	Pr	that
16.	服装	fúzhuāng	N	clothing, costume
17.	世界	shìjiè	N	world
18.	牌子	páizi	N	brand
19.	件	jiàn	M	piece
20.	T恤衫	T xù shān		T-shirt
21.	红	hóng	Adj	red
22.	白	bái	Adj	white
23.	顶	dǐng	M	a measure word for caps
24.	帽子	màozi	N	cap, hat
25.	双	shuāng	M	pair
26.	袜子	wàzi	N	socks
27.	运动	yùndòng	V	to do sport
28.	鞋	xié	N	shoes
29.	衬衣	chènyī	N	shirt
30.	毛衣	máoyī	N	pullover, jumper, sweater
31.	帽衫	màoshān	N	hoodie
32.	条	tiáo	M	a measure word for trousers or skirts
33.	裙子	qúnzi	N	skirt
34.	不过	búguò	Conj	however
35.	有点儿	yǒudiǎnr	Adv	a little bit
36.	老板	lǎobǎn	N	stall owner
37.	真	zhēn	Adj	real
38.	名牌	míngpái	N	name brand
39.	假	jiǎ	Adj	fake

专有名词　Proper Nouns

1.	李维斯	Lǐwéisī		Levi's

2. 阿迪达斯	**Ādídásī**	Adidas
3. 耐克	**Nàikè**	Nike
4. 锐步	**Ruìbù**	Reebok

注 释 Notes

1 你穿<u>多大</u>号的牛仔裤？

用"多 + 形容词"提问的疑问句：询问程度。例如：

The question using "多 + adjective": It is used to ask about the degree. For example,

① A：你弟弟穿多大的鞋？　　What size are your younger brother's shoes?
　 B：28 号的。　　　　　　 Size 28 .
② A：你哥哥多高？　　　　　How tall is your elder brother?
　 B：1 米 8。　　　　　　　180 centimeters.
③ A：这把香蕉多重？　　　　How much does this bunch of bananas weigh?
　 B：五斤。　　　　　　　　Five *jin*.

2 我穿 28 号的牛仔裤，她穿 <u>24 号的</u>。

"的"字短语："的"字前面是修饰、限制性的词语，后面省略了名词中心词的短语叫"的"字短语。"的"字短语相当于名词。名词、代词、动词、形容词都可以充当"的"字前面的修饰、限制性词语。例如：

The "的" phrase: The phrase that has a modifier before "的" with a noun as the main word omitted after "的" is known as the "的" phrase. It is equivalent to a noun. A noun, a pronoun, a verb or an adjective can be used before "的" as the modifier. For example,

① 我喜欢黑色的。（意思是：我喜欢黑色的牛仔裤　It means I like the black jeans.）
② 她穿 24 号的。（意思是：她穿 24 号的鞋　It means she wears the shoes of size 24.）
③ 我的书包是黑的。（意思是：我的书包是黑色的书包　It means my schoolbag is black.）
④ 他家的车是德国的。（意思是：他家的车是德国生产的车　It means the car of his family is made in Germany.）

有时"的"字后面省略的词语是什么，在具体上下文中是很清楚的。例如：
Sometimes it is very clear in the context what is the word omitted after "的". For example,

⑤ 我喜欢黑色的牛仔裤，她喜欢蓝色的。（蓝色的牛仔裤）
I like black jeans and she likes the blue ones.（blue jeans）

⑥ 他姐姐新买的车是蓝色的。（蓝色的车）
The car his elder sister just bought is blue.（blue car）

⑦ 我的猫是黄色的眼睛，她的猫是蓝色的。（蓝色的眼睛）
My cat's eyes are yellow, while her cat's eyes are blue.（blue eyes）

3 "李维斯"牌牛仔裤专卖店／"阿迪达斯"的 T 恤衫／"锐步"运动鞋

商品牌子的三种说法：
Three ways of saying the brands:

① 品牌名＋"的"＋名词。例如：
Brand name ＋ "的" ＋ noun. For example,

"阿迪达斯"的 T 恤衫　　　Adidas T-shirt

② 品牌名＋"牌"＋名词。例如：
Brand name ＋ "牌" ＋ noun. For example,

"耐克"牌帽子　　　　　　Nike cap

③ 品牌名＋名词。例如：
Brand name ＋ noun. For example,

"锐步"运动鞋　　　　　　Reebok sports shoes

4 不过有点儿贵。

"有点儿"＋形容词：表示不如意，"有点儿"后面的形容词常常带有贬义或消极意义。例如：
"有点儿" +adjective: It is used to express something unsatisfactory. The adjective after "有点儿" often has a derogatory or negative meaning. For example,

① 这条牛仔裤有点儿贵。　　This pair of jeans is a little bit too expensive.
② 我有点儿累。　　　　　　I am a little bit too tired.

有些形容词虽然不含贬义，也不是消极意义，但是用在"有点儿＋形容词"格式中也表示不如意。例如：
Although some adjectives are neither derogatory nor negative in meaning, they express the speaker's unsatisfaction when used in the structure "有点儿 +adjective". For example,

③ 这双鞋有点儿大。　　　　　　　This pair of shoes is a little bit too big.
④ 这条裤子有点儿长。　　　　　　This pair of trousers is a little bit too long.
⑤ 她的 T 恤衫有点儿红。　　　　　Her T-shirt is a little bit too red.

褒义形容词用在"有点儿 + 形容词"格式中时，要在形容词前面加"不"。例如：
When a commendatory adjective is used in "有点儿 +adjective", "不" is used before it. For example,

⑥ 今天我有点儿不舒服。　　　　　I don't feel very well today.
⑦ 他有点儿不高兴。　　　　　　　He is a bit unhappy.
⑧ 他朋友有点儿不满意他的房间。　His friend is a bit unsatisfied with his room.

15 王老师教你们什么

What does Mr. Wang teach you

课文 Text

我们班有三门汉语课：精读课、会话课和听力课。李老师教我们精读课，王老师教我们会话课，刘老师教我们听力课。

上精读课的时候，我们主要学习汉语语法知识。李老师还教我们写汉字，让我们两个星期写一篇汉语作文。现在我的汉语水平比较低，写汉语作文有点儿难，但是我喜欢写汉语作文。我们在上课的时候还做阅读练习。

会话课很有意思。上课的时候，同学们用汉语介绍自己的家庭、爱好等，练习口语。王老师喜欢我们大声地读生词、大声地回答问题。但是我怕自己的发音不标准，读生词和回答问题的时候声音都很小。不过，我喜欢上会话课。

我觉得听力课最难，因为速度太快，我常常听不懂。我很着急。每次上课我都问刘老师问题。刘老师每次都耐心地回答我的问题，让我别着急。我的同屋南希告诉我，现在听不懂没关系，两个星期以后会慢慢儿习惯。提高听力的好办法是每天听课文录音，或者听广播、看电视。她还送了我一套汉语课本的光盘。我很感谢她。

词语表 Vocabulary

1. 门	mén	M	*a measure word for fields of study or technical trainings*
2. 主要	zhǔyào	Adj	major, main
3. 语法	yǔfǎ	N	grammar
4. 知识	zhīshi	N	knowledge
5. 让	ràng	V	to ask, to let
6. 篇	piān	M	*a measure word for essays or articles*
7. 作文	zuòwén	N	composition
8. 水平	shuǐpíng	N	level
9. 低	dī	Adj	low

10.	阅读	yuèdú	V	to read
11.	介绍	jièshào	V	to introduce
12.	家庭	jiātíng	N	family
13.	口语	kǒuyǔ	N	spoken language
14.	大声	dà shēng		loudly
15.	地	de	StPt	used after an adjective or phrase to form an adverbial adjunct before the verb
16.	回答	huídá	V	to answer
17.	怕	pà	V	to be afraid of
18.	声音	shēngyīn	N	sound
19.	速度	sùdù	N	speed
20.	快	kuài	Adj	fast
21.	着急	zháojí	Adj	worried
22.	次	cì	M	time
23.	问	wèn	V	to ask
24.	耐心	nàixīn	Adj	patient
25.	别	bié	Adv	not
26.	告诉	gàosu	V	to tell
27.	没关系	méi guānxi		It doesn't matter
28.	慢慢儿	mànmānr	Adv	step by step
29.	习惯	xíguàn	V	to be used to
30.	提高	tígāo	V	to improve
31.	办法	bànfǎ	N	method
32.	录音	lùyīn	N	recording
33.	送	sòng	V	to give
34.	套	tào	M	set
35.	课本	kèběn	N	textbook
36.	感谢	gǎnxiè	V	to thank, to appreciate

专有名词　Proper Nouns

1.	王	Wáng	a family name
2.	刘	Liú	a family name

注　释　Notes

1 王老师教你们什么？

双宾语：指一个动词后面带两个宾语，一个是指人（或单位）的词语，叫"间接宾语"，因为离动词近，又叫"近宾语"；一个是指事物的词语，叫"直接宾语"，因为离动词远，又叫"远宾语"。汉语中能带双宾语的动词不太多，主要有"教"、"问"、"给"、"告诉"、"借"、"还"等。例如：

Double objects： It indicates that a verb is followed by two objects. The word referring to somebody (or a unit) is known as the "indirect object" or the "near object" because it is close to the verb; the word referring to something is known as the "direct object" or the "distant object" because it is distant from the verb. In Chinese, there are not many verbs that can be followed by double objects. The most commonly used ones are "教"，"问"，"给"，"告诉"，"借"，"还"，etc. For example,

① 李老师教我们精读课。　　Mr. Li teaches us intensive reading course.
② 我问了老师一个问题。　　I asked the teacher a question.
③ 老师告诉我明天没有课。　The teacher told me we won't have a class tomorrow.

2 上精读课的时候，我们主要学习汉语语法知识。

动宾短语做定语：动宾短语可以做定语，修饰、限制名词。例如：

The verb-object phrase as an attribute： The verb-object phrase can be used as an attribute to modify or restrict a noun. For example,

① 上课的时候　　　　　the time when somebody has a class
② 提高听力的好办法　　a good way to improve one's listening comprehension
③ 练习口语的教室　　　the classroom where somebody practices spoken Chinese

3 让我们两个星期写一篇汉语作文。

用"让"的兼语句："让"做兼语句中第一个动词，动词的使令意义更明显。例如：

The pivotal sentence using "让"： When "让" is the first verb of a pivotal sentence, the causative connotation of the verb is more obvious. For example,

① 老师让我好好儿休息。　　　　　My teacher told me to have a good rest.
② 我让同屋替我请假。　　　　　　I told my roommate to ask for leave for me.
③ 妈妈让我晚上给她打电话。　　　My mother asked me to call her in the evening.

4 王老师喜欢我们大声地读生词、大声地回答问题。

地：结构助词，用在状语后面、谓语前面。例如：

地：It is a structural particle used after the adverbial and before the predicate. For example,

① 黄老师耐心地回答了我的问题。　　Mr. Huang answered my question patiently.
② 我们认真地上课。　　　　　　　　We were attentive in class.
③ 大家开心地笑了。　　　　　　　　Everybody laughed happily.

5 让我别着急。

别：副词，用在动词前，表示安慰，或者劝阻不要发生这个动作。例如：

别：It is an adverb used before a verb to console somebody or dissuade somebody from doing something. For example,

① 别着急　　　　　　　　　don't worry
② 别担心　　　　　　　　　take it easy
③ 别怕　　　　　　　　　　don't be afraid
④ 别说话　　　　　　　　　don't talk
⑤ 别等他　　　　　　　　　don't wait for him
⑥ 别买这个牌子的牛仔裤　　don't buy the jeans of this brand

"别 + 动词 + 了"表示劝阻一个正在进行的动作。例如：

"别 + verb + 了" is used to dissuade someone from doing an ongoing action. For example,

⑦ 别唱了，大家都睡觉了。（正在"唱"）
　　Stop singing; everybody has gone to bed. (Somebody is "singing".)
⑧ 别说了，电影开始了。（正在"说"）
　　Stop talking; the movie has begun. (Somebody is "speaking".)
⑨ 别喝了，你已经喝了很多啤酒了。（正在"喝啤酒"）
　　Stop drinking; you have drunken too much beer. (Somebody is "drinking beer".)

16 今天冷还是昨天冷

Which day is colder, today or yesterday

课文 Text

现在我在北京留学。我还不习惯北京的天气。

北京空气很干燥，春天常常刮大风，夏天经常下大雨，温差很大，早晨和夜晚比中午凉。有时候早晚的温度比中午的低10℃（度），早上比中午凉多了。早上我去上课的时候常常忘了多穿衣服。昨天晚上我头疼、嗓子疼，浑身没劲儿，很不舒服，觉得很渴，不想吃饭，很想喝水，还不断地打喷嚏、流鼻涕。我觉得我感冒了。今天早上我让同屋替我请假。

下课以后，李老师来宿舍看我。她告诉我，北京温差

bǐ jiào dà, zǎo shang méi yǒu zhōng wǔ nuǎn huo。 xǔ duō wài guó xué sheng gāng lái běi jīng
比较大，早上没有中午暖和。许多外国学生刚来北京

dōu bù xí guàn běi jīng de tiān qì, róng yì gǎn mào。 tā ràng wǒ duō hē shuǐ, hǎo hāor
都不习惯北京的天气，容易感冒。她让我多喝水，好好儿

xiū xi。tóng wū hái gào su wǒ, tā gāng lái běi jīng de shí hou, cháng lā dù zi, yīn wèi
休息。同屋还告诉我，她刚来北京的时候，常拉肚子，因为

zhōng guó cài bǐ jiào yóu nì。 xiàn zài tā yǐ jīng xí guàn le。
中国菜比较油腻。现在她已经习惯了。

wǒ chī le gǎn mào yào, xiàn zài jué de bǐ zuó tiān hǎo diǎnr le。
我吃了感冒药，现在觉得比昨天好点儿了。

词语表 Vocabulary

1.	天气	tiānqì	N	weather
2.	空气	kōngqì	N	air
3.	干燥	gānzào	Adj	dry
4.	春天	chūntiān	N	spring
5.	刮	guā	V	to blow
6.	风	fēng	N	wind
7.	下	xià	V	(of rain, snow, etc.) to fall
8.	雨	yǔ	N	rain
9.	温差	wēnchā	N	difference in temperature
10.	早晨	zǎochen	N	morning
11.	夜晚	yèwǎn	N	night
12.	比	bǐ	Prep	than
13.	温度	wēndù	N	temperature
14.	度	dù	M	a measure word for temperature
15.	忘	wàng	V	to forget
16.	疼	téng	Adj	sore
17.	嗓子	sǎngzi	N	throat

18. 浑身	húnshēn	N	all over the body
19. 劲儿	jìnr	N	strength, energy
20. 舒服	shūfu	Adj	in good health
21. 渴	kě	Adj	thirsty
22. 喝	hē	V	to drink
23. 水	shuǐ	N	water
24. 不断	búduàn	Adv	one after another
25. 打	dǎ	V	to go through or perform (some physical actions)
26. 喷嚏	pēntì	N	sneeze
27. 流	liú	V	(of liquid) to flow
28. 鼻涕	bítì	N	(nasal) mucus
29. 感冒	gǎnmào	V	to catch a cold
30. 替	tì	Prep	on behalf of, for
31. 请假	qǐng jià	V//O	to ask for leave
32. 暖和	nuǎnhuo	Adj	warm
33. 刚	gāng	Adv	just, only a short while ago
34. 好好儿	hǎohāor	Adv	to one's heart's content
35. 拉肚子	lā dùzi		to have loose bowels
36. 油腻	yóunì	Adj	oily, greasy
37. 已经	yǐjīng	Adv	already
38. 药	yào	N	medicine

1 早晨和夜晚比中午凉。

　　A 比 B+ 形容词：比较 A、B 两事物，A 的程度比 B 的高。例如：

　　A 比 B+adjective: It is used to compare A and B, and A has a higher degree than B. For example,

109

① 今天比昨天热。　　　　　　　　Today is hotter than yesterday.
② 我比弟弟高。　　　　　　　　　I am taller than my younger brother.
③ 姐姐的房间比我的大。　　　　　My elder sister's room is bigger than mine.

2 有时候早晚的温度比中午的低10℃（度）。

温度的写法和读法：中国用摄氏计量温度，写做"～℃"，读做"～度"。例如：
Writing and reading temperature：China uses Celsius as a temperature measurement unit, which is written as "～℃" and read as "～度". For example,

　　20℃ → 二十度　　　　　　38℃ → 三十八度　　　　　　－5℃ → 零下五度

3 早上比中午凉多了。

A 比 B+ 形容词 + "一点儿" / "多了" / 数量补语：比较 A、B 两事物，并指出 A、B 之间的程度差别。例如：
A 比 B+adjective + "一点儿" / "多了" /quantifier complement：It is used to compare A and B and indicate the difference in degree between A and B. For example,

① 今天比昨天热一点儿。　　　　　Today is a bit hotter than yesterday.
② 姐姐的房间比我的大多了。　　　My elder sister's room is much bigger than mine.

4 早上我去上课的时候常常忘了多穿衣服。

忘：动词，后面常常是"忘"的内容。例如：
忘：It is a verb, which is often followed by something being forgotten. For example,

① 他忘了吃药。　　　　　　　　　He forgot to take his medicine.
② 昨天晚上我忘了给他打电话。　　I forgot to call him last night.
③ 我忘了今天有听写。　　　　　　I forgot we have a dictation today.
④ 我忘了她的电话号码。　　　　　I forgot her telephone number.

5 早上没有中午暖和。

A 没有 B+ 形容词：这是"A 比 B+ 形容词"的否定形式。例如：
A 没有 B+adjective：It is the negative form of "A 比 B + adjective". For example,

① 我没有弟弟高。　　　　　　　　I am not as tall as my younger brother.
② 他们的房租没有我们的贵。　　　Their rent is not as expensive as ours.

6 许多外国学生**刚**来北京都不习惯北京的天气。

刚：副词，用在动词前面，说明不久前发生的动作，也可以说"刚刚"。例如：

刚: It is an adverb used before a verb to indicate an action took place not long ago. It is equivalent to "刚刚". For example,

① 我朋友刚来北京。　　　　My friend has just come to Beijing.
② 他们班刚下课。　　　　　They have just finished their class.
③ 我同屋刚走。　　　　　　My roommate has just left.

7 句中语音停顿
The pause in a sentence

在朗读汉语句子或说汉语的时候，常常要在没有逗号的地方加上适当的停顿。这种停顿一般以双音节为基本单位。动态助词、结构助词跟着前面的词语一起读，形成一个一个的节拍群。例如：

When reading a Chinese sentence or speak the Chinese language, a pause is often made when no comma is used. Such a pause is generally disyllabic. The aspect particle and structural particle are read together with the preceding words, forming a rhythm group. For example,

① 他是//法国人。
② 我觉得//学习汉语//挺有//意思的。
③ 许多/外国学生//刚来/北京//都不/习惯//北京的/天气。

17 北京的天气跟东京的一样吗

Is the weather in Beijing the same as that in Tokyo

前天我感冒了，晚上朋友陪我坐出租车去医院看了病。大夫给我开了中药、西药，还给我打了针。吃了药以后，现在我头不疼了，嗓子也不疼了，也不发热了，但是还有点儿咳嗽。我打算明天去上课。

今天早上我给妈妈打电话了。我告诉妈妈，这儿的天气跟东京的不一样，一天的温度变化比较大。中午比早晨和夜晚暖和多了，许多刚来北京的留学生都不太习惯北京的天气。最近感冒的同学比较多。我不了解北京的气候特点，早晚没有多穿衣服，也感冒了。我还告诉妈妈，生

112

17 北京的天气跟东京的一样吗

病的时候特别想家，我在房间偷偷地哭了。但是我病了以后老师和同学们很关心我。他们来宿舍看我，送我水果和点心。现在我的感冒已经好了。我让妈妈别担心。

妈妈说，在国外生活跟在家里生活不一样，要自己照顾自己。她和爸爸最担心我生病。他们说，现在已经是秋天了，天气一天比一天冷了，要多注意身体，经常参加体育锻炼。

我给妈妈打电话的时候，爸爸、哥哥、弟弟也都在家，我也跟他们说了话，我很高兴。

词语表 Vocabulary

1.	一样	yíyàng	Adj	same
2.	前天	qiántiān	N	the day before yesterday
3.	了	le	MdPt	used to indicate the completion of an action or a change
4.	陪	péi	V	to accompany
5.	坐	zuò	V	to travel by (bus, train, taxi, etc.)
6.	出租车	chūzūchē	N	taxi, cab
7.	医院	yīyuàn	N	hospital
8.	看病	kàn bìng	V//O	to go to hospital
9.	大夫	dàifu	N	doctor

113

10.	开	kāi	V	to prescribe
11.	中药	zhōngyào	N	traditional Chinese medicine
12.	西药	xīyào	N	Western medicine
13.	打针	dǎ zhēn	V//O	to give or have an injection
14.	发热	fā rè	V//O	to have a fever
15.	咳嗽	késou	V	to cough
16.	打算	dǎsuàn	V	to plan
17.	变化	biànhuà	N	change
18.	最近	zuìjìn	N	recently
19.	了解	liǎojiě	V	to know
20.	气候	qìhòu	N	climate
21.	特点	tèdiǎn	N	characteristics
22.	生病	shēng bìng	V//O	to get sick
23.	偷偷	tōutōu	Adv	stealthily, secretly
24.	哭	kū	V	to cry
25.	关心	guān xīn	V//O	to care about
26.	担心	dān xīn	V//O	to worry
27.	国外	guó wài		abroad
28.	照顾	zhàogù	V	to look after
29.	秋天	qiūtiān	N	autumn
30.	注意	zhù yì	V//O	to pay attention to
31.	参加	cānjiā	V	to take part in
32.	体育	tǐyù	N	physical training
33.	锻炼	duànliàn	V	to exercise

注释 Notes

1 北京的天气跟东京的一样吗?

A 跟 B+ "一样/不一样":比较 A、B 两事物的异同。例如:

A 跟 B+ "一样/不一样": It is used to compare the similarity or difference between A and B. For example,

① 北京的天气跟东京的不一样。 The weather in Beijng is different from that in Tokyo.
② 他们班的课本跟我们班的一样。 The textbook they use in their class is the same as ours.
③ 他的牛仔裤的牌子跟我的一样。 The brand of his jeans is the same as that of mine.

这个句型也可以在后面加上形容词,即:A 跟 B + "一样/不一样" + 形容词。例如:

This sentence pattern can also be followed by an adjective, i.e.: A 跟 B + "一样/不一样" + adjective. For example,

④ 他的房租跟我的一样贵。 His rent is as expensive as mine.
⑤ 他的房租跟我的不一样贵。 His rent is not as expensive as mine.
⑥ 他们班的学生跟我们班的一样多。
  The number of students in their class is the same as that of ours.
⑦ 他们班的学生跟我们班的不一样多。
  The number of students in their class is not the same as that of ours.

2 前天我感冒了。

语气助词 "了$_2$":用在句子末尾,强调一个已经发生了的动作,表示情况有了变化。例如:

The modal particle "了$_2$": It is used at the end of a sentence to emphasize an action has taken place and indicate something has changed. For example,

① 现在我头不疼了。("头疼"这种情况有了变化)
  I don't have a headache now. (The state that I "had a headache" has changed.)
② 我的病好了。("病"的情况有了变化)
  I have recovered from the illness. (The state of "being ill" has changed.)
③ 他回宿舍了。("他在"的情况有了变化)
  He went back to his dormitory. (The state of "being here" has changed.)

3 现在我头不疼了。/ 早晚没有多穿衣服。/ 我让妈妈别担心。

辨析 Discrimination：不、没（没有）、别

这三个副词都可以用在动词前面表示否定，但是"不"否定的是发生在未来的动作，或者是一个由主观决定的动作。"没（没有）"否定的是发生在以前的动作，或者是一个由客观决定的动作。"别"是对动作的一种劝阻。例如：

All the three adverbs can be used before a verb to indicate negation. However, "不" is used to negate an action that will happen in the future, or a subjective action. "没（没有）" is used to negate an action that took place before, or an objective action. "别" is used to dissuade somebody from doing something. For example,

① 今天我不去上课。（在"上课前"说）
I won't go to class today.（It is said "before the class".）

② 昨天我没去上课。（在"上课后"说）
I didn't go to class yesterday.（It is said "after the class".）

③ 你发烧了，别去上课了。（劝阻"去上课"的发生）
Don't go to class. You have a fever.（It is used to "dissuade somebody from going to class".）

④ 妈妈不工作。（妈妈不想工作，是一种主观决定的动作）
My mother doesn't work.（My mother doesn't want to work, which is her own choice.）

⑤ 妈妈没工作。（妈妈想工作，但是没有找到工作，是一种客观决定的动作）
My mother doesn't have a job.（My mother wants to work, but she hasn't got a job, which is an objective situation.）

4 现在已经是秋天了，天气一天比一天冷了。

一天比一天：表示程度随着时间的延长而变化。后面常常是形容词。例如：

一天比一天：It indicates the degree changes as time goes by. It is often followed by an adjective. For example,

① 天气一天比一天冷了。　　It's getting colder day by day.
② 他的病一天比一天好了。　　He is getting better as time goes by.
③ 我认识的汉字一天比一天多了。
I know more and more Chinese characters with each passing day.

18 你最近怎么样
——给朋友的一封信
How are you doing these days — A letter to a friend

课文 Text

和子：

你好！好久没给你写信了。你最近怎么样？身体好吗？我很想你。我在北京挺愉快的。汉语老师很热情，外国同学很友好。我认识了许多新朋友，有中国人、美国人、德国人等。我现在很忙，从星期一到星期五，每天上午都有课。

上课的时候，各国同学用汉语介绍自己国家的情况，讨论大家都关心的事情，像爱好、习惯什么的，很有意思。

没有课的时候同学们也很忙，有的学拉二胡，有的学

117

画中国画儿。我喜欢一个人逛北京的胡同。我特别爱看胡同里的四合院。汉语老师告诉我们,学习语言要多听多说。在中国学习汉语跟在外国学习汉语不一样,学汉语的方法很多,比如说,看电视、听广播、买东西、逛大街、唱中国歌、交中国朋友等。所以没有课的时候同学们都有自己的安排。

下课以后我常常在大学的留学生餐厅吃午饭。晚上和周末去大学附近的小饭馆吃中国家常菜。中国菜比日本菜油腻多了,但是很好吃。我觉得我比刚来中国的时候胖多了。北京也有我们熟悉的快餐店,如麦当劳、必胜客等,还有不少外国风味的饭馆,像意大利的面条店、日本的寿司店、韩国的烤肉店什么的。

现在已经是北京的秋天了。秋天是北京最好的季节。天气很好,不冷也不热,不刮风也不下雨。天空又高又蓝,白云又轻又薄。有的树叶变黄了,有的树叶变红了,有的树叶还是绿的,非常漂亮,真像一幅美丽的图画。你们在日本也一定去看红叶了吧?

你的男朋友铃木最近工作一定很忙吧?问他好。

你的小狗"警察"好吗?它的样子真可爱——矮矮的,胖胖的,我也很想它。

下星期我们就要期中考试了。我得去复习了。

祝

身体好!

京美

10月 25 日

词语表 Vocabulary

1.	怎么样	zěnmeyàng	Pr	how
2.	封	fēng	M	a measure word for letters or telegrams, etc.
3.	信	xìn	N	letter
4.	好久	hǎojiǔ	Adj	a long time
5.	热情	rèqíng	Adj	warm-hearted
6.	友好	yǒuhǎo	Adj	friendly
7.	认识	rènshi	V	to get acquainted
8.	各	gè	Pr	each, every
9.	国家	guójiā	N	country
10.	情况	qíngkuàng	N	situation
11.	讨论	tǎolùn	V	to discuss
12.	事情	shìqing	N	thing, affair
13.	拉	lā	V	to play (a musical instrument)

14.	二胡	èrhú	N	*erhu*, a two-stringed bowed vertical musical instrument
15.	胡同	hútòng	N	alley, *hutong*
16.	四合院	sìhéyuàn	N	traditional, residential compound with houses at the four sides of a courtyard
17.	语言	yǔyán	N	language
18.	交	jiāo	V	to make (friends)
19.	安排	ānpái	V	to plan
20.	家常	jiācháng	N	home-style cooking
21.	胖	pàng	Adj	fat
22.	熟悉	shúxi	Adj	familiar
23.	快餐	kuàicān	N	fast food
24.	风味	fēngwèi	N	flavor
25.	寿司	shòusī	N	sushi
26.	烤	kǎo	V	to roast
27.	季节	jìjié	N	season
28.	天空	tiānkōng	N	sky
29.	云	yún	N	cloud
30.	轻	qīng	Adj	light
31.	薄	báo	Adj	thin
32.	树叶	shùyè	N	leaf
33.	绿	lǜ	Adj	green
34.	幅	fú	M	a measure word for pictures
35.	美丽	měilì	Adj	beautiful
36.	图画	túhuà	N	picture
37.	一定	yídìng	Adv	surely
38.	红叶	hóngyè	N	red leaf
39.	吧	ba	StPt	used the end of a sentence to indicate doubt or surmise
40.	男朋友	nánpéngyou	N	boyfriend

41.	问好	wèn hǎo	V//O	to say hello to sb.
42.	狗	gǒu	N	dog
43.	警察	jǐngchá	N	policeman
44.	它	tā	Pr	it
45.	样子	yàngzi	N	appearance
46.	可爱	kě'ài	Adj	lovely, cute
47.	矮	ǎi	Adj	(of stature) short
48.	就	jiù	Adv	at once
49.	要……了	yào……le		to be going to, to be about to
50.	期中	qīzhōng	N	mid-term
51.	考试	kǎo shì	V//O	to examine
52.	得	děi	OpV	must, have to
53.	祝	zhù	V	to wish

专有名词　Proper Nouns

1.	和子	Hézǐ	name of a Japanese
2.	麦当劳	Màidāngláo	McDonalds
3.	必胜客	Bìshèngkè	Pizza Hut
4.	意大利	Yìdàlì	Italy
5.	铃木	Língmù	name of a Japanese

1 你最近怎么样？

用"怎么样"提问的疑问句：用来询问事物的性质、状况，答句的谓语中心词常常是形容词。例如：

The question using "怎么样": It is used to ask about the property or condition of something. The main word in the predicate of the answer is often an adjective. For example,

① A：你身体怎么样？　　　　　　　How are you?
　 B：挺好的。　　　　　　　　　　Fine.
② A：这个菜怎么样？　　　　　　　How is this dish?
　 B：味道不错。　　　　　　　　　Not bad.
③ A：你朋友最近怎么样？　　　　　How is your friend recently?
　 B：他特别忙。　　　　　　　　　He is very busy.
④ A：她们新买的牛仔裤怎么样？　　How are the jeans they just bought?
　 B：非常合适。　　　　　　　　　Very nice.

辨析 Discrimination：什么、怎么、怎么样

用"什么"提问的疑问句，询问的是事物，一般用名词来回答。用"怎么"提问的疑问句，询问的是动作或动作的方式，一般用动词来回答。用"怎么样"提问的疑问句，询问的是性质、程度，一般用形容词来回答。例如：

A question with "什么" is used to ask about something and is generally answered by a noun. A question with "怎么" is used to ask about an action or the manner of doing something and is generally answered by a verb. A question with "怎么样" is used to ask about the property or degree of something and is generally answered by an adjective. For example,

⑤ A：你买什么？　　　　　　　　　What are you going to buy?
　 B：我买面包。　　　　　　　　　Some bread.
⑥ A：你们怎么介绍自己的爱好？　　How did you introduce your hobbies?
　 B：我们用汉语介绍自己的爱好。　We introduced our hobbies in Chinese.
⑦ A：他做的晚饭怎么样？　　　　　How is the supper he cooked?
　 B：非常简单。　　　　　　　　　Very simple.

2 各国同学用汉语介绍自己国家的情况，讨论大家都关心的事情，**像**爱好、习惯**什么的**。

像……什么的：表示列举，列举的事物放在"像"与"什么的"中间。例如：

像……什么的：It is used to enumerate things or people. The enumerated things or people are put between "像" and "什么的". For example,

① 北京外国风味的饭馆也不少，像意大利的面条店、日本的寿司店什么的。
There are many internationally flavored restaurants in Beijing, such as restaurants serving Italian spaghetti, restaurants serving Japanese sushi and so on.

② 我们学校有从各个国家来的留学生，像美国人、德国人什么的。
There are many international students in our school, such as Americans, Germans and so on.

③ 我很喜欢吃中国菜，像北京烤鸭、西红柿炒鸡蛋什么的，都很好吃。
I like Chinese dishes, like Beijing roast duck, stir-fried eggs with tomatoes and so on; they are all very delicious.

3 有的树叶还是绿的。

还：副词，表示情况和过去一样，没有变化。例如：

还：It is an adverb used to express that the state is unchanged and the same as before. For example,

① 我家还住那儿。　　　My family still live there.
② 她还在中国工作。　　She is still working in China.
③ 他还没听懂。　　　　He still doesn't understand what was said.

4 你的男朋友铃木最近工作一定很忙吧？

用"吧"提问的疑问句：这种疑问句是提出自己的推测以后，希望得到对方的确认。例如：

The question using "吧"：The speaker uses this question to put forward his speculation and hopes it will be confirmed by the other party. For example,

① 你一定很喜欢吃中国的家常菜吧？（说话人觉得"你"一定很喜欢）
You certainly like home-style Chinese food very much, don't you? (The speaker feels "you" certainly like it.)

② 他不是中国人吧？（说话人觉得"他"不是中国人）
He isn't Chinese, is he? (The speaker feels that "he" is not Chinese.)

③ 她是你们班的汉语老师吧？（说话人觉得"她"是你们班的汉语老师）
She is the Chinese teacher of your class, isn't she? (The speaker feels "she" is the Chinese teacher of your class.)

5 下星期我们就要期中考试了。

要……了：表示动作即将发生，动词用在"要"的后面。例如：

要……了：It is used to indicate an action is going to take place. The verb is used after "要". For example,

① 火车要开了。　　　　The train is leaving.
② 他要回国了。　　　　He is going back to his motherland.

"要"的前面也可以加上"就"、"快"、"马上"等词语。例如：

The word "就", "快" or "马上" can be put before "要". For example,

③ 我们就要放假了。　　We are going to have a holiday.

④ 快要下课了。　　　　　　　　The class will be dismissed soon.

⑤ 他的病快要好了。　　　　　　He will get well soon.

⑥ 他马上就要来了。　　　　　　He will come soon.

6 我**得**去复习了。

得 (děi)：能愿动词，用在动词前面，表示必须做某事。例如：

得：It is an optative verb used before a verb to indicate somebody has to do something. For example,

① 我得走了。　　　　　　　　　I have to go.

② 时间很晚了，我得回学校了。　It's so late. I have to go back to school.

③ 我明天得去银行取钱。

　　I need to withdraw some money from the bank tomorrow.

124

19 你学汉语多长时间了
How long have you been studying Chinese

课文 Text

我来中国学了三个多月的汉语了。我觉得自己的汉语水平有了很大的提高，学习也没有以前紧张了。课余时间我喜欢和中国朋友聊天儿，我希望了解中国一般老百姓的生活。我发现中国人一般都有睡午觉的习惯。他们吃了午饭以后都会休息休息，睡睡觉，一般睡一个多小时。也有的人只休息二十多分钟，或者半个小时，下午上班时精神很好。我认为中国人睡午觉的习惯不错，很有科学道理。我在公司工作的时候中午休息时间很短，一般只休息一个钟头，吃了午饭以后就只有二十多分钟了，没有时间睡午觉。下午上班的时候很困,总想喝喝茶、聊聊天儿。我有时候也偷偷睡十分钟或一刻钟。

现在在中国留学,我也有睡午觉的习惯了,真是"入乡随俗"。但是我有时候睡四个小时的"午觉",时间太长了,不是真正的"中国午觉",真不好意思。

中国朋友告诉我,现在中国人的生活节奏比以前快了,住在大城市的中国人、在公司工作的中国人也渐渐地不睡午觉了。我觉得很遗憾。

词语表 Vocabulary

1.	紧张	jǐnzhāng	Adj	intense, having a tight schedule
2.	课余	kèyú	N	after class
3.	时间	shíjiān	N	time
4.	希望	xīwàng	V	to hope
5.	一般	yìbān	Adj	ordinary, common
6.	老百姓	lǎobǎixìng	N	ordinary people
7.	发现	fāxiàn	V	to find
8.	午觉	wǔjiào	N	afternoon nap
9.	小时	xiǎoshí	N	hour
10.	只	zhǐ	Adv	only
11.	分钟	fēnzhōng	N	minute

12.	上班	shàng bān	V//O	to go to work
13.	精神	jīngshen	N	energy, spirit
14.	认为	rènwéi	V	to think
15.	科学	kēxué	Adj	scientific
16.	道理	dàoli	N	reason
17.	短	duǎn	Adj	short
18.	钟头	zhōngtóu	N	hour
19.	困	kùn	Adj	sleepy
20.	总	zǒng	Adv	always
21.	入乡随俗	rù xiāng suí sú		when in Rome, do as the Romans do
22.	长	cháng	Adj	long
23.	真正	zhēnzhèng	Adj	real
24.	不好意思	bù hǎoyìsi		to feel embarrassed
25.	节奏	jiézòu	N	tempo, rhythm
26.	城市	chéngshì	N	city
27.	渐渐	jiànjiàn	Adv	gradually
28.	遗憾	yíhàn	Adj	sorry, regrettable

1 你学汉语**多长时间**了？

时量补语：
· **The complement of duration:**

（1）时量补语是补充说明动作、状态持续的时间的词语。时量补语由时段短语充当。例如：
The complement of duration is used to indicate how long an action or a state lasts. A phrase indicating a period of time is used as the complement of duration. For example,

① 我中午只休息一个小时。 I only rested for an hour at noon.
② 我等了半个小时。 I have waited for half an hour.

③ 他们在上海住了三天。　　　　They have stayed in Shanghai for three days.
④ 她在国外生活了十年。　　　　She has lived abroad for ten years.

用"多长时间"询问时量补语。例如：
"多长时间" is used to enquire the complement of duration. For example,

⑤ A：你学了多长时间汉语了？　　How long have you been studying Chinese?
　 B：我学了半年汉语了。　　　　Half a year.
⑥ A：他在中国工作了多长时间？　How long has he been working in China?
　 B：他在中国已经工作了五年了。　Five years.

（2）动词带宾语时，时量补语放在动词和宾语中间，时量补语后面还可以用助词"的"。例如：
When a verb is followed by an object, the complement of duration is used between the verb and the object and can be followed by the particle "的". For example,

⑦ 他们睡了一个多小时觉。/他们睡了一个多小时的觉。
　 They have slept for more than an hour.
⑧ 他想学习半年汉语。/他想学习半年的汉语。
　 He wants to study Chinese for half a year.
⑨ 他们看了两个小时电视。/他们看了两个小时的电视。
　 They have watched TV for two hours.

（3）有时量补语的句子，句尾有语气助词"了$_2$"时，表示动作在持续；没有语气助词"了$_2$"时，表示动作已经结束。比较下面两组句子：
In a sentence with a complement of duration, the modal particle "了$_2$" is used at the end of a sentence, indicating the action is still going on. If the modal particle "了$_2$" is not used, it means the action is completed. Compare the following two groups of sentences:

A. 句尾没有"了$_2$"：
　 When "了$_2$" is not used at the end of a sentence:

⑩ 他学了半年汉语。（意思是：他现在不学汉语）
　 He has studied Chinese for half a year. (It means he is not studying Chinese now.)
⑪ 他们看了两个小时电视。（意思是：他们现在不看电视）
　 They have watched TV for two hours. (It means they are not watching TV now.)
⑫ 她睡了8个小时。（意思是：她现在没睡）
　 She has slept for 8 hours. (It means she is not sleeping now.)

B. 句尾有"了$_2$"：
　 When "了$_2$" is used at the end of a sentence：

128

⑬ 他学了半年汉语了。（意思是：他现在还在继续学汉语）

He has been studying Chinese for half a year. (It means he is still studying Chinese now.)

⑭ 他们看了两个小时电视了。（意思是：他们现在还在继续看电视）

They have been watching TV for two hours. (It means they are still watching TV now.)

⑮ 她睡了8个小时了。（意思是：她现在还在睡）

She has been sleeping for 8 hours. (It means she is still sleeping now.)

2 我发现中国人一般都有睡午觉的习惯。

一般：形容词，可以表示"普通"，也可以表示"通常"。表示"普通"的意思，常做定语；表示"通常"的意思，常做状语。例如：

一般：It is an adjective meaning "ordinary" or "usually". When it means "ordinary", it often serves as an attribute. When it means "usually", it often serves as an adverbial. For example,

① 我爸爸是公司一般职员。　　My father is an ordinary employee of the company.
② 我想了解一般中国人的生活。　　I want to learn about the life of ordinary Chinese people.
③ 中国人中午一般都睡午觉。　　Chinese people usually take a nap at noon.
④ 我一般早上7点起床。　　I usually get up at 7:00 in the morning.
⑤ 他一般一个星期给家里打一次电话。　　He usually calls his family every week.

3 他们吃了午饭以后都会休息休息，睡睡觉。

动词重叠：表示动作的时间缩短，程度减轻。单音节动词的重叠形式是：AA，如：看——看看；双音节动词的重叠形式是：ABAB，如：休息——休息休息。比较下面的句子：

Reduplication of a verb: The reduplication of a verb denotes an action lasts a shortened period of time or the degree is reduced. The reduplicative form of a monosyllabic verb is AA, such as "看——看看". While the reduplicative form of a disyllabic verb is ABAB, such as "休息——休息休息". Compare the following sentences:

A. 用重叠形式的句子：

The sentences with the reduplicative form of a verb:

① 睡觉前，我喜欢看看杂志，听听音乐。

I like reading a magazine or listening to the music before going to bed.

② 下课了，休息休息吧。

Class is over, let's take a break.

B. 不用重叠形式的句子：

The sentences without the reduplicative form of a verb:

③ 我每天下午 3 点到 5 点看书。
   I read books from 3:00 to 5:00 every afternoon.

④ 现在已经 12 点了，他休息了。
   It is 12:00 o'clock; he has taken a rest.

离合词的重叠形式是：AAB。例如：
The reduplicative form of a verb-object compound is AAB. For example,

⑤ 睡睡觉　　to have a sleep
⑥ 见见面　　to meet
⑦ 照照相　　to take a photo

有些表示心理活动、瞬间动作的动词不能重叠。例如：
The verbs indicating psychological activities or momentary actions cannot be reduplicated. For example,

⑧ 喜欢喜欢　（×）
⑨ 希望希望　（×）
⑩ 结结婚　　（×）

4 一般睡一个多小时。

时段短语：表示一段时间的词语叫时段短语。例如：

The phrase of duration: A word or phrase indicating a period of time is known as a phrase of duration. For example,

① 三个小时　　three hours
② 五天　　　　five days
③ 四个星期　　four weeks
④ 一个月　　　one month
⑤ 半年　　　　half a year

数词"半"放在时段短语中的量词后面、名词前面。例如：
The numeral "半" is used after the measure word and before the noun in the phrase of duration. For example,

⑥ 三个半小时　　three and a half hours
⑦ 一个半月　　　one and a half months

130

如果名词是"天"、"年",数词"半"必须在"天"、"年"的后面。例如:
If the noun is "天" or "年", the numeral "半" must be put after "天" or "年". For example,

⑧ 一天半　　　a day and a half
⑨ 两年半　　　two years and a half

5 吃了午饭以后就只有二十多分钟了,<u>没有时间睡午觉</u>。

"有/没有时间"+动词:表示有没有时间做某事。例如:

"有/没有时间"+verb: The structure means "having or not having time to do something". For example,

① 星期六晚上我有时间去看你。　　I will have time to visit you on Saturday evening.
② 今天晚上我没有时间陪你看电影。
　　I won't have time to see the movie with you tonight.
③ 明天下午你有时间打篮球吗?　　Will you have time to play basketball tomorrow afternoon?

20 tiān ān mén guǎng chǎng dà bu dà
天安门广场大不大
Is Tian'anmen Square large

课文 Text

天安门广场在北京城的中心，从南到北880米，从东到西500米，面积44万平方米，是世界上最大的广场，也是中国有名的名胜古迹。

天安门广场已经有五百多年历史了，广场北边的天安门城楼是明代的建筑物，也有五百多年了。天安门城楼后面就是举世闻名的故宫博物院。

现在天安门广场是人们游览、休闲的地方，也是中国举行重要政治活动的地方。

来北京以后，我一直想去天安门广场看看。星期六早上5点，我和中

132

20 天安门广场大不大

国朋友一起从学校骑自行车去逛天安门广场。早晨空气很新鲜，路上人很少，街道两旁干干净净的。我们骑了半个小时到了天安门广场。

天安门广场真大啊！天安门城楼在广场北边，正阳门在广场南边，人民大会堂在广场西边，国家博物馆在广场东边。广场中间是人民英雄纪念碑和毛主席纪念堂。

今天是晴天，头上是蓝蓝的天，白白的云，四周有红色的天安门城楼、灰色的正阳门、白色的国家博物馆等建筑物，天安门广场显得格外美。人们在广场上散步、游览、放风筝。

我觉得在天安门广场散步的感觉真好！

词语表 Vocabulary

1.	广场	guǎngchǎng	N	square
2.	中心	zhōngxīn	N	center
3.	南	nán	N	south
4.	北	běi	N	north

133

5.	米	mǐ	M	meter
6.	东	dōng	N	east
7.	西	xī	N	west
8.	面积	miànjī	N	area, space, surface area
9.	有名	yǒumíng	Adj	famous, well-known
10.	边	bian	Suf	*a suffix of a noun of locality*
11.	建筑物	jiànzhùwù	N	building
12.	后	hòu	N	back
13.	举世闻名	jǔshì wénmíng		world-famous
14.	休闲	xiūxián	V	to have leisure
15.	地方	dìfang	N	place
16.	举行	jǔxíng	V	to hold or have (a meeting, etc.)
17.	政治	zhèngzhì	N	politics
18.	活动	huódòng	N	activity
19.	一直	yìzhí	Adv	always
20.	路	lù	N	road
21.	街道	jiēdào	N	street
22.	旁	páng	N	side
23.	干净	gānjìng	Adj	clean
24.	真	zhēn	Adv	truly, really
25.	啊	a	MdPt	*used at the end of a sentence to express surprise or admiration*
26.	中间	zhōngjiān	N	middle
27.	晴	qíng	Adj	sunny
28.	头	tóu	N	head
29.	上	shang	N	above
30.	天	tiān	N	sky
31.	四周	sìzhōu	N	all around

32.	灰色	huīsè	N	gray
33.	显得	xiǎnde	V	to look, to appear
34.	格外	géwài	Adv	exceptionally, especially
35.	散步	sàn bù	V//O	to go for a walk
36.	放	fàng	V	to fly
37.	风筝	fēngzheng	N	kite
38.	感觉	gǎnjué	N	feeling

专有名词　Proper Nouns

1.	天安门广场	Tiān'ān Mén Guǎngchǎng	Tian'anmen Square
2.	天安门城楼	Tiān'ān Mén Chénglóu	Tian'anmen Gate Tower
3.	明代	Míngdài	Ming Dynasty (1368～1644)
4.	故宫博物院	Gù Gōng Bówùyuàn	the Palace Museum
5.	正阳门	Zhèngyáng Mén	Zhengyang Gate
6.	人民大会堂	Rénmín Dàhuìtáng	Great Hall of the People
7.	国家博物馆	Guójiā Bówùguǎn	National Museum
8.	人民英雄纪念碑	Rénmín Yīngxióng Jìniànbēi	the Monument to the People's Heroes
9.	毛主席纪念堂	Máo Zhǔxí Jìniàntáng	Chairman Mao's Memorial Hall

1 天安门广场大不大？

正反疑问句：谓语中心词的肯定、否定形式并列使用构成的疑问句是正反疑问句。例如：

The affirmative-negative question：A question that juxtaposes both the affirmative and negative forms of the main word in the predicate is known as an affirmative-negative question. For example,

① 你们班的韩国人多不多？　　Are there many Koreans in your class?

② 明天你去不去他家？　　　　　Will you go to his home tomorrow?

③ 你有没有哥哥？　　　　　　　Do you have an elder brother?

④ 你买不买这本词典？　　　　　Will you buy this dictionary?

⑤ 这个菜好吃不好吃？（"好吃不好吃"也可以说"好不好吃"）

Is this dish delicious?（"好吃不好吃" is equivalent to "好不好吃".）

⑥ 你了解不了解北京的气候？（"了解不了解"也可以说"了不了解"）

Do you know the weather in Beijing?（"了解不了解" can also be said as "了不了解".）

如果谓语中心词是动词，"动词＋不＋动词"和"动词＋没＋动词"意思不一样。例如：

If the main word in the predicate is a verb, "verb + 不 + verb" and "verb + 没 + verb" have different meanings. For example,

⑦ 你吃不吃早饭？　　　　　　Will you have breakfast?

（询问未来的动作　It is used to enquire an action that will happen in the future.）

⑧ 你吃没吃早饭？　　　　　　Did you have breakfast?

（询问过去的动作　It is used to enquire an action that happened in the past.）

⑨ 明天你去不去长城？　　　　Will you visit the Great Wall tomorrow?

（询问未来的动作　It is used to enquire the action that will happen in the future.）

⑩ 昨天你去没去长城？　　　　Did you visit the Great Wall yesterday?

（询问过去的动作　It is used to enquire an action that happened in the past.）

2　从南到北 880 米，从东到西 500 米。

方位词：方位词是表示方向、位置的词，可以分为两类：

The noun of locality：A noun of locality indicates the direction or position, which falls into the following two categories:

表示方向的词有 4 个：

There are 4 words indicating direction:

东、南、西、北

表示位置的词有 12 个：

There are 12 words indicating position:

上、下、前、后、左、右、里、外、内、中、旁、中间

方位词用在名词后面，组成方位短语。例如：

A noun of locality is used after a noun to make up a phrase of locality. For example,

广场上	on the square	学校里	in the school
教室外	out of the classroom	国外	abroad
国内	in the country		

方位词常和词尾"边"、"面"、"部"、"方"一起使用。例如：
A noun of locality is often used with a suffix like "边", "面", "部" or "方". For example,

西部	west	东部	east
北方	the North	南方	the South
左边	left side	右边	right side
上面	above	下面	below
旁边	next to sb. or sth.	里边	inside

3 来北京以后，我一直想去天安门广场看看。

一直：副词，用在动词或形容词前面，表示动作持续不断，或者状态保持不变。例如：

一直：It is an adverb used before a verb or an adjective to indicate an action is continuous or the state is kept unchanged. For example,

① 我家一直在这儿住。 My family have been living here.
② 开学以后我一直很忙。 I have been very busy since the beginning of this semester.
③ 他妈妈一直教音乐。 His mother has been teaching music.

4 街道两旁干干净净的。/ 头上是蓝蓝的天，白白的云。

形容词重叠：形容词重叠一般表示程度的加深，有描写作用。单音节形容词的重叠形式是 AA；双音节形容词的重叠形式是：AABB。重叠后的形容词可以修饰名词，充当定语，也可以做谓语。做谓语时，后面一般要用"的"。例如：

Reduplication of an adjective：Having a descriptive function, it is usually used to indicate the degree is growing. The reduplicative form of a monosyllabic adjective is AA; while that of a disyllabic adjective is AABB. The reduplicated adjective can be used as an attribute to modify a noun or used as the predicate. When used as the predicate, it is usually followed by "的". For example,

① 她高高的个子，大大的眼睛，黑黑的头发，非常漂亮。
   She is tall with big eyes and black hair. She is very pretty.
② 她的房间整整齐齐的。 Her room is very tidy.
③ 她今天穿的裙子简简单单的，但是非常漂亮。
   The skirt she wears today is simple, but very nice.

5 天安门广场真大啊！

感叹句：表示感叹的句子。句子开头或者末尾常用叹词"啊"。例如：

The exclamatory sentence：It indicates an exclamation. The interjection "啊" is often used at the beginning or the end of a sentence. For example,

① 他的房间真干净啊！　　His room is so clean!
② 啊，北京的自行车真多！　Oh, there are so many bicycles in Beijing!

6 天安门广场真大啊！

"啊"的音变："啊"因为受前面"大"的发音影响，也可以读 ya。

The change of the pronunciation of "啊"： Affected by the pronunciation of "大", "啊" is also read ya.

单元小结（11~20课）
Review (Lessons 11~20)

	语法项目	例　句
疑问句	1. 选择疑问句	这是咖啡还是可乐？
	2. 正反疑问句	留学生餐厅的菜贵不贵？
	3. 用"怎么"提问	苹果怎么卖？
	4. 用"怎么样"提问	他的汉语怎么样？
	5. 用"多+形容词"提问	你的房间多大？
	6. 询问时量补语的疑问句	你学了多长时间的汉语了？
	7. "……，对吗？"	这是你同屋的电脑，对吗？
	8. "……，好吗？"	中午吃包子，好吗？
	9. "……吧？"	你是韩国人吧？
比较句	1. A比B+形容词	今天比昨天冷。
	2. A比B+形容词+"一点儿"	今天比昨天冷一点儿。
	3. A比B+形容词+"多了"	今天比昨天冷多了。
	4. A比B+形容词+数量补语	今天的最高温度比昨天的高3℃。
	5. A没有B+形容词	今天没有昨天冷。
	6. A跟B+"一样/不一样"	东京的天气跟北京的不一样。
兼语句	主语+"让"+兼语+谓语+宾语	老师让我们写汉语作文。
感叹句	"……啊！"	她的房间真干净啊！

续表

语法项目		例　句
语法点	1. 动态助词"了₁"	昨天晚上我们喝了五瓶啤酒。
	2. 语气助词"了₂"	天气一天比一天冷了。
	3. "要……了"表示动作即将发生	我们就要上课了。
	4. 双宾语	李老师教我们听力课。
	5. 时量补语	他吃了一个小时的午饭。
	6. 动词重叠	周末，我喜欢听听音乐，看看书。
	7. 形容词重叠	今天天晴，蓝蓝的天上飘着白白的云。
	8. "有点儿"+形容词	这个菜有点儿贵。
	9. 主谓短语做定语	他买的裤子很合适。
	10. 动宾短语做定语	上课的时候，我们用汉语介绍自己的爱好。

语音知识：句中语音停顿	他是 // 法国人。

21 您要兑换什么
nín yào duì huàn shén me
What do you want to convert

课文 Text

人们在中国只能用人民币消费。外国人在中国必须用外币兑换人民币。我来中国留学没带外币现金，带的是旅行支票，因为带旅行支票比带现金更安全。听说学校附近的一家银行能兑换外国的旅行支票，我想去那儿看看。

银行的营业厅里整整齐齐、干干净净。一位年轻的女职员用英语对我说："我能帮助你吗？"我说："我要兑换旅行支票。"她告诉我，外国人在这儿可以兑换旅行支票，也可以用外币兑换人民币，不过要收手续费。这位小姐会说英语，也会说日语，对我很热情。我很高兴。我问她在中国的银行怎么取钱。她说，可以在银行窗口取钱，也可以用银行卡在自动取款机上取钱。但是一定要记住自己的密码。这位小姐告诉我，最好办一张银行卡，因为刷卡消费更方便，也更安全。现在有的银行卡在中国、外国都可以用。

听了她的介绍，我想我应该办一张这样在中国、在外国都可以用的银行卡。

这家银行在学校附近，银行职员服务很热情，也很耐心。以后我可以常来这儿换钱、存钱、取钱了。

词语表 Vocabulary

1.	要	yào	OpV	to want to, would like to, to need to
2.	兑换	duìhuàn	V	to exchange, to convert
3.	能	néng	OpV	can
4.	人民币	rénmínbì	N	RMB
5.	消费	xiāofèi	V	to consume
6.	必须	bìxū	Adv	must, to have to
7.	外币	wàibì	N	foreign currency
8.	带	dài	V	to take (sth. with sb.)
9.	现金	xiànjīn	N	cash
10.	旅行	lǚxíng	V	to travel

您要兑换什么

11.	支票	zhīpiào	N	cheque
12.	更	gèng	Adv	more, even more
13.	安全	ānquán	Adj	safe, secure
14.	听说	tīngshuō	V	to hear of, to be told
15.	银行	yínháng	N	bank
16.	营业	yíngyè	V	to do business
17.	整齐	zhěngqí	Adj	in apple-pie order, tidy
18.	年轻	niánqīng	Adj	young
19.	对	duì	Prep	to
20.	可以	kěyǐ	OpV	can
21.	收	shōu	V	to receive
22.	手续	shǒuxù	N	procedure
23.	费	fèi	N	fee, charge
24.	小姐	xiǎojie	N	Miss
25.	取	qǔ	V	to withdraw
26.	窗口	chuāngkǒu	N	the place where you pay or are served in a bank
27.	卡	kǎ	N	card
28.	自动取款机	zìdòng qǔkuǎnjī		ATM
	自动	zìdòng	Adj	automatic
29.	密码	mìmǎ	N	PIN
30.	办	bàn	V	to apply for (a card)
31.	刷卡	shuā kǎ	V//O	to swipe (a card)
32.	应该	yīnggāi	OpV	should, ought to
33.	服务	fúwù	V	to serve
34.	换	huàn	V	to exchange, to convert
35.	存	cún	V	to deposit

注释 Notes

1 您<u>要</u>兑换什么？/ 我<u>想</u>去那儿看看。

🔍 **辨析 Discrimination：想、要**

"想"与"要"都是能愿动词，用在动词前面，表示做某事的意愿。但是，"要"实现的可能性很大，"想"只是一种打算。例如：

Both "想" and "要" are optative verbs used before a verb to express one's wish. However, the action after "要" is more likely to be realized, while the action after "想" is just a plan. For example,

① 明年他要去中国工作。　　　　He will go to work in China next year.
② 下个月他要来北京旅游。　　　He will travel in Beijing next month.
③ 下午我要去银行换钱。　　　　I will change money in the bank this afternoon.
④ 他想去中国学习汉语。　　　　He wants to study Chinese in China.
⑤ 今天他想休息。　　　　　　　He wants to take today off.
⑥ 晚上我想看电影。　　　　　　I want to see the movie tonight.

"要"没有否定形式，也没有正反提问形式。"想"的否定形式是"不想"，可以用"想不想"提问。但是口语中也可以用"要不要＋动词"提问。例如：

"要" has neither a negative form nor an affirmative-negative form. The negative form of "想" is "不想", and "想不想" can be used to make a question. However, "要不要 + verb" is also used to make a question in spoken Chinese. For example,

⑦ 我不要去北京工作。　　　　　（×）
⑧ 你要不要去银行换钱？　　　　（×）
⑨ 我不想去北京工作。　　　　　I don't want to work in Beijing.
⑩ 你想不想去银行换钱？　　　　Do you want to change money in the bank?

"要"还表示需要的意思。例如：
"要" also means "need". For example,

⑪ 在银行换钱要收手续费。
　　You need to pay the procedure fee when changing money in the bank.
⑫ 从北京到上海坐飞机要两个小时。
　　It takes two hours to fly from Beijing to Shanghai.
⑬ 坐车要买票。　　You need to buy a ticket when taking a bus.

2 人们在中国只能用人民币消费。/ 外国人在这儿可以兑换旅行支票。

可以、能：能愿动词，都可以用在动词前，表示条件许可做某事。但是"可以"多用于客观条件许可做某事，"能"多用于主观意愿许可做某事。例如：

"可以" and "能": Both "可以" and "能" are optative verbs used before a verb to indicate somebody can do something under certain condition. However, in most cases, "可以" is used when somebody does something under objective conditions, while "能" is used when somebody does something out of subjective reasons. For example,

① 这儿可以吸烟。　　　　　　　You can smoke here.
② 超市也可以刷卡。　　　　　　You can also pay by card in the supermarket.
③ 这儿不可以照相。　　　　　　Taking photos is not permitted here.
④ 你可以进来了。　　　　　　　Please come in.
⑤ 我能出去打个电话吗？　　　　Can I go out to make a call?
⑥ 我能进来吗？　　　　　　　　May I come in?

3 人们在中国只能用人民币消费。/ 这位小姐会说英语，也会说日语。

会、能：能愿动词，都可以用在动词前面。

"会" and "能": Both "会" and "能" are optative verbs and can be used before a verb.

"会"表示经过学习掌握了一门技术、技能。否定形式是"不会"。例如：

"会" refers to having mastered some skill through learning. Its negative form is "不会". For example,

① 他会说汉语。　　　　　　　　He can speak Chinese.
② 我会开车。　　　　　　　　　I can drive.
③ 我不会发电子邮件。　　　　　I don't know how to send an email.
④ 她不会做饭。　　　　　　　　She doesn't know how to cook.

"能"指一种能力。否定形式是"不能"。例如：

"能" indicates one's ability. Its negative form is "不能". For example,

⑤ 他能写自己的汉语名字。　　　He can write his Chinese name.
⑥ 他的病好了，明天能去上课。
　　He has recovered from an illness and can go to class tomorrow.
⑦ 爷爷病了，不能出去散步了。　My grandfather is sick and cannot go out for a walk.
⑧ 我不能用汉语介绍我们公司。　I cannot use Chinese to introduce our company.

"会"与"能"都可以用正反形式提问。例如：
Both "会" and "能" can be used in affirmative-negative questions. For example,

145

⑨ 你会不会开飞机？　　　　　　　　Can you fly an airplane?
⑩ 你能不能告诉我银行在哪儿？　　　Can you tell me where the bank is?

4 听说学校附近的一家银行能兑换外国的旅行支票。

听说：动词，用来转述听到的内容。一般不用指出是听"谁"说的。例如：

听说：It is a verb used to tell what somebody heard. Usually there is no need to point out "who" said it. For example,

① 听说明天没有课。　　　It is said we won't have a class tomorrow.
② 听说他回国了。　　　　It is said he has gone back to his motherland.
③ 听说他感冒了。　　　　I hear he caught a cold.

5 一位年轻的女职员用英语对我说："我能帮助你吗？"

对：介词，后面常带表示人的名词做宾语，组成介宾短语修饰动词，说明动作关联的对象。例如：

对：It is a preposition followed by a noun indicating somebody as an object, forming a prepositional phrase. The phrase is used to modify the verb and explain the receiver of the action. For example,

① 他对我说"对不起"。　　　He said "sorry" to me.
② 他对我帮助很大。　　　　He helped to me a lot.
③ 我很想对她说"谢谢"。　　I really want to say "thank you" to her.

6 我想我应该办一张这样在中国、外国都可以用的银行卡。

应该：能愿动词，用在动词前面，表示按照道理、事理做某事。口语也说"该"。例如：

应该：It is an optative verb used before a verb, meaning "doing something because it is right or appropriate". "该" can also be said in spoken Chinese. For example,

① 你感冒了，应该休息。　　You've caught a cold and need to rest.
② 我大学毕业了，应该找工作了。
　　I've graduated from the university and I need to look for a job.
③ 下面该你介绍了。　　　　It is your turn to introduce yourself.

146

22 去中关村怎么坐车

How can I get to Zhongguancun by bus

课文 Text

我的中国朋友张文心家在中关村。她家最近买了一套新房子。她请我今天中午去她家吃饺子。

张文心给我画了一张去她家的图：先在学校东门坐公共汽车，到中关村下车。下车以后，不要换车，往前走一百米左右，过了红绿灯向右拐，再往前走5分钟，就会看见马路左边有一个住宅小区。那是大学教师住的小区。她家的新房子就在这个住宅小区，地址是中关村大街5号，中关园3区8号楼103。

上午我准备去她家的时候，她来了。她担心我不知道怎么去她家。她和我一块儿骑自行车去。我们一直向北骑，一边骑车，一边聊天儿，骑了40分钟后到张文心家。如果张文心不和我一块儿去她家，我可能会迷路。因为这个住宅小区有十座相同的住宅楼。

张文心家有三口人。她父亲是一家复印机公司的经理，她母亲是大学的数学教授。张文心很像她父亲。她父母热情地欢迎我去做客。中午我们吃了自己包的猪肉白菜馅儿饺子，味道真好。张文心母亲做的凉菜也很好吃。

这是我第一次在中国人家里吃饭。中国人习惯用筷子吃饭，我习惯用勺子、叉子、刀吃饭。可是我发现用筷子吃中国菜非常方便。以后我一定得学会用筷子吃中国菜。

词语表 Vocabulary

1.	图	tú	N	picture, drawing, diagram
2.	先	xiān	Adv	first
3.	不要	búyào	Adv	not
4.	换	huàn	V	to change, to transfer
5.	往	wǎng	Prep	to go towards

6.	前	qián	N	forward part or position
7.	左右	zuǒyòu	N	about, approximately
8.	过	guò	V	to cross
9.	红绿灯	hónglǜdēng	N	traffic light
10.	向	xiàng	Prep	towards
11.	右	yòu	N	right (side)
12.	拐	guǎi	V	to turn
13.	再	zài	Adv	*indicating that one action takes place after another*
14.	马路	mǎlù	N	road
15.	左	zuǒ	N	left (side)
16.	住宅	zhùzhái	N	residence
17.	小区	xiǎoqū	N	housing estate
18.	区	qū	N	area, district, region
19.	一块儿	yíkuàir	Adv	together
20.	一边……一边……	yìbiān……yìbiān……		at the same time
21.	如果	rúguǒ	Conj	if
22.	可能	kěnéng	Adv	maybe
23.	迷路	mí lù	V//O	to get lost, to lose one's way
24.	座	zuò	M	*a measuere word for large buildings*
25.	相同	xiāngtóng	Adj	same
26.	父亲	fùqin	N	father
27.	复印机	fùyìnjī	N	copier
	复印	fùyìn	V	to copy
28.	经理	jīnglǐ	N	manager
29.	母亲	mǔqin	N	mother
30.	数学	shùxué	N	math
31.	教授	jiàoshòu	N	professor
32.	父母	fùmǔ	N	parents

33.	做客	zuò kè	V//O	to be sb.'s guest
34.	包	bāo	V	to wrap
35.	猪肉	zhūròu	N	pork
36.	白菜	báicài	N	Chinese cabbage
37.	馅儿	xiànr	N	stuffing, filling
38.	第一次	dì yī cì		the first time
39.	筷子	kuàizi	N	chopsticks
40.	可是	kěshì	Conj	but, however
41.	勺子	sháozi	N	spoon
42.	叉子	chāzi	N	fork
43.	刀	dāo	N	knife

专有名词　Proper Nouns

1.	中关村	Zhōngguāncūn	a technology hub in Haidian District, Beijing
2.	张文心	Zhāng Wénxīn	name of a person
3.	中关园	Zhōngguānyuán	a residential area in Zhongguancun

注　释　Notes

1 往前走一百米左右，过了红绿灯向右拐。

往、向：介词，后面常带方位词做宾语，组成介宾短语修饰动词，说明动作的方向或经过的处所。例如：

"往" and "向"：They are both prepositions. They are often used as objects after nouns of locality, forming prepositional phrases to modify verbs, explaining the direction of somebody's action or the place somebody passes by. For example,

①下车后往前走五分钟。　　Get off the bus and walk ahead for five minutes.
②往北骑一公里就到了。　　Ride northwards for one kilometer, then you will get there.
③下车后向右拐。　　　　　Get off the bus and turn right.
④过了第一个红绿灯向左拐。　Turn left at the first traffic lights.

150

2 她家的新房子<u>就</u>在这个住宅小区。

就：副词，表示加强肯定，一般用在动词前面或其他状语前面。例如：

就：It is an adverb used to strengthen the affirmative statement. It is generally used before a verb or another adverbial. For example,

① 他就是我同屋。	He is my roommate.
② 这就是我新买的电脑。	This is the computer that I just bought.
③ 我就爱吃辣的。	I like eating spicy food.

3 地址是<u>中关村大街 5 号，中关园 3 区 8 号楼 103</u>。

地址的顺序：汉语表示地址的顺序是从大到小。

The order of expressing an address: An address is expressed in descending order in Chinese.

（1）城市（City）：~省 ~市 ~区 ~街/路 ~号 ~区（住宅区）~楼 ~号。例如：

① 北京市海淀区新街口外大街 19 号
   No. 19, Xinjiekouwai Street, Haidian District, Beijing

② 北京师范大学乐育区 19 楼 801 号
   Room 801, Building 19, Leyu Housing Estate, Beijing Normal University

（2）农村（Country）：~省 ~市 ~县 ~乡 ~村。例如：

③ 广东省中山市中山县高明乡陈家村
   Chenjia Village, Gaoming Township, Zhongshan County, Zhongshan City, Guangdong Province

4 我们一直向北骑，<u>一边</u>骑车，<u>一边</u>聊天儿。

一边……一边……：表示两种以上的动作同时进行。例如：

一边……一边……：It indicates somebody is doing two or more than two actions concurrently. For example,

| ① 他一边听音乐，一边看书。 | He listened to the music while reading a book. |
| ② 妈妈喜欢一边唱歌，一边做饭。 | My mother likes singing while cooking. |

有时也可以省略"一"，说成"边……边……"。例如：

Sometimes "一" is omitted and the above structure is changed into "边……边……". For example,

③ 他们边走边唱。	They sang songs while walking.
④ 他边看边吃。	He ate while watching.
⑤ 她边说边笑。	She smiled while speaking.

5 **如果**张文心不和我一块儿去她家，我可能会迷路。

如果：连词，表示一种假设的情况，用在假设的小句前面。例如：

如果：It is a conjunction used before a hypothetical clause to indicate a hypothetical situation. For example,

① 如果明天有时间，我一定给你打电话。
　　If I have time tomorrow, I will surely call you.

② 如果我有很多钱，我会买很大很漂亮的房子。
　　If I have a lot of money, I will buy a big and beautiful house.

③ 如果你不舒服，可以回房间休息。
　　If you are not feeling well, you can go back to your room to have a rest.

23 客厅后边是什么
What is behind the sitting room

课文 Text

这是我家的照片。

我家的房子朝南,是一栋两层的日式建筑。楼下进门是客厅。客厅是家里最大的房间,也是最重要的房间。客厅里有桌子、椅子、沙发,还有电视、空调等电器。我们一般在客厅吃饭、聊天儿、看电视什么的。客厅的玻璃窗户又高又大,在客厅里可以看见外面漂亮的小花园。书房在客厅左边,楼梯在客厅右边,客厅后边是厨房。楼梯旁边是卫生间,书房后边是客房,里面也有一个卫生间。

楼上有三间卧室,左边的是我的,右边的是弟弟的,爸爸妈妈的卧室在中间。哥哥在外面租房子住,所以家

153

里没有他的卧室。三间卧室的对面是阳台。阳台很大，夏天的傍晚，我们全家人喜欢在那儿喝茶、乘凉，有时候爸爸喜欢在那儿抽烟。阳台下面是车库。

房子前面有一个小花园。里面有花儿、有草、有树，春天花园很漂亮。房子后面有超市、邮局、银行。附近有一所小学，还有一所中学。这栋房子离地铁站也不远，生活挺方便的。

我家在这儿住了二十多年了。房子虽然有点儿旧了，但是我和哥哥、弟弟都是在这儿出生、长大的，我们对它很有感情。

词语表 Vocabulary

1.	朝	cháo	V	to face
2.	栋	dòng	M	a measure word for buildings
3.	式	shì	Suf	style
4.	楼下	lóu xià		downstairs
5.	客厅	kètīng	N	sitting room, parlor
6.	里	li	N	in
7.	沙发	shāfā	N	sofa
8.	玻璃	bōli	N	glass

9.	窗户	chuānghu	N	window
10.	外面	wàimian	N	outside
11.	花园	huāyuán	N	garden
12.	书房	shūfáng	N	study, especially in sb.'s home, used for reading and writing
13.	楼梯	lóutī	N	stairs
14.	厨房	chúfáng	N	kitchen
15.	卫生间	wèishēngjiān	N	rest room
16.	客房	kèfáng	N	guest room
17.	里面	lǐmian	N	inside
18.	楼上	lóu shàng		upstairs
19.	卧室	wòshì	N	bedroom
20.	对面	duìmiàn	N	opposite
21.	阳台	yángtái	N	balcony
22.	傍晚	bàngwǎn	N	evening
23.	乘凉	chéng liáng	V//O	to relax in a cool place
24.	抽	chōu	V	to smoke
25.	烟	yān	N	tobacco
26.	车库	chēkù	N	garage
27.	花儿	huār	N	flower
28.	草	cǎo	N	grass
29.	树	shù	N	tree
30.	超市	chāoshì	N	supermarket
31.	邮局	yóujú	N	post office
32.	所	suǒ	M	*a measure word for schools, colleges, hospitals or other institutions*
33.	离	lí	V	to be from
34.	地铁	dìtiě	N	underground (railway), subway
35.	站	zhàn	N	station
36.	远	yuǎn	Adj	far

37.	虽然……但是……	suīrán……dànshì……		although
38.	旧	jiù	Adj	old
39.	出生	chūshēng	V	to be born
40.	长大	zhǎngdà	V	to grow up
41.	感情	gǎnqíng	N	affection

1 客厅后边是什么？

方位短语：指由名词和方位词构成的短语。方位短语表示地点。例如：

The phrase of locality: It is a phrase made up of a noun and a noun of locality. A phrase of locality indicates place. For example,

① 客厅右边　　　　on the right side of the sitting room
② 学校后边　　　　behind the school
③ 桌子上　　　　　on the table
④ 他左边　　　　　on his left side
⑤ 房间里边　　　　in the room

注意："客厅右边"和"客厅的右边"意思不一样。"客厅右边"在客厅外，"客厅的右边"在客厅里。

Note: "客厅右边" and "客厅的右边" have different meanings. The former refers to the right side out of the sitting room, while the latter refers to the right side in the sitting room.

2 楼下进门是客厅。/ 客厅里有桌子、椅子、沙发。/ 书房在客厅左边。

存在句：表示某处存在某物的句子是存在句。按谓语中心词的不同，可以分为三种。

The sentence indicating existence: A sentence indicating existence of something in some place is known as a sentence indicating existence. It is divided into three categories based on the different main word in the predicate.

（1）"是"字句：某处＋"是"＋某物。例如：

The "是" sentence：some place ＋ "是" ＋ something. For example,

① 客厅左边是楼梯。　　　　　　　　The stairs are on the left side of the sitting room.
② 我旁边是山下京美。　　　　　　　I am beside Yamashita Kyomi.
③ 桌子上是老师的书。　　　　　　　My teacher's book is on the desk.

（2）"有"字句：某处＋"有"＋某物。例如：

The "有" sentence：some place ＋ "有" ＋ something. For example,

④ 楼上有三间卧室。　　　　　　　　There are three bedrooms upstairs.
⑤ 教室里有很多人。　　　　　　　　There are many people in the classroom.
⑥ 学校大门外边有银行、车站、商店。
　　There is a bank, a bus station and a shop out of the school gate.

（3）"在"字句：某物＋"在"＋某处。例如：

The "在" sentence：something ＋ "在" ＋ some place. For example,

⑦ 书房在客厅左边。　　　　　　　　The study is on the left side of the sitting room.
⑧ 电视在卧室里。　　　　　　　　　The TV set is in the bedroom.
⑨ 车站在马路对面。　　　　　　　　The bus station is across the road.

3 这栋房子**离**地铁站也不远。

离：动词，用在地点名词或者时间词前面，表示两个地点之间的距离，或者两个时点之间的距离。例如：

离：It is a verb used before a noun of place or a noun of time. It indicates the distance in time or space. For example,

① 我家离学校很远。　　　　　　　　I live very far away from the school.
② 中国离韩国不远。　　　　　　　　China is not far away from Korea.
③ 我的宿舍离教室很近。　　　　　　My dormitory is near the classroom.
④ 现在离下课还有五分钟。　　　　　The class will be over in five minutes.
⑤ 今天离放假还有两个星期。　　　　There are still two weeks before the vacation.
⑥ 圣诞节离新年很近。　　　　　　　Christmas is near the New Year.

4 房子**虽然**有点儿旧了，**但是**我和哥哥、弟弟都是在这儿出生、长大的。

虽然……但是……：表示转折关系，用在转折复句中。如果两个分句的主语相同，主语出现在"虽然"的前面。例如：

157

虽然……但是……: It is used in a transitional compound sentence, indicating a transitional relationship. If the subject in the two clauses is the same one, it is used before "虽然". For example,

① 她虽然很漂亮，但是不太聪明。　　She is pretty, but not very smart.
② 我们的汉语课虽然有点儿难，但是很有意思。
　　Although our Chinese courses are a bit difficult, they are very interesting.
③ 中国菜虽然很好吃，但是很油腻。　　Chinese dishes are delicious, but very oily.

如果两个分句的主语不相同，两个主语应分别出现在"虽然"、"但是"的后面。例如：
If the two clauses have different subjects, the subjects appear after "虽然" and "但是" respectively. For example,

④ 虽然他有汉语名字，但是大家喜欢叫他的英语名字。
　　Although he has a Chinese name, everyone calls his English name.
⑤ 虽然这条牛仔裤很便宜，但是我不想买。
　　Although this pair of jeans is inexpensive, I don't want to buy it.
⑥ 虽然中国菜很油腻，但是留学生都很爱吃。
　　Although Chinese dishes are oily, all the international students like them.

"虽然"常常可以省略，只用"但是"或"可是"。例如：
"虽然" is often omitted, and only "但是" or "可是" is used in a sentence. For example,

⑦ 这个菜很好吃，但是比较贵。　　This dish is delicious, but it is comparatively expensive.
⑧ 我感冒了，但是没发热。　　I caught a cold, but I didn't run a fever.
⑨ 我会说的汉语句子不少，可是认识的汉字很少。
　　I can speak many Chinese sentences, but I read few Chinese characters.

24 这是谁送你的生日礼物

Who gave you this birthday gift

课文 Text

下个月5号是我20岁生日。昨天是星期天,我去邮局取了妈妈寄来的包裹。邮局里人很多。有买邮票的,有看杂志的,也有寄包裹的。我等了一会儿。这个包裹是个大纸箱子。虽然比较大,但是不太重。我取了包裹就回学校了。我想马上打开包裹,看看里面的东西。

包裹里主要是家里人送给我的生日礼物:爸爸送我的一本日汉电子词典、妈妈送我的一条金项链、哥哥送我的一套西服、弟弟送我的三张流行音乐光盘,还有奶奶送我的一件和服。我的这件和服是深蓝色的,上面有

159

浅黄色的花儿，非常漂亮。这是奶奶自己做的和服。奶奶做和服做得很好。我的这件和服奶奶做得特别合适。除了生日礼物以外，还有一些我喜欢吃的零食、甜点等休闲食品。

今天我在会话课上介绍了和服。因为我现在的汉语是初级水平，我觉得我介绍得不太详细，但是同学们听得十分认真。他们让我穿穿这件和服，他们想看看我穿和服的样子。我说我不会穿和服，要妈妈帮我穿。大家听了，笑得特别开心。乔治说："你已经是大学生了，怎么还要妈妈帮你穿衣服呢？"我告诉他们，和服是日本的传统服装，现在日本人平时不穿和服，只有节日或有重要活动的时候才穿，比如说，新年、结婚典礼等，所以很多年轻人都不会穿和服了。现在，日本还有教穿和服的学习班呢。

词语表 Vocabulary

| 1. | 生日 | shēngrì | N | birthday |
| 2. | 礼物 | lǐwù | N | present, gift |

160

这是谁送你的生日礼物

3.	寄	jì	V	to send by post, to mail
4.	包裹	bāoguǒ	N	parcel
5.	邮票	yóupiào	N	stamp
6.	杂志	zázhì	N	magazine
7.	等	děng	V	to wait
8.	一会儿	yíhuìr	Q	a short while, a moment
9.	纸	zhǐ	N	cardboard, paper
10.	箱子	xiāngzi	N	box
11.	重	zhòng	Adj	heavy
12.	马上	mǎshàng	Adv	right away, at once
13.	本	běn	M	*a measure word for books*
14.	电子	diànzǐ	N	electron
15.	词典	cídiǎn	N	dictionary
16.	金	jīn	N	gold
17.	项链	xiàngliàn	N	necklace
18.	西服	xīfú	N	Western suit
19.	奶奶	nǎinai	N	(paternal) grandmother
20.	和服	héfú	N	kimono
21.	深	shēn	Adj	(of color) deep, dark
22.	浅	qiǎn	Adj	(of color) light
23.	得	de	StPt	*used after a verb or an adjective to introduce a complement of result or degree*
24.	除了……以外，还/也……	chúle……yǐwài, hái / yě……		*used together with "还", "也" to mean "besides"*
25.	一些	yìxiē	Q	some
26.	零食	língshí	N	snack
27.	甜点	tiándiǎn	N	dessert
28.	食品	shípǐn	N	food

161

29.	初	chū		elementary, rudimentary
30.	详细	xiángxì	Adj	detailed
31.	认真	rènzhēn	Adj	careful, attentive
32.	笑	xiào	V	to laugh
33.	开心	kāixīn	Adj	happy
34.	传统	chuántǒng	Adj	traditional
35.	平时	píngshí	N	in ordinary times
36.	只有……才……	zhǐyǒu……cái……		only then
37.	节日	jiérì	N	festival
38.	新年	xīnnián	N	New Year
39.	结婚	jié hūn	V//O	to marry
40.	典礼	diǎnlǐ	N	ceremony
41.	呢	ne	MdPt	used at the end of a statement to give emphasis

补充词语　Complementary Word

	一点儿	yìdiǎnr	Q	a bit, a little

1 这是谁送你的生日礼物？/ 奶奶做和服做得很好。

辨析 Discrimination：的、地、得

　　这三个词都是结构助词。"的"用在定语和中心词中间，后面常常是名词。基本结构：定语 + "的" + 名词。例如：

All the three words are structural particles. "的" is used between the attribute and the main word and is often followed by a noun. The structure is: attribute + "的" + noun. For example,

　　① 这是朋友的电脑。　　　　This is my friend's computer.

162

② 我新买的牛仔裤很合适。　　My newly-bought jeans fit me very well.

"地"用在状语和谓语中间，后面常常是动词或形容词。基本结构：状语 + "地" + 谓语。例如：
"地" is used between the adverbial and the predicate and is often followed by a verb or an adjective. The basic structure is: adverbial + "地" + predicate. For example,

③ 她详细地介绍了包饺子的方法。
　　She told us how to make dumplings in detail.
④ 饭馆的服务员热情地介绍他们的拿手菜。
　　The waitress of the restaurant cordially recommended their specialty.

"得"用在谓语和补语中间，前面常常是动词。基本结构：动词 + "得" + 补语。例如：
"得" is used between the predicate and the complement and is often preceded by a verb. The basic structure is: verb + "得" + complement. For example,

⑤ 她笑得很开心。　　　　　　She laughed happily.
⑥ 他说汉语说得非常流利。　　He speaks Chinese very fluently.

2 奶奶做和服做得很好。

状态补语（带宾语）：动词后面既有宾语又有状态补语时，有两种格式：
The complement of state (with an object): When a verb is followed by an object and a complement of state, there are two patterns:

（1）动词 + 宾语 + 动词 + "得" + 状态补语。例如：
　　 Verb + object + verb + "得" + complement of state. For example,

① 他说汉语说得很流利。　　He speaks Chinese very fluently.
② 她写汉字写得很漂亮。　　She writes Chinese characters beautifully.
③ 他洗衣服洗得不太干净。　He doesn't wash clothes well.

（2）宾语 + 动词 + "得" + 状态补语。例如：
　　 Object + verb + "得" + complement of state. For example,

④ 他汉语说得很流利。　　He speaks Chinese very fluently.
⑤ 她汉字写得很漂亮。　　She writes Chinese characters beautifully.
⑥ 他衣服洗得不太干净。　He doesn't wash clothes well.

3 **除了**生日礼物**以外**，**还**有一些我喜欢吃的零食、甜点等休闲食品。

除了……以外，还 / 也……：表示排除已知，补充其他相同的情况。主语可以出现在"除了"前面，也可以出现在"还 / 也"前面。有时也可以省略"以外"。例如：

除了……以外，还 / 也……：They are used to exclude something already known and complement other similar situations. The subject can be used either before "除了" or before "还 / 也". "以外" is omitted sometimes. For example,

① 除了会话课以外，我们还有精读课、听力课。
　　In addition to speaking course, we also have intensive reading and listening.

② 我们班除了日本人以外，还有美国人、英国人。
　　Besides Japanese, there are Americans and Englishmen in our class.

③ 她除了会说英语以外，还会说法语、德语、西班牙语。
　　In addition to English, she can speak French, German and Spanish.

④ 除了白色，我也喜欢黑色。
　　Besides white, I like black.

⑤ 我们家除了她不吃猪肉，我也不吃猪肉。
　　In our family I don't eat pork besides her.

4 还有**一些**我喜欢吃的零食、甜点等休闲食品。

一些：数量词，表示少量。前面有"有"时，常说"有些"。例如：

一些：It is a quantifier, meaning "a small amount". "有些" is often used when it is preceded by "有". For example,

① 下午我去商店买了一些吃的。
　　I went to buy some food in the store in the afternoon.

② 我在北京认识了一些新朋友。　　I made some new friends in Beijing.
③ 我有些词不认识。　　There are some words I don't know.
④ 他有些朋友在国外上大学。　　He has some friends studying in universities abroad.
⑤ 外面有些人在照相。　　Some people are taking photos outside.

辨析 Discrimination：一些、一点儿

"一些"与"一点儿"都表示数量，也可以表示程度。"一些"表示的数量、程度比"一点儿"表示的要多、深。

Both "一些" and "一点儿" indicate the quantity or degree. The former indicates a larger quantity or higher degree than the latter. For example,

⑥ 我买了一些吃的。　　I bought some food.
⑦ 我买了一点儿吃的。　　I bought a little food.

⑧ 今天比昨天冷一些。　　　　　Today is colder than yesterday.
⑨ 今天比昨天冷一点儿。　　　　Today is a bit colder than yesterday.
⑩ 来中国的时候，我带了一些感冒药，现在只有一点儿了。
　　I took some cold medicine with me when coming to China, but now there is only a little left.

5 我觉得我介绍得不太详细，但是同学们听得十分认真。

状态补语（不带宾语）：用在动词后面补充说明动作状态的词语叫状态补语。基本结构：动词＋"得"＋状态补语。例如：

The complement of state (without an object): The words used after a verb to complement and explain the action or state are known as the complement of state. The basic structure is: verb +"得"+ complement of state. For example,

① 他们听得很认真。　　　　They listened carefully.
② 他介绍得很详细。　　　　He gave a detailed introduction.
③ 她说得很快。　　　　　　She speaks very fast.
④ 他写得不太好。　　　　　He didn't write it very well.

6 现在日本人平时不穿和服，只有节日或有重要活动的时候才穿。

只有……才……：表示唯一的条件关系。例如：

只有……才……：It indicates "under only one condition". For example,

① 只有多听多说，才能学好语言。
　　Only by extensively listening and speaking can we learn a language well.
② 只有去中国，才能真正了解中国。
　　Only by going to China can we really know China.
③ 现在日本人只有参加重要活动才穿和服。
　　Only when participating in important activities do Japanese wear kimonos.

7 日本还有教穿和服的学习班呢。

呢：陈述句句尾用"呢"表示加强确认。例如：

呢：It is used at the end of a declarative sentence to strengthen affirmation. For example,

① 她已经工作十年了呢。　　She has already been working for ten years.
② 他是经理呢。　　　　　　He is a manager.

25 生日晚会几点开始
When will the birthday party begin

课文 Text

昨天晚上我去参加了张文心的生日晚会。张文心是我在北京认识的中国朋友。她高高的个子、白白的皮肤、大大的眼睛,爱看英文小说,喜欢唱歌跳舞,除了中国民歌,美国电影中的英文插曲她也唱得很好听。我们每个星期在一起学习一次,我教她英语,她教我汉语。她说汉语像唱歌一样好听,和她在一起学习汉语很愉快。现在张文心是大学外语系英语专业四年级的学生,明年夏天就要大学毕业了。她打算毕业以后当翻译。

我进门的时候,张文心正和她男朋友聊天儿呢。她男

25 生日晚会几点开始

朋友是英国文学专业的博士生，高高的，瘦瘦的，戴着一副眼镜，长得很帅。昨天张文心穿着一条浅绿色的连衣裙，特别漂亮。我送她一束鲜花，祝她永远像鲜花一样美丽。

昨天是张文心的22岁生日。来参加晚会的客人很多，除了我以外，都是中国人，主要是张文心的同学和朋友。人们在客厅里喝着茶，聊着天儿。7点钟生日晚会开始了，大家吃了生日蛋糕，祝张文心生日快乐。

9点晚会结束了。我坐公共汽车回学校时，宿舍楼里安安静静的，我的同屋正在认真地做作业呢。

词语表 Vocabulary

1.	晚会	wǎnhuì	N	party
2.	眼睛	yǎnjing	N	eye
3.	跳舞	tiào wǔ	V//O	to dance
4.	插曲	chāqǔ	N	song in a film or play
5.	像……一样	xiàng……yíyàng		like, as... as
6.	好听	hǎotīng	Adj	pleasant to hear
7.	年级	niánjí	N	year, grade
8.	毕业	bì yè	V//O	to graduate

167

9.	当	dāng	V	to be, to work as
10.	翻译	fānyì	N	translator, interpreter
11.	正……呢	zhèng……ne		to be doing
12.	文学	wénxué	N	literature
13.	博士生	bóshìshēng	N	PhD candidate
14.	瘦	shòu	Adj	thin
15.	戴	dài	V	to wear
16.	着	zhe	AsPt	*used to indicate a state*
17.	副	fù	M	pair
18.	眼镜	yǎnjìng	N	glasses
19.	帅	shuài	Adj	handsome
20.	连衣裙	liányīqún	N	dress
21.	束	shù	M	bunch
22.	鲜花	xiānhuā	N	flower
23.	永远	yǒngyuǎn	Adv	forever
24.	除了……以外，都……	chúle……yǐwài, dōu……		except
25.	点钟	diǎnzhōng	N	o'clock
26.	蛋糕	dàngāo	N	cake
27.	快乐	kuàilè	Adj	happy
28.	结束	jiéshù	V	to finish, to end
29.	公共汽车	gōnggòng qìchē		bus
	汽车	qìchē	N	car
30.	安静	ānjìng	Adj	quiet
31.	正在	zhèngzài	Adv	to be doing

注释 Notes

1 她说汉语像唱歌一样好听。

"像……一样"+形容词：一种比较句，表示比况，说明比较的两事物某一点相似或相同。例如：

"像……一样"+adjective: It is a comparative sentence, indicating the two things being compared are similar or in common in some aspect. For example,

① 她像小鸟一样快乐。　　　　　She is as happy as a bird.
② 他像他爸爸一样不爱说话。　　He doesn't like talking, just like his father.
③ 她像她妈妈一样漂亮。　　　　She is as beautiful as her mother.
④ 他说汉语像中国人说的一样流利。　He speaks Chinese as fluently as Chinese people.

2 我进门的时候，张文心正和她男朋友聊天儿呢。

正在/正/在……（呢）：这种格式表示动作的进行状态。动词放在"正在/正/在"的后面。例如：

正在/正/在……（呢）: This pattern indicates an action is going on. The verb is used after "正在/正/在". For example,

① 昨天你给我打电话的时候，我在洗衣服。
　　I was washing clothes when you called me yesterday.
② 现在我洗澡呢。　　　　I am taking a bath now.
③ 他们正上听力课呢。　　They are having their listening course.

3 戴着一副眼镜，长得很帅。

着：动态助词，用在动词后面，表示动作的持续状态。例如：

着: It is an aspect particle used after a verb to indicate the continuation of an action. For example,

① 她穿着一条连衣裙。　　　　She is wearing a dress.
② 穿着旗袍走不快。　　　　　You cannot walk fast when you wear a cheongsam.
③ 他笑着说："请。"　　　　　"Please," he said with a smile.
④ 她喜欢躺着看书。　　　　　She likes reading a book while lying on the bed.

4 来参加晚会的客人很多，除了我以外，都是中国人。

除了……以外，都……：表示排除特殊，强调一致。"特殊"的情况放在"除了"后面。主语可以在"除了"的前面，也可以在"都"的前面。"以外"可以省略。例如：

169

除了……以外,都……: It means "being the same except somebody or something". The exceptional case is used after "除了". The subject can precede either "除了" or "都". "以外" can be omitted. For example,

① 我们除了星期六、星期天以外,每天都有课。
We have classes every day except Saturday and Sunday.

② 除了导游以外,他们都不会说汉语。
They cannot speak Chinese except the tourist guide.

③ 除了香菜,别的她都吃。 She eats everything but coriander.

5 汉语的句调
The intonation of Chinese sentences

说汉语的时候,除了要注意汉字的读音以外,还要注意汉语句子的语调,这样才能更好、更准确地表达自己的意思。汉语句子语调的一般规律是:

When speaking Chinese, you need not only pay attention to the pronunciation of characters, but also to the intonation of sentences, so as to accurately express what you mean. The general rules of the intonation of Chinese sentences are:

(1) 陈述句句尾下降。例如:

Using a falling tone at the end of a declarative sentence. For example,

① 我是中国人。   I am Chinese.
② 这就是我朋友。   This is my friend.
③ 明天星期天。   Tomorrow is Sunday.

(2) 有疑问语气词的疑问句,句尾下降。例如:

Using a falling tone at the end of a question with an interrogative modal particle. For example,

④ 你是留学生吗?   Are you an international student?
⑤ 他是你同屋吧?   Is he your roommate?
⑥ 我的精读课本呢?   Where is my intensive reading textbook?

(3) 没有疑问语气词的疑问句,句尾上扬。例如:

Using a rising tone at the end of the questions without an interrogative modal particle. For example,

⑦ 他是谁?   Who is he?
⑧ 你喜欢听什么音乐?   What kind of music do you like?
⑨ 你住哪儿?   Where do you live?

（4）长句中间有逗号（ , ）、顿号（ 、）、冒号（ ：）的地方，读平调。例如：

Using a level tone when a comma, slight-pause mark or colon is used in a long sentence. For example,

⑩ 我们每个星期在一起学习一次，我教她英语，她教我汉语。
We study together once a week. I teach her English, and she teaches me Chinese.

⑪ 她家有三口人：爸爸、妈妈和她。
There are three people in her family: her father, her mother and she.

注意：汉语句子的语调不能改变汉字本身的声调。句调是在汉字声调基础上的下降或上扬。

Note：The intonation of a Chinese sentence cannot change the tone of a character. The intonation falls or rises based on the tones of characters.

你参加过汉语水平考试（HSK）吗

Did you take HSK

课文 Text

这几天，我听了汉语水平考试辅导班的课，我想参加五月举行的汉语水平考试。下午我和班里的三四个同学一起去留学生办公室报名。负责汉语水平考试的陈老师告诉我们，每人需要交两张黑白或者彩色照片、护照和报名费。十天左右来办公室取准考证。陈老师还告诉我们，考试那天，同学们必须带护照、准考证和2B铅笔进考场。如果迟到35分钟，就不能参加考试了。大概考试结束三个月以后，考试中心会通知考试成绩，发汉语

水平等级证书。这个证书长期有效。同学们也可以自己上网查成绩，或者打电话问成绩。

我发现在办公室报名的同学大部分是韩国人或者日本人，其他国家的同学很少。我觉得有点儿奇怪。

有些年轻的同学对我考HSK不太理解。他们认为我已经不用找工作了，为什么还要参加HSK呢？我告诉他们，两年前我在国内参加过一次汉语水平考试，但是成绩不理想，因此我想再考一次。这次我希望得到六级水平的证书。

我发现我还没有一张满意的照片。我打算晚上理了发去照相馆照一张彩色照片。

1.	过	guo	AsPt	indicating the completion of an action
2.	辅导	fǔdǎo	V	to give guidance in study or training
3.	办公室	bànggōngshì	N	office
4.	报名	bào míng	V//O	to register
5.	负责	fùzé	V	to be responsible
6.	需要	xūyào	V	to require, to need

7.	交	jiāo	V	to hand in
8.	黑白	hēibái	N	black-and-white
9.	护照	hùzhào	N	passport
10.	准考证	zhǔnkǎozhèng	N	admission card for an examination
11.	铅笔	qiānbǐ	N	pencil
12.	进	jìn	V	to enter
13.	考场	kǎochǎng	N	examination room, test site
14.	迟到	chídào	V	to be late
15.	大概	dàgài	Adv	approximately
16.	通知	tōngzhī	V	to inform
17.	成绩	chéngjì	N	result, score
18.	等级	děngjí	N	level
19.	证书	zhèngshū	N	certificate
20.	长期	chángqī	N	long term
21.	有效	yǒuxiào	V	to be valid
22.	查	chá	V	to check
23.	部分	bùfen	N	part
24.	其他	qítā	Pr	other
25.	奇怪	qíguài	Adj	strange
26.	理解	lǐjiě	V	to understand
27.	不用	búyòng	Adv	need not
28.	为什么	wèi shénme		why
29.	国内	guó nèi		in one's country
30.	理想	lǐxiǎng	Adj	ideal
31.	因此	yīncǐ	Conj	so, therefore
32.	得到	dédào	V	to get
33.	理发	lǐ fà	V//O	to have a haircut

专有名词 Proper Nouns

1. 汉语水平考试　　Hànyǔ Shuǐpíng Kǎoshì　　HSK, Chinese Proficiency Test
2. 陈　　　　　　　Chén　　　　　　　　　　a family name

1 你参加过汉语水平考试吗？

过：动态助词，用在动词后面，表示动作的经历状态，说明以前有某种经验。这种经验对现在或将来有作用。例如：

过：It is an aspect particle used after a verb to indicate the state of an action. It means somebody has experienced something, which still influences the present and the future. For example,

① 爸爸以前来中国工作过，他比较了解中国的情况。
My father used to work in China, so he knows the country's conditions pretty well.

② 她吃过北京烤鸭，知道怎么吃。
She has eaten Beijing roast duck, so she knows how to eat it.

否定式是："没"＋动词＋"过"。例如：
Its negative form is: "没" + verb + 过. For example,

③ 我没吃过饺子。　　　I haven't had dumplings.
④ 我没去过上海。　　　I haven't been to Shanghai.
⑤ 我没考过HSK。　　　I haven't taken HSK.

2 你参加过汉语水平考试吗？

汉语水平考试（HSK）：这是这中国政府举行的测试母语非汉语者的汉语水平的标准化考试。缩写为HSK。

Chinese Proficiency Test (HSK): It is a standard test held by Chinese government, testing the Chinese proficiency of people whose mother tongue is not Chinese. It is abbreviated HSK.

175

3 下午我和班里的<u>三四个</u>同学一起去留学生办公室报名。/ <u>十天左右</u>来办公室取准考证。/ <u>大概</u>考试结束三个月以后，……

概数：概数是一个不确定的数目。汉语常用的表示概数的方法有下面几种：

The approximate number: It refers to an uncertain number. In Chinese, the following ways are usually used to indicate an approximate number:

（1）两个相邻的数字连用，但是"九"、"十"不能连用。例如：
Except "九" and "十", two adjacent numbers are used. For example,

① 四五天　　　　　four or five days
② 六七岁　　　　　six or seven years old
③ 两三点钟　　　　two or three o'clock
④ 三四十岁　　　　in one's thirties or forties

（2）在数词或数量短语后面加表示大概意思的词语，如"左右"、"上下"、"多"等。例如：
A word indicating approximation like "左右", "上下" or "多", etc., is used after a numeral or a quantifier phrase. For example,

⑤ 十天左右　　　　about ten days
⑥ 五十岁上下　　　about fifty years old
⑦ 一年多　　　　　more than a year

（3）在数词或数量短语前面用"大概"、"可能"等词语限制数量短语。例如：
A modifying word like "大概" or "可能" is used before a numeral or a quantifier phrase. For example,

⑧ 他大概两个月以后回北京。　　He will return to Beijing in about two months.
⑨ 我们大概10点钟到车站。　　　We will arrive at the station at about 10 o'clock.
⑩ 这辆自行车可能要2000块。　　This bicycle may cost you 2,000 *kuai*.

（4）在数词后面用"几"。例如：
"几" is used after a numeral. For example,

⑪ 十几个人　　　　more than ten people
⑫ 四十几岁　　　　more than forty years old

4 <u>为什么</u>还要参加 HSK 呢？

用"为什么"提问的疑问句：询问原因。例如：
The question using "为什么": It is used to enquire the cause or reason. For example,

① A：你今天为什么没来上课？　　Why didn't you come to class today?
　 B：因为我生病了。　　　　　　Because I was sick.
② A：你为什么学汉语？　　　　　Why do you study Chinese?
　 B：我觉得说汉语很好听。　　　I think Chinese sounds pleasing.
③ A：你为什么喜欢白色？　　　　Why do you like white?
　 B：我觉得白色显得干净。　　　I think white looks pure.

5 两年前我在国内参加过一次汉语水平考试。

动量词：动词后面表示动作数量的词叫动量词。常用的动量词有"次"、"趟"、"遍"等。例如：

The verbal measure word: A verbal measure word is used after a verb to indicate the number of occurrence of an action. The commonly used ones include "次", "趟", "遍" and so on. For example,

① 他来过三趟北京。　　　　He has been to Beijing three times.
② 请你再说一遍。　　　　　Please say it again.

6 两年前我在国内参加过一次汉语水平考试，但是成绩不理想，因此我想再考一次。

因此：连词，用在表示结果或结论的句子前面。例如：

因此: It is a conjunction used before a clause indicating a result or conclusion. For example,

① 我不了解北京的天气特点，因此刚来时常常感冒。
　 I didn't know the weather conditions of Beijing, so I often caught a cold when I just arrived.
② 日本也用汉字，因此，日本留学生学习汉字没有问题。
　 Chinese characters are also used in Japan, so students from Japan have no problems in learning the characters.
③ 她爸爸是德国人，妈妈是法国人，因此，她会说德语和法语。
　 Her father is German and her mother is French, so she can speak German and French.

27 你怎么又来办延长手续了

Why do you come to extend your programme again

课文 Text

前天留学生办公室出了一个通知。通知上说，希望延长留学时间的同学请在本月20号以前来办公室办手续。

我已经学了三个多月的汉语了。我觉得这所大学条件不错，老师们很热情，课余生活很丰富，留学生办公室经常安排各种各样的了解中国文化的活动，比如，看京剧、唱中国歌、用汉语讲故事、中式服装表演等。我觉得在这儿学习汉语进步很快，我感到自己的汉语水平有了明显的提高。我刚来中国的时候，连"你好"也不会说，

27 你怎么又来办延长手续了

现在我能用汉语进行日常生活会话了。

开学已经三个多月了,我渐渐习惯了在北京的留学生活。我认识了不少新朋友,也有了在国外的生活经验,现在一个人在中国生活没问题了。我觉得半年的留学时间太短了,我想延长一个学期,再学半年,明年二月回国。爸爸妈妈同意了我的要求。

通知还说,办延长签证的手续需要填延长申请表,说明延长签证的理由和时间,还要交护照和手续费。一个星期以后自己再去办公室取护照。刚才我去了一趟办公室,因为忘了带照片,只好又去了一趟。

以前我总以为办延长签证手续很复杂,其实很简单。

词语表 Vocabulary

1.	又	yòu	Adv	again
2.	延长	yáncháng	V	to extend
3.	出	chū	V	to issue
4.	通知	tōngzhī	N	notice, notification

179

5.	条件	tiáojiàn	N	condition
6.	丰富	fēngfù	Adj	rich and varied
7.	各种各样	gè zhǒng gè yàng		all kinds of, various
8.	文化	wénhuà	N	culture
9.	京剧	jīngjù	N	Beijing opera
10.	表演	biǎoyǎn	V	to perform, to act
11.	进步	jìnbù	V	to make progress
12.	感到	gǎndào	V	to feel
13.	明显	míngxiǎn	Adj	noticeable, significant
14.	连……也……	lián……yě……		even
15.	进行	jìnxíng	V	to carry out
16.	日常	rìcháng	Adj	daily
17.	开学	kāi xué	V//O	to start a new term
18.	经验	jīngyàn	N	experience
19.	没问题	méi wèntí		no problem
20.	学期	xuéqī	N	term, semester
21.	明年	míngnián	N	next year
22.	同意	tóngyì	V	to agree
23.	要求	yāoqiú	N	request
24.	签证	qiānzhèng	N	visa
25.	填	tián	V	to fill in
26.	申请	shēnqǐng	V	to apply
27.	表	biǎo	N	form
28.	说明	shuōmíng	V	to explain
29.	理由	lǐyóu	N	reason
30.	刚才	gāngcái	N	just now
31.	趟	tàng	M	*a measure word for a round trip, etc., or train or bus service*
32.	只好	zhǐhǎo	Adv	cannot... but, have to

33.	以为	yǐwéi	V	to think, to consider
34.	复杂	fùzá	Adj	complicated
35.	其实	qíshí	Adv	in fact, actually

注释 Notes

1 你怎么**又**来办延长手续了？/ 我想延长一个学期，**再**学半年。

辨析 Discrimination：再、又

"再"和"又"都是副词，都可以修饰动词，表示动作的重复。但是，"再"修饰的动作还没重复，"又"修饰的动作已经重复了。例如：

Both "再" and "又" are adverbs and can be used to modify verbs, indicating the repetition of an action. However, the action modified by "再" has not yet been repeated, while the action modified by "又" has already been repeated. For example,

① 我想再考一次HSK。（还没"考"）

I want to take HSK again. (It means I haven't "taken the examination" yet.)

② 我要再去一次办公室。（还没"去"）

I will go to the office again. (It means I haven't "gone" to the office.)

③ 请再说一遍。（还没"说"）

Please say it again. (It means I haven't "said" it yet.)

④ 我又说了一遍。（已经"说"了）   I said it again. (It means I already "said" it.)

⑤ 这种啤酒味道不错，我又买了一瓶。（已经"买"了）

The beer tastes good, so I bought another bottle. (It means I already "bought" it.)

⑥ 他今天又迟到了。（已经"迟到"了）

Today he is late again. (It means he "came late".)

2 **通知上说**，希望延长留学时间的同学请在本月20号以前来办公室办手续。

通知上说：用来转引通知上的话或主要内容。例如：

通知上说：It is used to quote the notice or the main content of the notice. For example,

① 通知上说，明天早上8点在东门上车去游览长城。

The notice says we will meet at the east gate to take the bus at 8 o'clock tomorrow morning to visit

the Great Wall.

② 通知上说，下星期一全校开运动会。
The notice says our school will hold a sports meeting next Monday.

③ 通知上说，国庆节放一个星期假。
The notice says we will have seven days off for the National Day.

类似的还有："报纸上说"，用来转引报纸上某一条新闻的主要内容；"电视上说"，用来转引电视报道中的主要内容。例如：

Similar expressions include "报纸上说", which is used to quote the main content of a piece of news in a newspaper; and "电视上说", which is used to quote the main content of a TV report. For example,

④ 今天的报纸上说，明天有马拉松比赛。
Today's newspaper says a marathon game will be held tomorrow.

⑤ 电视上说，晚上 10 点有重要新闻。
The TV says some important news will be announced at 10:00 p.m.

3 我刚来中国的时候，连"你好"也不会说。

连……也……：强调这个短语前面的句子的意思，应该选择最能起强调作用的词语放在"连"的后面。例如：

连……也……： It is used to emphasize the meaning of the preceding clause. The word or phrase that functions the best in emphasizing the preceding clause is used after "连". For example,

① 参加晚会的人很多，连校长也来了。（强调"参加晚会的人很多"）
Many people, even the headmaster, went to the party. (It emphasizes "many people went to the party.")

② 他不舒服，连饭也不想吃。（强调"他不舒服"）
He is not feeling well, so he does not even want to eat his meal. (It emphasizes "he is not feeling well.")

③ 他的汉语水平很高，连中文新闻广播也听得懂。（强调"他的汉语水平很高"）
He has a high level of proficiency in Chinese language, and he can even understand Chinese news broadcast on radio. (It emphasizes "he has a high level of proficiency in Chinese language.")

4 刚才我去了一趟办公室。

辨析 Discrimination：刚才、刚

"刚才"是名词，指说话以前不久的时间。可以用在主语前面，也可以用在主语后面。"刚"是副词，表示发生在不久前，只能用在谓语动词前面。"刚才"后面可以有动词的否定形式，"刚"后面不能有动词的否定形式。"刚才"的肯定句末尾可以用语气助词"了₂"，"刚"不行。例如：

"刚才" is a noun, indicating "just before somebody speaks". It can be used before or after the subject. "刚" is an adverb, meaning "not long ago". It is only used before the predicate verb. "刚才" can be followed by the negative form of a noun, while "刚" cannot. If "刚才" is used in an affirmative sentence, the modal particle "了₂" can be used at the end of the sentence; if "刚" is used in an affirmative sentence, the modal particle "了₂" cannot be used. For example,

① 刚才我去办公室了。　　　　　　　　I went to the office just now.
② 刚才我看见你同屋在这儿抽烟。　　　I saw your roommate smoking here just now.
③ 我刚才没买牛奶。　　　　　　　　　I didn't buy milk just now.
④ 老师刚才让我们介绍自己的爱好了。
　　The teacher asked us to introduce our hobbies just now.
⑤ 他刚来一个星期。　　　　　　　　　He just arrived a week ago.
⑥ 我刚打三分钟电话。　　　　　　　　I just had a three-minute conversation on the phone.
⑦ 我们刚下课。　　　　　　　　　　　We have just finished our class.

5 因为忘了带照片，<u>只好</u>又去了一趟。

只好：副词，表示因为某种原因必须这样做，但是这样做常常不是最好的选择。用在动词前面。例如：

只好：It is an adverb, meaning "having to do something for some reason", but it is often not the best option to do so. It is used before a verb. For example,

① 我感冒了，明天只好不去上课。
　　I've caught a cold, so I cannot go to class tomorrow.
② 他找到了工作，只好提前回国。
　　He has found a job, so he has to return to his mother country ahead of schedule.
③ 他生病了，又不会说汉语，我只好陪他去医院。
　　He is sick and doesn't know how to speak Chinese. So I have to go to the hospital with him.

6 以前我总以为办延长签证手续很复杂，<u>其实</u>很简单。

其实：副词，表示后面说的情况是真实的。常常与"以为"一起使用，引出和"以为"后面的情况不一样的情况。例如：

其实：It is an adverb, indicating what follows is true. It is often used with "以为", introducing a situation different from the one following "以为". For example,

① 我以为她是日本人，其实她是中国人。
　　I thought she was Japanese, but she is actually Chinese.
② 我们都以为他不会说英语，其实他的英语很好。
　　We all thought he could not speak English, but he actually speaks English very well.

28 你喜欢看哪个频道的电视节目

Which TV channel do you like to watch

课文 Text

乔治和汉斯是同屋，他们俩不但喜欢踢足球，而且都是足球迷。他们非常喜欢看足球比赛，特别爱看电视台现场直播的足球比赛。昨天晚上11点他们看了一场很好看的足球比赛。参加比赛的是英国队和巴西队。比赛开始3分钟后，英国队就进了一个球，43分钟时，英国队又进了一个球。下半场20分钟时，巴西队才进了一个球。比赛就要结束了，巴西队又进了一个球。最后比分是2比2。球场上双方运动员都踢得很勇敢，观众们也很热

28 你喜欢看哪个频道的电视节目

情,比赛紧张而精彩。但是他们俩最喜欢的足球运动员都没参加这场比赛,他们觉得有点儿美中不足。

白天他们要上课,没有时间看电视。不过没关系,他们爱看的电视节目大部分都在晚上。如4频道的儿童动画片、9频道的"成语故事"、"动物世界"和教育频道的"学汉语"等。这些节目的内容都不复杂,特别是有的动画片过去他们在国内看过英语的,或者看过英语的书,内容已经很熟悉了,比如《米老鼠和唐老鸭》,虽然他们现在是初级汉语水平,也比较容易看懂。他们坚持每天看中文电视,现在他们能看懂的电视节目越来越多了,他们也越来越爱看中文电视了。

周末他们还喜欢在房间看一些中国电影的光盘。他们觉得看中国电影不但能提高汉语水平,而且还能了解中国文化。

词语表 Vocabulary

1.	频道	píndào	N	channel
2.	节目	jiémù	N	programme

185

3.	不但……而且……	búdàn……érqiě……		not only… but also
4.	踢	tī	V	to kick, to play
5.	足球	zúqiú	N	football, soccer
6.	迷	mí	Suf	fan, enthusiast
7.	比赛	bǐsài	N	game, match
8.	电视台	diànshìtái	N	TV station
9.	现场	xiànchǎng	N	site, spot
10.	直播	zhíbō	V	to make a live broadcast or live telecast
11.	好看	hǎokàn	Adj	good
12.	就	jiù	Adv	as soon as, right after
13.	下半场	xiàbànchǎng	N	second half (of a game)
14.	才	cái	Adv	used to indicate something happens later than expected
15.	比分	bǐfēn	N	score
16.	比	bǐ	V	to (in a score)
17.	球场	qiúchǎng	N	ground or court for a ball game
18.	双方	shuāngfāng	N	both sides
19.	勇敢	yǒnggǎn	Adj	brave
20.	观众	guānzhòng	N	audience
21.	而	ér	Conj	and
22.	精彩	jīngcǎi	Adj	wonderful
23.	美中不足	měi zhōng bù zú		flaw in sth. otherwise perfect
24.	白天	báitiān	N	day, daytime
25.	儿童	értóng	N	children, kids
26.	动画片	dònghuàpiàn	N	cartoon
27.	成语	chéngyǔ	N	idiom
28.	动物	dòngwù	N	animal
29.	坚持	jiānchí	V	to pesist in, to uphold

| 30. | 越来越 | yuè lái yuè | more and more |

专有名词 Proper Nouns

1.	汉斯	Hànsī	name of a person
2.	巴西	Bāxī	Brazil
3.	《米老鼠和唐老鸭》	《Mǐlǎoshǔ hé Tánglǎoyā》	Mickey Mouse and Donald Duck

1 他们俩**不但**喜欢踢足球，**而且**都是足球迷。

不但……而且……：表示递进关系。如果两个分句的主语相同，主语在"不但"前面；如果两个分句的主语不相同，两个主语分别出现在"不但"、"而且"前面。例如：

不但……而且……: It indicates a progressive relationship. If the subject in the two clauses is the same one, it is used before "不但"; if the subjects in the two clauses are different from each other, they are used before "不但" and "而且" respectively. For example,

① 他不但喜欢吃中国菜，而且还会做中国菜。
   He not only likes Chinese dishes, but also knows how to cook them.

② 南希不但很漂亮，而且很聪明。
   Nancy is not only pretty, but also smart.

③ 昨天不但刮大风，而且下大雨。
   It was not only windy, but also rainy yesterday.

④ 不但他来过中国，而且他爸爸也来过中国。
   He has been to China. So has his father.

⑤ 不但我听不懂广东话，而且很多中国人也听不懂。
   I don't understand Cantonese. Neither do many Chinese people.

⑥ 不但我感冒了，而且我的同屋也感冒了。
   I caught a cold. So did my roommate.

2 比赛开始3分钟后，英国队**就**进了一个球。

就：副词，用在动词前面，表示动作发生得早、快、顺利。例如：

就: It is an adverb used before a verb, indicating something happens earlier, quicker or more successful than expected. For example,

① 我等了三分钟，汽车就来了。　　　I waited for 3 minutes before the bus came.

② 我们8点上课，她7点就到教室了。
　　Our lecture begins at 8:00, and she got to the classroom at 7:00.

③ 他20岁就结婚了。　　　He got married at only 20 years old.

3 下半场20分钟时，巴西队才进了一个球。

才：副词，用在动词前面，表示动作发生得晚、慢、不顺利。例如：

才: It is an adverb used before a verb, indicating that something happens later, slower or less successful than expected. For example,

① 我等了20分钟，汽车才来。　　　I waited for 20 minutes before the bus came.

② 我们8点上课，他8点20才进教室。
　　Our lecture began at 8:00, and he didn't come until 8:20.

③ 他45岁才结婚。　　　He didn't get married until 45 years old.

4 最后比分是2比2。

体育比赛比分的写法和读法：许多体育比赛的比分写做"~：~"，读做"~比~"。例如：

Writing and reading the score of a sports game: The scores of many sports games are written as: "~：~"; and read as "~ 比 ~". For example,

篮球比赛	basketball game	82：92	→	82 比 92
排球比赛	volleyball game	13：14	→	13 比 14
足球比赛	football game	1：1	→	1 比 1、1 平

5 比赛紧张而精彩。

而：连词，用来连接形容词。例如：

而: It is a conjunction used to connect adjectives. For example,

① 她的房间干净而整齐。　　　Her room is clean and neat.

② 他汉语说得流利而标准。　　　He speaks Chinese fluently and accurately.

③ 老师每次都耐心而详细地回答我的问题。
　　My teacher answers my questions patiently and elaborately every time.

6 现在他们能看懂的电视节目<u>越来越</u>多了，他们也<u>越来越</u>爱看中文电视了。

越来越：用在动词、形容词前面，表示程度随着时间的延长而变化，而且程度的起点比较高。例如：

越来越：It is used before a verb or an adjective, indicating the degree changes as time goes by and the beginning level of the degree is relatively high. For example,

① 我越来越喜欢这座城市了。　　　　　I like this city more and more.
② 我越来越习惯北京的天气了。　　　　I'm getting used to the weather in Beijing.
③ 天气越来越冷了。　　　　　　　　　It is getting colder and colder.
④ 她女儿越来越漂亮了。　　　　　　　Her daughter is getting more and more beautiful.

辨析 Discrimination：越来越、一天比一天

这两个短语都表示程度随着时间的推移而加深。但是，"越来越"的起点比较高，"一天比一天"的起点比较低。例如：

Both phrases indicate the degree gets higher with the passage of time. However, the beginning level of the former phrase is higher than that of the latter one. For example,

⑤ 现在是 9 月，北京的天气一天比一天凉了。

　　It is September, and the weather in Beijing is getting cooler and cooler.

⑥ 现在是 11 月，北京的天气越来越冷了。

　　It is November, and the weather in Beijing is getting colder and colder.

29 你是一个人去旅游的吗
Did you travel alone

日 记

12月14日　　　　星期一　　　　阴天

上星期五到星期天我去西安旅游了。我是星期五下午1点从学校出发的。因为只有三天时间,我没有提前订火车票。我是坐飞机去、坐飞机回的。我坐的是中国国际航空公司的飞机。从北京到西安坐飞机大概需要一个半小时。下午六点多我到了西安。出发之前我没有和西安的朋友们联系,没让他们来机场接我。我怕她们周末陪我在西安玩儿两天太累了。我一到饭店就给弟弟打了电话,他对西安的名胜古迹很感兴趣,因为日本的京都、奈良就是仿照西安建造的。

西安是一座文化古城，已经有三千多年历史了。西安在历史上又叫长安，做过周代、秦代、汉代、唐代等十三个朝代的首都，名胜古迹很多。西安的街道像北京的一样又直又宽。听说西安的饺子很有名，晚上我吃了真正的西安饺子。西安的饺子皮儿薄、馅儿多，的确很好吃。我吃了很多，吃得很饱。

第二天上午我参观了兵马俑博物馆。那不但是中国人的伟大创举，而且也是人类的奇迹，真让人吃惊。

这次我是一个人去西安旅游的，虽然有些寂寞，但是行动自由。我住的饭店离市中心很近，下午我没有游览名胜古迹，带着一张西安地图，一个人去逛街，照了很多照片，吃了各种各样的西安小吃，还和热情的西安人合影留念，逛得很开心。

我是第一次去西安旅游。我喜欢这座中国历史文化名城。如果有时间，回国之前我一定要再去一次。

词语表 Vocabulary

1.	旅游	lǚyóu	V	to travel
2.	日记	rìjì	N	diary
3.	阴天	yīntiān	N	cloudy day
4.	出发	chūfā	V	to set out
5.	提前	tíqián	V	to be in advance
6.	订	dìng	V	to book
7.	火车	huǒchē	N	train
8.	票	piào	N	ticket
9.	飞机	fēijī	N	airplane
10.	国际	guójì	N	international
11.	航空	hángkōng	V	to design, build or fly an aircraft
12.	之	zhī	StPt	used to connect the modifier and the word modified
13.	联系	liánxì	V	to contact
14.	机场	jīchǎng	N	airport
15.	接	jiē	V	to meet
16.	累	lèi	Adj	tired
17.	一……就……	yī……jiù……		as soon as
18.	饭店	fàndiàn	N	hotel
19.	感兴趣	gǎn xìngqù		to be interested in
20.	仿照	fǎngzhào	V	to follow, to be after the pattern of
21.	古城	gǔ chéng		old city, ancient city
22.	朝代	cháodài	N	dynasty
23.	直	zhí	Adj	straight
24.	宽	kuān	Adj	broad, wide
25.	皮儿	pír	N	(dumpling) wrapper
26.	的确	díquè	Adv	indeed

27.	饱	bǎo	Adj	full, having had enough to eat
28.	伟大	wěidà	Adj	great
29.	创举	chuàngjǔ	N	pioneering work
30.	人类	rénlèi	N	mankind
31.	奇迹	qíjì	N	miracle
32.	吃惊	chī jīng	V//O	to be surprised
33.	寂寞	jìmò	Adj	lonely
34.	行动	xíngdòng	N	activity
35.	自由	zìyóu	Adj	free
36.	近	jìn	Adj	near
37.	地图	dìtú	N	map
38.	小吃	xiǎochī	N	snack
39.	合影	hé yǐng	V//O	to have a group photo
40.	留念	liúniàn	V	to keep as a souvenir
41.	名城	míng chéng		famous city

专有名词　Proper Nouns

1.	西安	Xī'ān	capital of Shaanxi Province
2.	中国国际航空公司	Zhōngguó Guójì Hángkōng Gōngsī	Air China
3.	京都	Jīngdū	a city of Japan
4.	奈良	Nàiliáng	a city of Japan
5.	长安	Cháng'ān	an ancient capital for more than ten dynasties in Chinese history, presently known as Xi'an
6.	周代	Zhōudài	Zhou Dynasty (1046 BC~256 BC) includes Western Zhou Dynasty (1046 BC~771 BC) and Eastern Zhou Dynasty (770 BC~256 BC). Xi'an is the capital of Western Zhou Dynasty
7.	秦代	Qíndài	Qin Dynasty (221 BC~206 BC)
8.	汉代	Hàndài	Han Dynasty (206 BC~220)

| 9. | 唐代 | Tángdài | Tang Dynasty (618~907) |
| 10. | 兵马俑博物馆 | Bīngmǎyǒng Bówùguǎn | Museum of the Terracotta Warriors and Horses |

注释 Notes

1 你是一个人去旅游的吗？

"是……的"句式：强调已经完成的动作发生的地点、时间、方式等，被强调的部分放在"是"与"的"中间，要重读。例如：

The sentence pattern "是……的": It emphasizes the place, time or manner of a completed action. The emphasized part is used between "是" and "的" and needs to be pronounced with stress. For example,

① 我是星期五下午1点出发的。（强调时间）

I set out at 1 o'clock Friday afternoon. (It emphasizes the time.)

② 我是坐飞机去的。（强调方式）

I went there by plane. (It emphasizes the means.)

③ 我是跟同学一起去的。（强调方式）

I went there with my classmates. (It emphasizes the manner.)

④ 我是从北京去的。（强调地点）

I went there from Beijing. (It emphasizes the place.)

2 我没有提前订火车票。

提前：动词，后面要用动词性的词语。例如：

提前：It is a verb followed by a verb or verbal phrase. For example,

① 提前买飞机票可以打折。

One can get a discount if he purchases a plane ticket in advance.

② 我们会提前通知你。　　We will inform you in advance.

③ 我同屋要提前回国。

My roommate will return to his mother country ahead of schedule.

194

3 我**一**到饭店**就**给弟弟打了电话。

一……就……：表示两个动作紧接着发生。两个动词分别放在"一"和"就"的后面。如果两个动作是同一个主语发出的，主语只出现一次，在"一"的前面。例如：

一……就……: It indicates one action follows right after another. The two verbs are used after "一" and "就" respectively. If the subject of the two verbs is the same one, it is used before "一". For example,

① 他一看就学会了。　　　　　　　He learned it at a glance.
② 他一听音乐就想跳舞。　　　　　He wants to dance whenever he hears music.
③ 他一到周末就给朋友打电话。　　He calls his friends once the weekend comes.

如果两个动作不是同一个主语发出的，两个主语分别放在"一"和"就"前面。例如：

If the two actions are not performed by the same subject, the two subjects are used before "一" and "就" respectively. For example,

④ 爸爸一抽烟，妈妈就不高兴。　　My mother is unhappy whenever my father smokes.
⑤ 她一哭，我就很紧张。　　　　　I get nervous whenever she cries.
⑥ 我一开车，她就让我慢点儿。　　She asks me to slow down whenever I drive.

4 他**对**西安的名胜古迹很**感兴趣**。

对……感兴趣：表示喜欢什么，感兴趣的事物放在"对"的后面。例如：

对……感兴趣: It means "to be interested in something". Something that somebody is interested in is put after "对". For example,

① 我对计算机很感兴趣。　　　　　I am very interested in computer.
② 她对中国民歌非常感兴趣。　　　She is extremely interested in Chinese folk songs.
③ 他对京剧特别感兴趣。　　　　　He is particularly interested in Beijing opera.

30 姓钱和有钱有关系吗

Does the surname Qian have anything to do with money

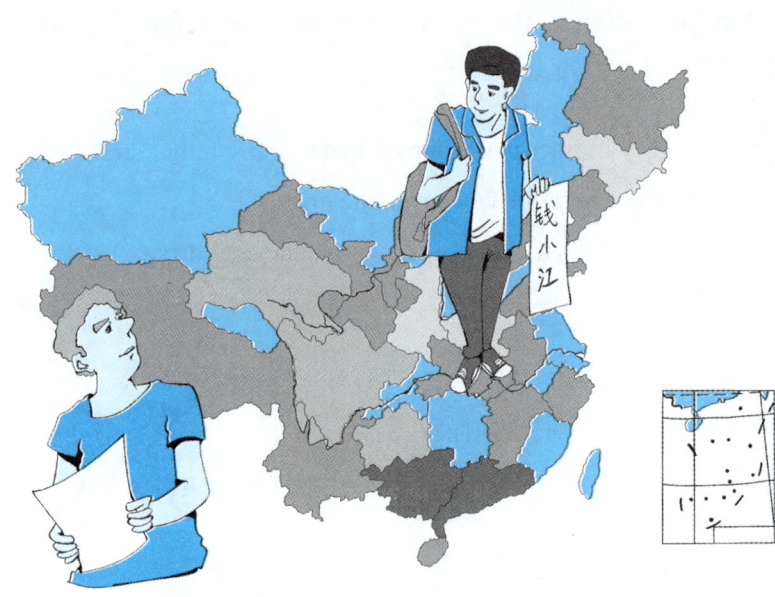

我是乔治的朋友。我姓钱,叫小江。姓钱的"钱"和金钱的"钱"虽然是同一个汉字,但是姓"钱"和有"钱"没有关系。中国人很早就有姓,最早的姓代表一个部落。中国人的姓很多,据说中国人历史上用过的姓有两万多个,现在还有三千五百多个姓仍然在使用。据统计,"李"、"王"、"陈"、"张"、"刘"是中国人用得最多的五个姓,其中姓李的最多。中国人的姓大多数是一个汉字,一个汉字的姓叫单姓。两个汉字的姓叫复姓,如"欧阳"、"司马"等。现在姓复姓的人已经非常少了。

30 姓钱和有钱有关系吗

过去中国姑娘结婚后,都要在自己的姓前面加上丈夫的姓。比如,一个叫"张玉花"的姑娘和一个叫"王大春"的小伙子结婚后,名字就得改成"王张玉花"。现在中国姑娘结婚以后,仍然姓自己的姓,不用在自己的姓前面加上丈夫的姓了。

按照中国人的习惯,孩子一般姓父亲的姓。我父亲姓钱,我当然也姓钱。中国人的姓没有意义,但是名字有意义。人们一般爱用声音响亮、意义美好的字给孩子起名字。中国人的名字中用得最多的八个汉字是:英、华、玉、明、文、国、春、平。父母或长辈在给孩子起名字的时候,总是要表达他们对孩子、对生活的一种希望。例如,我的名字是"小江",是我爷爷给我起的。因为我是在长江边的武汉市出生的,爷爷希望我像一条小江,朝着远大的目标,日夜奔流,永远进步。

词语表 Vocabulary

| 1. | 金钱 | jīnqián | N | money |
| 2. | 代表 | dàibiǎo | V | to represent |

3.	部落	bùluò	N	tribe
4.	据说	jùshuō	V	It is said that…
5.	仍然	réngrán	Adv	still
6.	统计	tǒngjì	V	to count, to add up
7.	其中	qízhōng	N	among
8.	单姓	dānxìng	N	surname composed of one character
9.	复姓	fùxìng	N	surname composed of two characters
10.	姑娘	gūniang	N	girl
11.	丈夫	zhàngfu	N	husband
12.	小伙子	xiǎohuǒzi	N	young man
13.	按照	ànzhào	Prep	according to
14.	当然	dāngrán	Adv	certainly
15.	意义	yìyì	N	meaning
16.	响亮	xiǎngliàng	Adj	loud and clear
17.	美好	měihǎo	Adj	good, fine
18.	起	qǐ	V	to give
19.	华	huá		prosperous, magnificent
20.	玉	yù	N	jade
21.	平	píng	Adj	level, smooth
22.	长辈	zhǎngbèi	N	senior member of the older generation
23.	总是	zǒngshì	Adv	always
24.	表达	biǎodá	V	to express
25.	例如	lìrú	V	to give an example
26.	爷爷	yéye	N	(paternal) grandfather
27.	市	shì	N	city
28.	远大	yuǎndà	Adj	lofty
29.	目标	mùbiāo	N	aim, goal
30.	奔流	bēnliú	V	to flow at great speed

专有名词　Proper Nouns

1.	钱小江	Qián Xiǎojiāng	name of a person
2.	欧阳	Ōuyáng	a family name
3.	司马	Sīmǎ	a family name
4.	长江	Cháng Jiāng	Yangtze River
5.	武汉	Wǔhàn	capital of Hubei Province, China

注　释　Notes

1 姓钱和有钱有关系吗？

A 和 B 有 / 没有关系：说明两种事物之间的关系。例如：

A 和 B 有 / 没有关系：It indicates the relationship between two things. For example,

① 他这次考得不好和他生病有关系。
His poor performance in the examination has something to do with his illness.

② 她口语能力差和她的性格有关系。
Her command of spoken Chinese is poor, which has a bearing on her disposition.

③ 他和这件事没有关系。　　He has nothing to do with it.

2 现在还有三千五百多个姓仍然在使用。

仍然：副词，表示情况没有改变。充当状语，用在谓语前面。例如：

仍然：It is an adverb, indicating the situation is still unchanged. It is used as an adverbial before the predicate. For example,

① 他家仍然住那儿。　　His family still lives there.
② 他仍然在那家银行工作。　　He is still working in that bank.
③ 妈妈已经四十多岁了，仍然很漂亮。
My mother is still very pretty although she is over forty years old.

3 其中姓李的最多。

其中：名词，指上文提到的事物中的一部分。例如：

199

其中: It is a noun, referring to a part of what was mentioned above. For example,

① 她喜欢看电影，其中最喜欢看美国电影。
She likes seeing movies, among which she likes American movies the most.

② 他的朋友很多，其中最好的朋友是钱小江。
He has many friends, and Qian Xiaojiang is his best among them.

③ 在北京出门玩儿的时候，可以坐公共汽车、骑自行车，也可以坐出租车，其中坐出租车最方便。
In Beijing, you can go out to enjoy yourself by bus, bike or taxi, among which the last means of transportation is the most convenient.

4 按照中国人的习惯，孩子一般姓父亲的姓。

按照：介词，用在动词前，表示遵照某种标准或习惯。例如：

按照: It is a preposition used before a verb, meaning "following certain standard or habit". For example,

① 他正在按照说明书装计算机。
He is assembling the computer following the manual.

② 按照他家的习惯，春节必须回家。
He must go home on the Spring Festival according to the customs of his family.

③ 按照中国人的习惯，圣诞节不休息。
Chinese people don't take a day off on Christmas according to their customs.

5 我父亲姓钱，我当然也姓钱。

当然：副词，表示符合一般事理或一般规律，充当状语。常常用在主语后面。例如：

当然: It is an adverb, meaning "following the general logic or rule". It is often used as an adverbial after the subject. For example,

① 他爱人是中国人，他汉语口语当然不错。
His wife is Chinese, so he has a good command of spoken Chinese.

② 大学毕业后我当然要找工作。
Of course I will look for a job after graduating from the college.

③ 明天会下大雪，我们的旅游计划当然应该取消。
It will snow heavily tomorrow, so our travel plan will certainly be cancelled.

单元小结（21~30课）
Review (Lessons 21~30)

语法项目		例句
常用句型	1. 存在句（"有"、"在"、"是"）	马路对面有银行。
		书房在客厅左边。
		阳台下面是车库。
	2. "是……的" 句式	他是坐飞机去上海的。
		他是一个人去上海的。
		他是昨天去上海的。
	3. 用 "为什么" 提问的疑问句	你为什么要参加汉语水平考试？
常用短语	1. 除了……以外，都……	除了绿色以外，我都喜欢。
	2. 除了……以外，还/也……	除了绿色以外，我还喜欢白色、黑色。
		除了绿色以外，我也喜欢白色、黑色。
	3. 连……也……	他的汉语水平很低，连"你好"也不会说。
	4. 一……就……	我一到北京就给家里打了电话。
	5. 对……感兴趣	我对中国历史很感兴趣。
	6. 像……一样 + 形容词	她说汉语像唱歌一样好听。
	7. 越来越	他的发音越来越好了。
	8. 一天比一天	他认识的汉字一天比一天多了。
	9. 一边……一边……	我们一边聊天儿，一边喝咖啡。
	10. 虽然……但是……	这个菜虽然有点儿贵，但是很好吃。
	11. 不但……而且……	这个菜不但贵，而且不好吃。

续表

语法项目		例　句
动作的时态	1. 动作的进行态	你给我打手机的时候，我正在上课呢。
	2. 动作的持续态	她今天穿着一条蓝色的连衣裙。
	3. 动作的经历态	他吃过北京烤鸭。
状态补语		他走得很快。
		他说汉语说得很快。
		他汉语说得很流利。
常用介词、动词	1. 离	我家离地铁站不远。
	2. 往	你一直往前走就到了。
	3. 向	过了红绿灯向右拐，再走五分钟就到了。
	4. 对	汉语老师对我们很热情。
能愿动词	1. 要	明年我要去中国学习汉语。
	2. 想	以后我想去中国工作。
	3. 能	我能用汉字写自己的中文名字。
	4. 会	他会开车。
	5. 可以	这儿可以吸烟。
	6. 应该	你感冒了，应该休息。
常用副词	1. 再	明天我要再去一趟办公室。
	2. 又	下午我又去了一趟办公室。
	3. 就	我们等了三分钟，她就来了。
	4. 才	我们等了半个小时，她才来。

语音知识		例　句
句调	句尾下降	我是留学生。
	句尾上扬	你是留学生吗？
	句尾拉平	我的房间大，弟弟的房间小。

附录 1 Appendix 1

汉语拼音方案
hàn yǔ pīn yīn fāng àn
Scheme for the Chinese phonetic alphabets

一、字母表

字母	Aa	Bb	Cc	Dd	Ee	Ff	Gg
名称	ㄚ	ㄅㄝ	ㄘㄝ	ㄉㄝ	ㄜ	ㄝㄈ	ㄍㄝ
	Hh	Ii	Jj	Kk	Ll	Mm	Nn
	ㄏㄚ	丨	ㄐ丨ㄝ	ㄎㄝ	ㄝㄌ	ㄝㄇ	ㄋㄝ
	Oo	Pp	Qq	Rr	Ss	Tt	
	ㄛ	ㄆㄝ	ㄑ丨ㄡ	ㄚㄦ	ㄝㄙ	ㄊㄝ	
	Uu	Vv	Ww	Xx	Yy	Zz	
	ㄨ	ㄪㄝ	ㄨㄚ	ㄒ丨	丨ㄚ	ㄗㄝ	

V 只用来拼写外来语、少数民族语言和方言。字母的手写体依照拉丁字母的一般书写习惯。

二、声母表

b ㄅ玻	p ㄆ坡	m ㄇ摸	f ㄈ佛	d ㄉ得	t ㄊ特	n ㄋ讷	l ㄌ勒
g ㄍ哥	k ㄎ科	h ㄏ喝		j ㄐ基	q ㄑ欺	x ㄒ希	
zh ㄓ知	ch ㄔ蚩	sh ㄕ诗	r ㄖ日	z ㄗ资	c ㄘ雌	s ㄙ思	

在给汉字注音的时候,为了使拼式简短,zh ch sh 可以省作 ẑ ĉ ŝ。

三、韵母表

	i 衣	u 乌	ü 迂
a ㄚ 啊	ia 丨ㄚ 呀	ua ㄨㄚ 蛙	
o ㄛ 喔		uo ㄨㄛ 窝	
e ㄜ 鹅	ie 丨ㄝ 耶		üe ㄩㄝ 约
ai ㄞ 哀		uai ㄨㄞ 歪	
ei ㄟ 欸		uei ㄨㄟ 威	
ao ㄠ 熬	iao 丨ㄠ 腰		
ou ㄡ 欧	iou 丨ㄡ 忧		
an ㄢ 安	ian 丨ㄢ 烟	uan ㄨㄢ 弯	üan ㄩㄢ 冤
en ㄣ 恩	in 丨ㄣ 因	uen ㄨㄣ 温	ün ㄩㄣ 晕
ang ㄤ 昂	iang 丨ㄤ 央	uang ㄨㄤ 汪	
eng ㄥ 亨的韵母	ing 丨ㄥ 英	ueng ㄨㄥ 翁	
ong (ㄨㄥ) 轰的韵母	iong ㄩㄥ 雍		

(1) "知、蚩、诗、日、资、雌、思"等七个音节的韵母用 i,即:知、蚩、诗、日、资、雌、思等字拼作 zhi, chi, shi, ri, zi, ci, si。

(2) 韵母儿写成 er,用作韵尾的时候写成 r。例如:"儿童"拼作 ertong,"花儿"拼作 huar。

(3) 韵母ㄝ单用的时候写成 ê。

(4) i 行的韵母,前面没有声母的时候,写成 yi (衣),ya (呀),ye (耶),yao (腰),you (忧),yan (烟),yin (因),yang (央),ying (英),yong (雍)。

u 行的韵母,前面没有声母的时候,写成 wu (乌),wa (蛙),wo (窝),wai (歪),wei (威),wan (弯),wen (温),wang (汪),weng (翁)。

ü 行的韵母,前面没有声母的时候,写成 yu (迂),yue (约),yuan (冤),yun (晕),yong (雍);ü 上两点省略。

ü 行的韵母跟声母 j,q,x 拼的时候,写成 ju (居),qu (区),xu (虚),ü 上两点也省略;但是跟声母 n,l 拼的时候,仍然写成 nü (女),lü (吕)。

(5) iou,uei,uen 前面加声母的时候,写成 iu,ui,un。例如 niu (牛),gui (归),lun (论)。

(6) 在给汉字注音的时候,为了使拼式简短,ng 可以省作 ŋ。

四、声调符号

阴平	阳平	上声	去声
ˉ	ˊ	ˇ	ˋ

声调符号标在音节的主要母音上。轻声不标。例如:

妈 mā	麻 má	马 mǎ	骂 mà	吗 ma
(阴平)	(阳平)	(上声)	(去声)	(轻声)

五、隔音符号

a,o,e 开头的音节连接在其他音节后面的时候,如果音节的界限发生混淆,用隔音符号(')隔开,例如:pi'ao (皮袄)。

附录 2 Appendix 2

汉语音节表
hàn yǔ yīn jié biǎo
List of Chinese syllables

声母\韵母	-i [ɿ]	-i [ʅ]	a	o	e	ai	ei	ao	ou	an	en	ang	eng	er	i	ia	ie	iao	iou	ian	in	iang	ing	iong
b			ba	bo		bai	bei	bao		ban	ben	bang	beng		bi		bie	biao		bian	bin		bing	
p			pa	po		pai	pei	pao	pou	pan	pen	pang	peng		pi		pie	piao		pian	pin		ping	
m			ma	mo	me	mai	mei	mao	mou	man	men	mang	meng		mi		mie	miao	miu	mian	min		ming	
f			fa	fo			fei		fou	fan	fen	fang	feng											
d			da		de	dai	dei	dao	dou	dan	den	dang	deng		di		die	diao	diu	dian			ding	
t			ta		te	tai	tei	tao	tou	tan		tang	teng		ti		tie	tiao		tian			ting	
n			na		ne	nai	nei	nao	nou	nan	nen	nang	neng		ni		nie	niao	niu	nian	nin	niang	ning	
l			la		le	lai	lei	lao	lou	lan		lang	leng		li	lia	lie	liao	liu	lian	lin	liang	ling	
g			ga		ge	gai	gei	gao	gou	gan	gen	gang	geng											
k			ka		ke	kai	kei	kao	kou	kan	ken	kang	keng											
h			ha		he	hai	hei	hao	hou	han	hen	hang	heng											
j															ji	jia	jie	jiao	jiu	jian	jin	jiang	jing	jiong
q															qi	qia	qie	qiao	qiu	qian	qin	qiang	qing	qiong
x															xi	xia	xie	xiao	xiu	xian	xin	xiang	xing	xiong
zh	zhi		zha		zhe	zhai	zhei	zhao	zhou	zhan	zhen	zhang	zheng											
ch	chi		cha		che	chai		chao	chou	chan	chen	chang	cheng											
sh	shi		sha		she	shai	shei	shao	shou	shan	shen	shang	sheng											
r	ri				re			rao	rou	ran	ren	rang	reng											
z		zi	za		ze	zai	zei	zao	zou	zan	zen	zang	zeng											
c		ci	ca		ce	cai		cao	cou	can	cen	cang	ceng											
s		si	sa		se	sai		sao	sou	san	sen	sang	seng											
0			a	o	e	ai		ao	ou	an	en	ang	eng	er	yi	ya	ye	yao	you	yan	yin	yang	ying	yong

续表

声母\韵母	u	ua	uo	uai	uei	uan	uen	uang	ueng	ong	ü	üe	üan	ün
b	bu													
p	pu													
m	mu													
f	fu													
d	du		duo		dui	duan	dun			dong				
t	tu		tuo		tui	tuan	tun			tong				
n	nu		nuo			nuan				nong	nü	nüe		
l	lu		luo			luan	lun			long	lü	lüe		
g	gu	gua	guo	guai	gui	guan	gun	guang		gong				
k	ku	kua	kuo	kuai	kui	kuan	kun	kuang		kong				
h	hu	hua	huo	huai	hui	huan	hun	huang		hong				
j											ju	jue	juan	jun
q											qu	jue	quan	qun
x											xu	xue	xuan	xun
zh	zhu	zhua	zhuo	zhuai	zhui	zhuan	zhun	zhuang		zhong				
ch	chu	chua	chuo	chuai	chui	chuan	chun	chuang		chong				
sh	shu	shua	shuo	shuai	shui	shuan	shun	shuang						
r	ru	rua	ruo		rui	ruan	run			rong				
z	zu		zuo		zui	zuan	zun			zong				
c	cu		cuo		cui	cuan	cun			cong				
s	su		suo		sui	suan	sun			song				
0	wu	wa	wo	wai	wei	wan	wen	wang	weng		yu	yue	yuan	yun

附录 3　Appendix 3

汉语句子成分
Chinese sentence elements

hàn yǔ jù zi chéng fèn

一、句子成分名称
Sentence elements

1	主语	zhǔyǔ	subject
2	谓语	wèiyǔ	predicate
3	宾语	bīnyǔ	object
4	定语	dìngyǔ	attribute
5	状语	zhuàngyǔ	adverbial
6	补语	bǔyǔ	complement

二、各成分之间的关系
Relationship between the elements

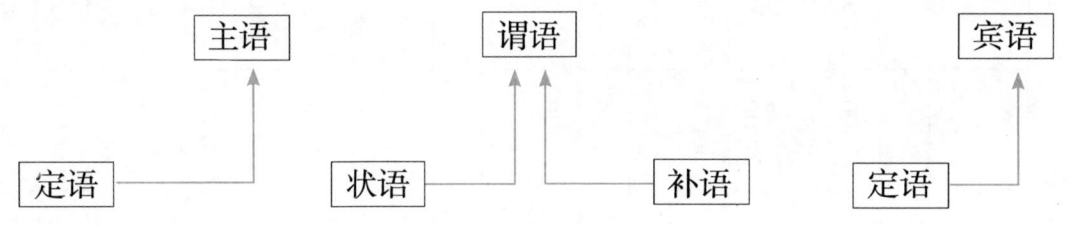

例如：

（她）姐姐［已经］学了＜五年＞（中国）历史了。

定语　主语　状语　谓语　补语　　定语　宾语

附录 4　Appendix 4

常用汉字笔画名称
cháng yòng hàn zì bǐ huà míng chēng
Commonly used strokes of Chinese characters

笔画形状 Shape of strokes	笔画名称 Strokes	例字 Examples
丶	点（diǎn）　the dot	六
一	横（héng）　the horizontal stroke	三
丨	竖（shù）　the vertical stroke	十
丿	撇（piě）　the left-falling stroke	八
乀	捺（nà）　the right-falling stroke	人
⼂	提（tí）　the diagonal stroke, rising from left to right	虫
㇕	折（zhé）　the turning stroke	买
亅	钩（gōu）　the hook	水
㇂	斜钩（xiégōu）　the slanting hook stroke	我
㇜	撇折（piězhé）　the left-falling turning stroke	云
㇆	横折（héngzhé）　the horizontal turning stroke	国
㇛	撇点（piědiǎn）　the left-falling dot stroke	女
㇙	竖提（shùtí）　the vertical rising stroke	很
㇊	横折提（héngzhétí）　the horizontal turning-and-rising stroke	语
㇅	横折钩（héngzhégōu）　the horizontal turning hook	月
㇌	横折折撇（héngzhé zhépiě）　the horizontal turning-and-turning left-falling stroke	建

附录 5　Appendix 5

汉字笔顺规则
hàn zì bǐ shùn guī zé
Rules of writing Chinese characters

笔顺规则 Rules of stroke order	例字 Examples	笔顺演示 Stroke order demonstration
先横后竖　xiān héng hòu shù the horizontal stroke before the vertical stroke	十	一 十
先撇后捺　xiān piě hòu nà the left-falling stroke before the right-falling stroke	人	丿 人
从上到下　cóng shàng dào xià the upper stroke before the lower stroke	三	一 二 三
从左到右　cóng zuǒ dào yòu from left to right	你	丿 亻 亻 你 你 你
从外到内　cóng wài dào nèi the outer strokes before the inner strokes	月	丿 刀 月 月
先里头后封口　xiān lǐtou hòu fēng kǒu the enclosing strokes before the enclosed strokes	四	丨 冂 叼 四 四
先中间后两边　xiān zhōngjiān hòu liǎngbiān the strokes in the middle before the strokes on both sides	小	亅 小 小
主笔最后出　zhǔ bǐ zuìhòu chū the main stroke written at last	中	丨 冂 口 中

附录 6　Appendix 6

常用汉字部首名称
cháng yòng hàn zì bù shǒu míng chēng
Commonly used radicals of Chinese characters

序号 No.	形旁 Semantic radicals	名称 Names	例字 Examples			意义 Meanings
1	扌	提手旁（tíshǒupáng）	打	抄	找	跟手有关　Related to one's hand
2	亻	单人旁（dānrénpáng）	你	他	们	跟人有关　Related to a person
3	氵	三点水（sāndiǎnshuǐ）	江	河	汤	跟水有关　Related to water
4	木	木字旁（mùzìpáng）	椅	树	桌	跟树有关　Related to a tree
5	忄、心	心字旁（xīnzìpáng）	忙	快	想	跟心理活动有关　Related to one's psychological activities
6	口	口字旁（kǒuzìpáng）	吃	喝	唱	跟嘴巴有关 Related to one's mouth
7	艹	草字头（cǎozìtóu）	草	茶	花	跟草有关　Related to grass
8	纟	绞丝旁（jiǎosīpáng）	红	绿	纸	跟丝有关　Related to silk
9	讠	言字旁（yánzìpáng）	说	话	语	跟说话有关　Related to speech
10	月	月字旁（yuèzìpáng）	期	肚	胖	跟月亮或身体有关 Related to the moon or body
11	土	提土旁（títǔpáng）	地	城	场	跟土有关　Related to soil
12	辶	走之儿（zǒuzhīr）	迎	进	远	跟走路有关　Related to walking
13	日	日字旁（rìzìpáng）	时	昨	早	跟太阳、时间有关 Related to the sun or time
14	宀	宝盖头（bǎogàitóu）	家	室	安	跟房屋有关　Related to a house
15	衤	衣字旁（yīzìpáng）	裤	衫	袜	跟衣服有关　Related to clothes
16	刂	立刀旁（lìdāopáng）	刻	别	列	跟刀有关　Related to a knife
17	火	火字旁（huǒzìpáng）	灯	炒	烟	跟火有关　Related to fire
18	钅	金字旁（jīnzìpáng）	钱	银	钟	跟金属有关　Related to metal
19	女	女字旁（nǚzìpáng）	妈	她	妻	跟女性有关　Related to female
20	贝	贝字旁（bèizìpáng）	贵	贫	费	跟钱有关　Related to money
21	目	目字旁（mùzìpáng）	看	睡	眼	跟眼睛有关　Related to one's eyes

附录7　Appendix 7

常用形近字对照
cháng yòng xíng jìn zì duì zhào
Comparison of commonly used characters similar in form

是（shì）	足（zú）	爱（ài）	受（shòu）	杯（bēi）	坏（huài）
了（le）	子（zǐ）	电（diàn）	申（shēn）	业（yè）	亚（yà）
他（tā）	地（dì）	直（zhí）	真（zhēn）	男（nán）	另（lìng）
我（wǒ）	找（zhǎo）	住（zhù）	往（wǎng）	特（tè）	持（chí）
着（zhe）	看（kàn）	四（sì）	西（xī）	止（zhǐ）	正（zhèng）
大（dà）	太（tài）	凡（fán）	风（fēng）	头（tóu）	斗（dòu）
夫（fū）	天（tiān）	土（tǔ）	上（shàng）	友（yǒu）	发（fā）
各（gè）	名（míng）	木（mù）	本（běn）	及（jí）	乃（nǎi）
使（shǐ）	便（biàn）	学（xué）	字（zì）	北（běi）	比（bǐ）
八（bā）	人（rén）	工（gōng）	王（wáng）	此（cǐ）	比（bǐ）
入（rù）	人（rén）	手（shǒu）	毛（máo）	为（wèi）	办（bàn）
已（yǐ）	己（jǐ）	来（lái）	米（mǐ）	刀（dāo）	力（lì）
日（rì）	目（mù）	没（méi）	设（shè）	并（bìng）	井（jǐng）
口（kǒu）	日（rì）	古（gǔ）	占（zhàn）	开（kāi）	井（jǐng）
问（wèn）	向（xiàng）	无（wú）	元（yuán）	运（yùn）	远（yuǎn）
问（wèn）	间（jiān）	末（mò）	未（wèi）	雨（yǔ）	两（liǎng）
几（jǐ）	儿（ér）	今（jīn）	令（lìng）	弟（dì）	第（dì）
几（jǐ）	九（jiǔ）	林（lín）	材（cái）	夏（xià）	复（fù）
百（bǎi）	白（bái）	材（cái）	村（cūn）	由（yóu）	田（tián）
白（bái）	自（zì）	同（tóng）	周（zhōu）	由（yóu）	曲（qǔ）
必（bì）	心（xīn）	车（chē）	东（dōng）	每（měi）	母（mǔ）

续表

主（zhǔ）	王（wáng）	公（gōng）	么（me）	体（tǐ）	休（xiū）
部（bù）	陪（péi）	买（mǎi）	卖（mài）	睛（jīng）	晴（qíng）
老（lǎo）	考（kǎo）	买（mǎi）	实（shí）	李（lǐ）	季（jì）
外（wài）	处（chù）	音（yīn）	意（yì）	午（wǔ）	牛（niú）
月（yuè）	用（yòng）	共（gòng）	其（qí）	明（míng）	朋（péng）
万（wàn）	方（fāng）	又（yòu）	义（yì）	下（xià）	上（shàng）
金（jīn）	全（quán）	干（gān/gàn）	千（qiān）	官（guān）	宫（gōng）
小（xiǎo）	少（shǎo）	干（gān/gàn）	于（yú）	写（xiě）	马（mǎ）

附录8　Appendix 8

常用同音字
cháng yòng tóng yīn zì

Commonly used homophones

#	pinyin	characters	#	pinyin	characters
1	bān	班 般 搬	24	gǎn	赶 敢 感
2	bàn	办 半 伴	25	gāo	高 膏 糕
3	bǎo	饱 宝 保	26	gē	哥 歌
4	bì	币 必 毕	27	gè	个 各
5	biàn	变 便 遍	28	gōng	工 公 功
6	bù	不 步 部	29	gǔ	古 谷 骨
7	cái	才 材 裁	30	guā	瓜 刮
8	cè	册 厕 测	31	guān	关 观
9	chá	茶 查 察	32	guì	柜 贵
10	cháng	长 尝 常	33	guǒ	果 裹
11	chéng	成 城 乘	34	háng	行 航
12	dài	代 带 戴	35	hào	号 好
13	dàn	但 淡 蛋	36	hé	和 河 盒
14	de	地 的 得	37	hòu	后 候
15	dì	地 弟 第	38	huà	划 画 话
16	diàn	电 店 垫	39	jī	机 鸡 积
17	dìng	订 定	40	jí	及 级 急
18	dōng	东 冬	41	jì	计 记 季
19	duì	队 对 兑	42	jiā	加 家
20	fàn	饭 范 贩	43	jiān	尖 间 兼
21	fēi	飞 非	44	jiàn	见 件 建
22	fēng	丰 风	45	jiāo	交 教
23	fù	父 负 复	46	jiào	叫 觉 较

续表

47	jīn	斤 今 金		73	rèn	认 任
48	jìn	进 近		74	shān	山 衫
49	jīng	京 经 精		75	shēn	申 身 深
50	jìng	净 静 镜		76	shí	十 时 食
51	jiǔ	九 久 酒		77	shì	市 事 是 室
52	jiù	旧 就		78	shǒu	手 首
53	jù	句 具 据		79	shù	束 树 数
54	jué	决 觉 绝		80	sù	诉 速 宿
55	kè	刻 客 课		81	tài	太 态
56	kuài	块 快 筷		82	tí	提 题
57	lán	栏 蓝 篮		83	tián	甜 填
58	lèi	泪 类 累		84	tīng	厅 听
59	lǐ	李 里 理		85	tóng	同 童
60	lì	历 丽 例		86	wǎn	晚 碗
61	liáng	良 凉 粮		87	wǎng	网 往
62	liàng	亮 辆 量		88	wàng	忘 望
63	liú	留 流		89	wèi	为 位 喂
64	měi	每 美		90	wén	文 闻
65	míng	名 明		91	wǔ	五 午 舞
66	nán	男 南 难		92	xī	西 希 息
67	qī	七 妻 期		93	xǐ	洗 喜
68	qí	齐 奇 骑		94	xià	下 夏
69	qì	气 汽 器		95	xiān	先 鲜
70	qián	前 钱		96	xiāng	相 香 箱
71	qīng	青 轻 清		97	xiàng	向 巷 像
72	qíng	情 晴		98	xīn	新 心

续表

99	xìng	兴 性 姓		109	yuè	月 乐 越
100	yào	药 要		110	zài	再 在
101	yè	业 页 夜		111	zǎo	早 澡
102	yī	一 衣 医		112	zhèng	正 政 挣
103	yǐ	已 以 椅		113	zhī	之 支 只 知
104	yì	亿 译 易		114	zhǐ	只 址 纸
105	yīn	因 阴 音		115	zhōng	中 终 钟
106	yǒng	永 泳 勇		116	zhù	助 住 祝 筑
107	yóu	邮 油 游		117	zì	自 字
108	yǒu	友 有		118	zuò	作 坐 做

附录9　Appendix 9

cháng yòng duō yīn zì
常　用　多　音　字
Commonly used polyphones

1	长	① cháng	长城	② zhǎng	成长		
2	重	① chóng	重叠	② zhòng	重要		
3	大	① dà	大学	② dài	大夫		
4	得	① dé	得到	② de	说得好	③ děi	得走了
5	发	① fā	发现	② fà	头发		
6	给	① gěi	给他打电话	② jǐ	供给		
7	还	① hái	还是	② huán	还书		
8	行	① háng	银行	② xíng	不行		
9	好	① hǎo	很好	② hào	爱好		
10	和	① hé	我和他	② huó	活面	③ huo	暖和
11	会	① huì	会说汉语	② kuài	会计		
12	系	① jì	系领带	② xì	数学系		
13	教	① jiāo	教汉语	② jiào	教室		
14	觉	① jiào	睡觉	② jué	觉得		
15	校	① jiào	校对	② xiào	学校		
16	卷	① juǎn	卷发	② juàn	卷子		
17	看	① kān	看门	② kàn	看电视		
18	落	① là	落了一本书	② luò	落后		
19	乐	① lè	快乐	② yuè	音乐		
20	了	① le	吃了饭	② liǎo	了解		
21	色	① sè	颜色	② shǎi	掉色儿		
22	少	① shǎo	很少	② shào	少年		
23	着	① zháo	着急	② zhe	笑着说	③ zhuó	穿着
24	只	① zhī	一只鞋	② zhǐ	只有		
25	种	① zhǒng	一种外语	② zhòng	种树		

附录 10　Appendix 10

语法点索引
Index of grammatical points

语法项目 Grammatical item	课号 Lesson
A	
A 比 B ＋形容词	16
A 比 B ＋形容词＋一点儿 / 多了 / 数量补语	16
A 跟 B＋ 一样 / 不一样	17
A 和 B 有 / 没有关系	30
A 没有 B ＋形容词	16
"啊"的音变	20
按照（介词）	30
B	
吧（用于是非疑问句）	18
百分数的读法	10
比较（副词）	8
比如（动词）	10
别（副词）	15
宾语	1
不但……而且……	28
"不"、"没（有）"与"别"	17
C	
才（副词）	28
除了……以外，都……	25
除了……以外，还 / 也……	24
从……到……（表时间）	8

216

续表

存在句（"有"、"在"、"是"）	23
D	
当然（副词）	30
地（结构助词）	15
的（结构助词）	4
"的"、"地"与"得"	24
"的"字短语	14
得（děi）（能愿动词）	18
等（助词，表列举）	10
"等＋名词"表示列举	11
地址的顺序	22
电话号码的表示	6
定语	2
动宾短语做定语	15
动词重叠	19
动词谓语句	3
动量词	26
都（副词）	3
对（介词）	21
对……感兴趣	29
对吗	13
多＋形容词（用于特指疑问句）	14
多少（用于特指疑问句）	3
E	
而（连词）	28
"二"与"两"	6

F	
方位词	20
方位短语	23
房间号的表示	6
G	
概数的表示法	26
感叹句	20
刚（副词）	16
"刚才"与"刚"	27
过（动态助词，表动作的经历）	26
H	
还（副词，表示数量增加、范围扩大）	6
还（副词，表示情况没有变化）	18
"还"与"也"	6
好吗	13
会+动词	7
"会"与"能"	21
"或者"与"还是"	6
J	
集合名词	13
几（用于特指疑问句）	2、3
兼语句（"请"带兼语）	4
兼语句（"让"带兼语）	15
"教师"与"老师"	5
介宾短语	5
"经常"与"常常"	7
就（副词，加强肯定）	22

续表

就（副词，表示动作发生得早、快、顺利）	28
觉得（动词）	9
L	
了₁（动态助词，表动作的完成）	12
了₂（语气助词）	17
离（动词）	23
离合词	13
俩（数量词）	7
连……也……	27
楼号的表示	6
M	
吗（用于是非疑问句）	1
名词谓语句	7
名量词	3
N	
哪（用于特指疑问句）	7
哪儿（用于特指疑问句）	3
那（指示代词）	5
……呢（表示确认）	24
Q	
其实（副词）	27
去+地点+动词	3
R	
人民币的写法和读法	13
仍然（副词）	30
如果（连词）	22

续表

S	
商品牌子的三种说法	14
谁（用于特指疑问句）	5
谁的（用于特指疑问句）	6
什么（用于特指疑问句）	9
"什么"、"怎么"与"怎么样"	18
时段短语	19
时间的顺序	8
时间状语	8
时量补语	19
"是……的"句式	29
（是）……还是……（用于选择疑问句）	11
"是"字句（表判断）	1
双宾语	15
虽然……但是……	23

T	
特别（副词）	9
提前（动词）	29
听说（动词）	21
挺……的	10
通知上说	27

W	
往（介词）	22
忘（动词）	16
为什么（用于特指疑问句）	26
谓语	1

续表

	续表
温度的写法和读法	16
X	
喜欢＋动词	7
想＋人/动物	5
"想"与"要"	21
向（介词）	22
像（动词）	10
像……什么的	18
像……一样＋形容词	25
形容词重叠	20
形容词谓语句	4
序数词	4
询问年龄	7
Y	
要……了（表动作即将发生）	18
也（副词）	2
一……就……	29
一共（副词）	13
以后（名词）	8、9
以前（名词）	9
100以上的称数法	10
100以下的称数法	3
一边……一边……	22
一般（形容词）	19
一些（数量词）	24
一天比一天	17
一直（副词）	20

续表

因此（连词）	26
因为……所以……	12
应该（能愿动词）	21
有点儿＋形容词	14
有/没有时间＋动词	19
有时候……有时候……	8
"有"字句（表领有）	2
又……又……	11
"越来越"与"一天比一天"	28
Z	
"再"与"又"	27
"在"与"给"	5
怎么（用于特指疑问句）	13
怎么样（用于特指疑问句）	18
这（指示代词）	5
着（动态助词，表动作的持续）	25
正反疑问句	20
正在/正/在……呢（表动作的进行）	25
只好（副词）	27
只有……才……	24
钟点的读法	8
主谓短语做定语	11
主谓谓语句	5
主语	1
状态补语（不带宾语）	24
状态补语（带宾语）	24
状语	2
最（副词）	11

词语总表 Vocabulary

【说明】"等级1"为该词语在《高等学校外国留学生汉语言专业教学大纲》和《汉语水平词汇与汉字等级大纲》中的对应等级;"等级2"为该词语在2010年出版的《汉语国际教育用音节汉字词汇等级划分》中的对应等级。空白表示该词语未收入上述大纲。

【Note】Level (1), i.e., "等级1", indicates the word or expression level in *Teaching Syllabus of Chinese for Foreign Students of Higher Educational Institutions* and *Syllabus of Graded Words and Characters for Chinese Proficiency*. Level (2), i.e., "等级2", indicates the word or expression level in *The Graded Chinese Syllables, Characters and Words for the Application of Teaching Chinese to the Speakers of Other Languages* published in 2010. Blanks indicate that the words or expressions are not included in the above syllabuses.

序号	词语	拼音	词性	等级1	等级2	课号
			A			
1	啊	a	MdPt	一/1	一②	20
2	矮	ǎi	Adj	一/1	二	18
3	爱	ài	V	一/1	一②	5
4	爱	ài	V	一/1	一②	11
5	爱好	àihào	N	一/1	一②	9
6	安静	ānjìng	Adj	一/1	一②	25
7	安排	ānpái	V	一/1	一③	18
8	安全	ānquán	Adj	一/2	一①	21
9	按照	ànzhào	Prep	一/2	一③	30
			B			
10	把	bǎ	M	一/1	一②	6
11	爸爸	bàba	N	一/1	一①	2
12	吧	ba	StPt	一/1	一①	18
13	白	bái	Adj	一/1	一①	14
14	白菜	báicài	N	一/2	一③	22
15	白天	báitiān	N	一/2	一①	28
16	班	bān	N	一/1	一①	3
17	办	bàn	V	一/1	一②	21
18	办法	bànfǎ	N	一/1	一②	15

223

19	办公室	bàngōngshì	N	一/1	一②	26
20	半	bàn	Nu	一/1	一①	13
21	拌	bàn	V	二	三	12
22	帮助	bāngzhù	V	一/1	一①	7
23	傍晚	bàngwǎn	N	一/2	二	23
24	包	bāo	V	一/2	一①	22
25	包裹	bāoguǒ	N	三、四	三	24
26	包子	bāozi	N	一/2	一②	11
27	薄	báo	Adj	一/2	二	18
28	饱	bǎo	Adj	一/1	二	29
29	报名	bào míng	V//O	一/2	一②	26
30	报纸	bàozhǐ	N	一/2	一②	8
31	杯	bēi	N	一/1	一②	11
32	北	běi	N	一/1	一①	20
33	奔流	bēnliú	V			30
34	本	běn	M	一/1	一①	24
35	鼻涕	bítì	N	丁	三	16
36	比	bǐ	Prep	一/1	一①	16
37	比	bǐ	V	一/1	一①	28
38	比分	bǐfēn	N	三、四	二	28
39	比较	bǐjiào	Adv	一/1	一②	8
40	比如	bǐrú	V	一/1	一③	10
41	比赛	bǐsài	N	一/1	一②	28
42	必须	bìxū	Adv	一/1	一②	21
43	毕业	bì yè	V//O	一/1	二	25
44	边	bian	Suf	一/1	一②	20
45	变化	biànhuà	N	一/1	一③	17
46	标准	biāozhǔn	Adj	一/2	一③	10
47	表	biǎo	N	一/1	一②	27
48	表达	biǎodá	V	一/2	一③	30
49	表演	biǎoyǎn	V	一/1	一②	27
50	别	bié	Adv	一/1	一①	15
51	玻璃	bōli	N	一/2	二	23
52	博士生	bóshìshēng	N			25

53	不错	búcuò	Adj	一/1	一②	4
54	不但……而且……	búdàn……érqiě……		一/1	一②	28
55	不断	búduàn	Adv	一/2	一②	16
56	不过	búguò	Conj	一/2	一③	14
57	不要	búyào	Adv	一/1	一②	22
58	不用	búyòng	Adv	一/1	一②	26
59	不好意思	bù hǎoyìsi		一/2	一②	19
60	部	bù	M	一/2	一③	6
61	部分	bùfen	N	一/1	一②	26
62	部落	bùluò	N			30

C

63	才	cái	Adv	一/1	一①	28
64	彩色电视	cǎisè diànshì				6
65	菜	cài	N	一/1	一①	11
66	参加	cānjiā	V	一/1	一②	17
67	餐厅	cāntīng	N	一/2	二	11
68	操场	cāochǎng	N		二	8
69	草	cǎo	N	一/1	一②	23
70	草莓	cǎoméi	N			13
71	层	céng	M	一/1	一②	6
72	叉子	chāzi	N	一/1	二	22
73	插曲	chāqǔ	N			25
74	茶	chá	N	一/1	一①	11
75	查	chá	V	一/1	一②	26
76	长	cháng	Adj	一/1	一①	19
77	长期	chángqī	N	一/2	一②	26
78	常	cháng	Adv	一/1	一①	8
79	常常	chángcháng	Adv	一/1	一①	5
80	唱	chàng	V	一/1	一①	10
81	抄写	chāoxiě	V	乙	二	4
82	超市	chāoshì	N		一②	23
83	朝	cháo	V	一/1	一③	23
84	朝代	cháodài	N	三、四	附	29
85	炒	chǎo	V	二	二	12

86	车库	chēkù	N			23
87	衬衣	chènyī	N	一/1	二	14
88	成绩	chéngjì	N	一/1	一②	26
89	成语	chéngyǔ	N	二	二	28
90	城市	chéngshì	N	一/1	一②	19
91	乘凉	chéng liáng	V//O	三、四		23
92	橙子	chéngzi	N			13
93	吃	chī	V	一/1	一①	8
94	吃惊	chī jīng	V//O	二	二	29
95	迟到	chídào	V	一/1	二	26
96	抽	chōu	V	一/1	二	23
97	出	chū	V	一/1	一①	27
98	出发	chūfā	V	一/1	一②	29
99	出来	chūlai	V	一/1	一①	13
100	出生	chūshēng	V	一/2	一②	23
101	出租车	chūzūchē	N		一②	17
102	初	chū		一/2	一③	24
103	除了……以外，都……	chúle……yǐwài, dōu……		一/1	一②	25
104	除了……以外，还/也……	chúle……yǐwài, hái/yě……		一/1	一②	24
105	厨房	chúfáng	N	一/2	二	23
106	穿	chuān	V	一/1	一①	14
107	传统	chuántǒng	Adj	一/2	二	24
108	窗户	chuānghu	N	一/1	二	23
109	窗口	chuāngkǒu	N	二	二	21
110	床	chuáng	N	一/1	一②	6
111	创举	chuàngjǔ	N			29
112	春天	chūntiān	N	一/1	一②	16
113	词典	cídiǎn	N	一/1	一②	24
114	次	cì	M	一/1	一①	15
115	葱	cōng	N	三、四	三	12
116	聪明	cōngming	Adj	一/2	二	9

117	从……到……	cóng……dào……		一/1		8
118	醋	cù	N	一/2	二	12
119	存	cún	V	一/2	一②	21

D

120	打	dǎ	V	一/1	一①	5
121	打	dǎ	V	一/1	一①	16
122	打算	dǎsuàn	V	一/1	一②	17
123	打针	dǎ zhēn	V//O	乙	二	17
124	大概	dàgài	Adv	一/1	一②	26
125	大家	dàjiā	Pr	一/1	一①	6
126	大声	dà shēng		一/1	一②	15
127	大学生	dàxuéshēng	N	一/1	一①	5
128	大夫	dàifu	N	一/1	一②	17
129	代表	dàibiǎo	V	一/1	一②	30
130	带	dài	V	一/1	一②	21
131	戴	dài	V	一/1	二	25
132	担心	dān xīn	V//O	一/2	二	17
133	单姓	dānxìng	N			30
134	但是	dànshì	Conj	一/1	一①	8
135	蛋糕	dàngāo	N	一/2	二	25
136	当	dāng	V	一/1	一①	25
137	当然	dāngrán	Adv	一/1	一①	30
138	刀	dāo	N	一/1	一②	22
139	道理	dàoli	N	一/2	一②	19
140	得到	dédào	V	一/1	一①	26
141	德语（德文）	Déyǔ (Déwén)	N	一/2	二	7
142	地	de	StPt	一/1	一①	15
143	的	de	StPt	一/1	一①	4
144	得	de	StPt	一/1	一①	24
145	得	děi	OpV	一/1	二	18
146	等	děng	Pt	一/1	一②	10
147	等	děng	V	一/1	一①	24
148	等级	děngjí	N	三、四	二	26
149	低	dī	Adj	一/1	一②	15

150	的确	díquè	Adv	乙	二	29
151	地方	dìfang	N	一/1	一①	20
152	地铁	dìtiě	N	一/1	一②	23
153	地图	dìtú	N	一/2	一②	29
154	地址	dìzhǐ	N	一/2	二	9
155	弟弟	dìdi	N	一/1	一②	2
156	第	dì	Pref	一/1	一②	4
157	第一次	dì yī cì				22
158	典礼	diǎnlǐ	N	二	二	24
159	点	diǎn	M	一/1	一①	8
160	点	diǎn	V	一/1	一①	12
161	点心	diǎnxin	N	一/1	三	12
162	点钟	diǎnzhōng	N	一/1	二	25
163	电话	diànhuà	N	一/1	一①	5
164	电脑	diànnǎo	N	二	一①	6
165	电视台	diànshìtái	N	一/2	一③	28
166	电影	diànyǐng	N	一/1	一②	7
167	电子	diànzǐ	N	二		24
168	电子邮件	diànzǐ yóujiàn		一/2	一③	6
169	顶	dǐng	M	二	二	14
170	订	dìng	V	一/2	二	29
171	东	dōng	N	一/1	一①	20
172	东部	dōngbù	N	一/2	一③	10
173	东西	dōngxi	N	一/1	一①	8
174	冬天	dōngtiān	N	一/1	一②	7
175	懂	dǒng	V	一/1	一②	9
176	动画片	dònghuàpiàn	N	二	二	28
177	动物	dòngwù	N	一/1	一②	28
178	栋	dòng	M	丁	三	23
179	都	dōu	Adv	一/1	一①	3
180	豆腐	dòufu	N	一/2	二	12
181	读	dú	V	一/1	一②	4
182	度	dù	M	一/2	一②	16
183	短	duǎn	Adj	一/1	一②	19

184	锻炼	duànliàn	V	一/1	二	17
185	队	duì	N	一/2	一②	9
186	队员	duìyuán	N	丙	一②	9
187	对	duì	Prep	一/1	一①	21
188	对面	duìmiàn	N	一/2	一②	23
189	兑换	duìhuàn	V	二	三	21
190	顿	dùn	M	一/1	一②	11
191	多	duō	Adj	一/1	一①	4
192	多数	duōshù	N	一/2	一③	10

E

193	儿童	értóng	N	一/2	二	28
194	而	ér	Conj	一/2	二	28
195	二胡	èrhú	N			18

F

196	发	fā	V	一/2	一②	6
197	发热	fā rè	V//O	丁	三	17
198	发现	fāxiàn	V	一/2	一②	19
199	发音	fāyīn	N			4
200	法语(法文)	Fǎyǔ (Fǎwén)	N	一/1	二	7
201	翻译	fānyì	N	一/1	二	25
202	饭店	fàndiàn	N	一/1	一①	29
203	饭馆	fànguǎn	N	一/2	二	11
204	方便	fāngbiàn	Adj	一/1	一①	11
205	方便面	fāngbiànmiàn	N		一①	11
206	方言	fāngyán	N		三	10
207	房间	fángjiān	N	一/1	一①	6
208	房租	fángzū	N	三、四	二	7
209	仿照	fǎngzhào	V			29
210	放	fàng	V	一/1	一①	20
211	飞机	fēijī	N	一/1	一①	29
212	非常	fēicháng	Adv	一/1	一①	14
213	费	fèi	N	一/2	一③	21
214	分钟	fēnzhōng	N		一②	19
215	丰富	fēngfù	Adj	一/1	一③	27

216	风	fēng	N	一/1	一②	16
217	风味	fēngwèi	N	三、四	三	18
218	风筝	fēngzheng	N	丁	三	20
219	封	fēng	M	一/1	一②	18
220	服务	fúwù	V	一/1	一②	21
221	服装	fúzhuāng	N	丁	一③	14
222	幅	fú	M	一/2	二	18
223	辅导	fǔdǎo	V	一/1	三	26
224	父母	fùmǔ	N	一/1	一②	22
225	父亲	fùqin	N	一/1	一③	22
226	负责	fùzé	V	一/1	一②	26
227	附近	fùjìn	N	一/1	二	12
228	复习	fùxí	V	一/1	二	8
229	复姓	fùxìng	N			30
230	复印	fùyìn	V	一/2	一②	22
231	复印机	fùyìnjī	N			22
232	复杂	fùzá	Adj	一/1	一③	27
233	副	fù	M	一/2	二	25

G

234	咖喱	gālí	N			11
235	干净	gānjìng	Adj	一/1	一①	20
236	干燥	gānzào	Adj	一/2	三	16
237	感到	gǎndào	V	一/1	一②	27
238	感觉	gǎnjué	N	一/2	一②	20
239	感冒	gǎnmào	V	一/1	二	16
240	感情	gǎnqíng	N	一/2	一③	23
241	感谢	gǎnxiè	V	一/1	一②	15
242	感兴趣	gǎn xìngqù		一/2	二	29
243	刚	gāng	Adv	一/1	一①	16
244	刚才	gāngcái	N	一/1	一①	27
245	钢琴	gāngqín	N	丁	二	9
246	高	gāo	Adj		一①	5
247	高兴	gāoxìng	Adj		一①	12
248	告诉	gàosu	V	一/1	一②	15

249	哥哥	gēge	N	一/1	一①	2
250	歌	gē	N	一/1	一①	10
251	格外	géwài	Adv	二	二	20
252	个	gè	M	一/1	一①	3
253	个子	gèzi	N	一/2	三	5
254	各	gè	Pr	一/1	一②	18
255	各种各样	gè zhǒng gè yàng				27
256	给	gěi	Prep	一/1	一①	5
257	跟	gēn	Prep	一/1	一①	4
258	更	gèng	Adv	一/1	一①	21
259	工作	gōngzuò	N	一/1	一①	5
260	公共汽车	gōnggòng qìchē		一/1	一②	25
261	公里	gōnglǐ	M	一/1	一②	10
262	公司	gōngsī	N	一/2	一②	5
263	公寓	gōngyù	N	一/1	三	7
264	狗	gǒu	N	一/2	二	18
265	姑娘	gūniang	N	一/2	一②	30
266	古城	gǔ chéng				29
267	古典	gǔdiǎn	Adj	丙	二	9
268	古国	gǔ guó				10
269	故事	gùshi	N	一/1	一②	9
270	刮	guā	V	一/1	二	16
271	拐	guǎi	V	一/2	二	22
272	关心	guān xīn	V//O	一/1	一②	17
273	观众	guānzhòng	N	一/2	一②	28
274	光盘	guāngpán	N		二	9
275	广播	guǎngbō	N	一/1	一②	10
276	广场	guǎngchǎng	N	一/2	一②	20
277	逛	guàng	V		二	14
278	贵	guì	Adj	一/1	一①	7
279	国际	guójì	N	一/2	一②	29
280	国家	guójiā	N	一/1	一①	18
281	国内	guó nèi			一②	26
282	国外	guó wài			一②	17

283	果汁	guǒzhī	N		二	12
284	过	guò	V	一/1	一①	22
285	过	guo	AsPt	一/1	一①	26
		H				
286	还	hái	Adv	一/1	一①	6
287	还是	háishi	Conj	一/1	一①	11
288	汉堡包	hànbǎobāo	N			11
289	汉语（中文）	Hànyǔ (Zhōngwén)	N	一/1	一①	3
290	汉字	Hànzì	N	一/1	一①	4
291	汉族	Hànzú	N			10
292	航空	hángkōng	V	一/1	二	29
293	好	hǎo	Adj	一/1	一①	1
294	好吃	hǎochī	Adj	一/1	一①	12
295	好好儿	hǎohāor	Adv	一/2	二	16
296	好喝	hǎohē	Adj			12
297	好久	hǎojiǔ	Adj	一/2	一②	18
298	好看	hǎokàn	Adj	一/1	一①	28
299	好听	hǎotīng	Adj	一/2	一①	25
300	号	hào	M	一/1	一①	6
301	号	hào	N	一/1	一①	14
302	号码	hàomǎ	N	一/1	二	6
303	喝	hē	V	一/1	一①	16
304	合适	héshì	Adj	一/1	一②	14
305	合影	hé yǐng	V//O		三	29
306	和	hé	Conj	一/1	一①	2
307	和	hé	Prep	一/1	一①	9
308	和服	héfú	N			24
309	黑	hēi	Adj	一/1	一①	10
310	黑白	hēibái	N	丁	三	26
311	黑色	hēisè	N		一③	14
312	很	hěn	Adv	一/1	一①	4
313	红	hóng	Adj	一/1	一②	14
314	红绿灯	hónglǜdēng	N			22
315	红叶	hóngyè	N			18

316	后	hòu	N	一/1	一①	20
317	胡同	hútòng	N	一/2	二	18
318	护照	hùzhào	N	一/2	一②	26
319	花	huā	V	一/1	一②	13
320	花儿	huār	N	一/1	一①	23
321	花园	huāyuán	N	一/2	一②	23
322	华	huá				30
323	画	huà	V	一/1	一②	10
324	画儿	huàr	N	一/1	一②	10
325	话	huà	N	一/1	一③	10
326	欢迎	huānyíng	V	一/1	一②	6
327	换	huàn	V	一/1	一②	21
328	换	huàn	V	一/1	一②	22
329	黄	huáng	Adj	一/1	一②	10
330	黄瓜	huánggua	N	一/2	二	12
331	灰色	huīsè	N		二	20
332	回答	huídá	V	一/1	一①	15
333	会	huì	OpV	一/1	一①	7
334	会话	huìhuà	N	一/1		8
335	浑身	húnshēn	N	丙	三	16
336	活动	huódòng	N	一/1	一①	20
337	火车	huǒchē	N	一/1	一①	29
338	火腿	huǒtuǐ	N			11
339	或者	huòzhě	Conj	一/1	一②	6

J

340	机场	jīchǎng	N	一/1	一①	29
341	鸡蛋	jīdàn	N	一/1	一①	12
342	几	jǐ	Nu	一/1	一①	2
343	计算机	jìsuànjī	N	一/2	一②	5
344	记录	jìlù	V	一/2	一③	10
345	记住	jìzhù	V		一①	9
346	纪念	jìniàn	N		一③	13
347	技术	jìshù	N	一/1	一③	7
348	季节	jìjié	N	一/2	二	18

233

349	寄	jì	V	一/1	一②	24
350	寂寞	jìmò	Adj	丙	三	29
351	夹	jiā	V	一/2	二	11
352	家	jiā	N	一/1	一①	2
353	家	jiā	M	一/1	一①	5
354	家常	jiācháng	N	三、四		18
355	家庭	jiātíng	N	一/1	一②	15
356	假	jiǎ	Adj	一/2	一①	14
357	价格	jiàgé	N	一/2	一②	12
358	坚持	jiānchí	V	一/1	一②	28
359	简单	jiǎndān	Adj	一/1	一②	11
360	件	jiàn	M	一/1	一②	14
361	建筑物	jiànzhùwù	N		三	20
362	渐渐	jiànjiàn	Adv	一/2	二	19
363	交	jiāo	V	一/1	一②	18
364	交	jiāo	V	一/1	一②	26
365	教	jiāo	V	一/1	一①	5
366	饺子	jiǎozi	N	一/1	一②	11
367	叫	jiào	V	一/1	一①	1
368	教师	jiàoshī	N	一/2	一②	5
369	教室	jiàoshì	N	一/1	一②	3
370	教授	jiàoshòu	N	一/2	二	22
371	教育	jiàoyù	N	一/1	一②	7
372	接	jiē	V	一/1	一②	29
373	街道	jiēdào	N	一/2	二	20
374	节	jié	M	一/1	一②	8
375	节目	jiémù	N	一/1	一②	28
376	节日	jiérì	N	一/1	一②	24
377	节奏	jiézòu	N	三、四	二	19
378	结婚	jié hūn	V//O	二	一②	24
379	结束	jiéshù	V	一/1	一②	25
380	结账	jié zhàng	V//O			12
381	姐姐	jiějie	N	一/1	一①	2
382	介绍	jièshào	V	一/1	一②	15

383	斤	jīn	M	一/1	一②	13
384	今天	jīntiān	N	一/1	一①	4
385	金	jīn	N	一/2	一③	24
386	金钱	jīnqián	N	丁	二	30
387	紧张	jǐnzhāng	Adj	一/1	一②	19
388	进	jìn	V	一/1	一①	26
389	进步	jìnbù	V	一/2	一②	27
390	进口	jìn kǒu	V//O	一/2	一③	13
391	进行	jìnxíng	V	一/1	一②	27
392	近	jìn	Adj	一/1	一②	29
393	劲儿	jìnr	N		二	16
394	京剧	jīngjù	N	一/2	一②	27
395	经常	jīngcháng	Adv	一/1	一②	7
396	经济	jīngjì	N	一/1	一③	5
397	经理	jīnglǐ	N	一/1	一②	22
398	经验	jīngyàn	N	一/1	一②	27
399	精彩	jīngcǎi	Adj	一/1	一②	28
400	精读	jīngdú	V			4
401	精神	jīngshen	N	一/2	一②	19
402	警察	jǐngchá	N	一/2	一②	18
403	旧	jiù	Adj	一/1	一②	23
404	就	jiù	Adv	一/1	一①	18
405	就	jiù	Adv	一/1	一①	28
406	举世闻名	jǔshì wénmíng		二	附	20
407	举行	jǔxíng	V	一/2	一②	20
408	句子	jùzi	N	一/1	一②	4
409	据说	jùshuō	V	一/2	一③	30
410	觉得	juéde	V	一/1	一①	9

K

411	咖啡	kāfēi	N	一/1	二	11
412	卡	kǎ	N	丁	一②	21
413	卡拉OK	kǎlā-OK				12
414	开	kāi	V	一/1	一①	17
415	开始	kāishǐ	V	一/1	一②	8

416	开心	kāixīn	Adj	三、四	一②	24
417	开学	kāi xué	V//O	一/1	一③	27
418	看	kàn	V	一/1	一①	6
419	看病	kàn bìng	V//O	甲	一①	17
420	看见	kànjiàn	V	一/1	一①	14
421	考场	kǎochǎng	N		二	26
422	考试	kǎo shì	V//O	一/1	一②	18
423	烤	kǎo	V	一/2	三	18
424	科学	kēxué	Adj	一/1	一②	19
425	咳嗽	késou	V	一/1	三	17
426	可爱	kě'ài	Adj	一/1	一②	18
427	可乐	kělè	N			11
428	可能	kěnéng	Adv	一/1	一①	22
429	可是	kěshì	Conj	一/1	一①	22
430	可以	kěyǐ	OpV	一/1	一①	21
431	渴	kě	Adj	一/1	一①	16
432	客房	kèfáng	N		三	23
433	客厅	kètīng	N	二	二	23
434	课	kè	N	一/1	一①	4
435	课本	kèběn	N	一/1	一①	15
436	课文	kèwén	N	一/1	一②	4
437	课余	kèyú	N			19
438	空气	kōngqì	N	一/1	一②	16
439	空调	kōngtiáo	N	丁	一②	7
440	口	kǒu	M	一/1	一①	2
441	口语	kǒuyǔ	M	一/1	二	15
442	哭	kū	V	一/1	一②	17
443	块（元）	kuài (yuán)	M	一/1	一①	13
444	快	kuài	Adj	一/1	一①	15
445	快餐	kuàicān	N	一/2	一②	18
446	快乐	kuàilè	Adj	一/2	一②	25
447	筷子	kuàizi	N	一/1		22
448	宽	kuān	Adj	一/2	二	29
449	困	kùn	Adj	一/2	一③	19

			L			
450	拉	lā	V	一/1	一②	18
451	拉肚子	lā dùzi				16
452	来	lái	V	一/1	一①	6
453	蓝色	lánsè	N		一③	14
454	篮球	lánqiú	N	一/1	一②	9
455	老	lǎo	Adv	一/2	一②	12
456	老百姓	lǎobǎixìng	N	乙	一③	19
457	老板	lǎobǎn	N	一/2	一②	14
458	老师	lǎoshī	N	一/1	一①	3
459	了	le	AsPt	一/1	一①	12
460	了	le	MdPt	一/1	一①	17
461	累	lèi	Adj	一/1	一①	29
462	冷	lěng	Adj	一/1	一①	7
463	离	lí	V	一/1	一②	23
464	离开	líkāi	V	一/1	一②	11
465	梨	lí	N	一/2	三	13
466	礼物	lǐwù	N	一/1	一②	24
467	里面	lǐmian	N	一/1	一①	23
468	理发	lǐ fà	V//O	一/2	二	26
469	理解	lǐjiě	V	一/2	一③	26
470	理想	lǐxiǎng	Adj	一/2	一②	26
471	理由	lǐyóu	N	一/2	一②	27
472	里	li	N	一/1	一①	23
473	历史	lìshǐ	N	一/1	一②	6
474	例如	lìrú	V	一/1	一②	30
475	俩	liǎ	Q	一/1	二	7
476	连……也……	lián……yě……		一/1		27
477	连衣裙	liányīqún	N			25
478	联系	liánxì	V	一/1	一②	29
479	练习	liànxí	N/V	一/1	一②	4
480	凉菜	liángcài	N			12
481	两	liǎng	Nu	一/1	一①	6
482	聊天儿	liáo tiānr	V//O	一/1	二	9

237

483	了解	liǎojiě	V	一/1	一②	17
484	零食	língshí	N		二	24
485	留念	liúniàn	V	一/1	三	29
486	留学	liú xué	V//O	一/2	一③	9
487	留学生	liúxuéshēng	N	一/1	一②	1
488	流	liú	V	一/1	一②	16
489	流行	liúxíng	V	二	一②	9
490	楼	lóu	N	一/1	一①	6
491	楼上	lóu shàng			一②	23
492	楼梯	lóutī	N	一/2	二	23
493	楼下	lóu xià			一②	23
494	录音	lùyīn	N	一/1	一③	15
495	路	lù	N	一/1	一①	20
496	旅行	lǚxíng	V	一/1	一②	21
497	旅游	lǚyóu	V	二	一②	29
498	绿	lǜ	Adj	一/1	一②	18

M

499	妈妈	māma	N	一/1	一①	2
500	麻婆豆腐	mápó dòufu				12
501	马路	mǎlù	N	一/1	一①	22
502	马上	mǎshàng	Adv	一/1	一①	24
503	吗	ma	MdPt	一/1	一①	1
504	买	mǎi	V	一/1	一①	8
505	卖	mài	V	一/1	一②	11
506	满意	mǎnyì	Adj	一/1	一②	7
507	慢慢儿	mànmānr	Adv		二	15
508	芒果	mángguǒ	N			13
509	忙	máng	Adj	一/1	一①	5
510	毛(角)	máo (jiǎo)	M	一/1	一②	13
511	毛衣	máoyī	N		二	14
512	帽衫	màoshān	N			14
513	帽子	màozi	N		二	14
514	没关系	méi guānxi		一/1	一①	15
515	没问题	méi wèntí				27

516	没有	méiyǒu	V	一/1	一①	2
517	每	měi	Pr	一/1	一②	6
518	美好	měihǎo	Adj	一/2	一③	30
519	美丽	měilì	Adj	一/2	二	18
520	美元	měiyuán	N	一/2	一②	7
521	美中不足	měi zhōng bù zú		三、四	附	28
522	妹妹	mèimei	N	一/1	一②	2
523	门	mén	M	一/1	一①	15
524	门口	ménkǒu	N	一/1	一①	13
525	们	men	Suf	一/1	一①	3
526	迷	mí	Suf	三、四		28
527	迷路	mí lù	V//O		三	22
528	猕猴桃	míhóutáo	N			13
529	米	mǐ	M	一/1	一②	20
530	米饭	mǐfàn	N	一/1	一②	11
531	密码	mìmǎ	N		二	21
532	面包	miànbāo	N	一/1	一①	11
533	面粉	miànfěn	N	丙	三	12
534	面积	miànjī	N	一/2	一③	20
535	面条	miàntiáo	N	一/1	一②	11
536	民族	mínzú	N	一/1	一③	9
537	名城	míng chéng				29
538	名牌	míngpái	N	二	二	14
539	名胜古迹	míngshèng gǔjì				7
540	名字	míngzi	N	一/1	一①	6
541	明年	míngnián	N	一/1	一①	27
542	明天	míngtiān	N	一/1	一①	4
543	明显	míngxiǎn	Adj	一/2	一③	27
544	母亲	mǔqin	N		一③	22
545	目标	mùbiāo	N	一/2	一②	30

N

546	哪	nǎ / něi	Pr	一/1	一①	7
547	哪儿	nǎr	Pr	一/1	一①	3
548	那	nà	Pr	一/1	一①	5

549	那个	nàge	Pr	一/1	二	14
550	那儿	nàr	Pr	一/1	一①	12
551	奶酪	nǎilào	N			11
552	奶奶	nǎinai	N	一/2	一②	24
553	耐心	nàixīn	Adj	一/2	二	15
554	男	nán	Adj	一/1	一①	3
555	男朋友	nánpéngyou	N		一①	18
556	南	nán	N	一/1	一①	20
557	难	nán	Adj	一/1	一①	4
558	呢	ne	MdPt	一/1	一①	24
559	内容	nèiróng	N	一/1	一③	11
560	能	néng	OpV	一/1	一①	21
561	你	nǐ	Pr	一/1	一①	1
562	年级	niánjí	N	一/1	一②	25
563	年轻	niánqīng	Adj	一/1	一②	21
564	牛	niú	N	一/1	一①	11
565	牛奶	niúnǎi	N	一/1	一①	11
566	牛仔裤	niúzǎikù	N		二	14
567	女	nǚ	Adj	一/1	一①	3
568	暖和	nuǎnhuo	Adj	一/1	一②	16

P

569	怕	pà	V	一/1	一①	15
570	牌子	páizi	N	二	一②	14
571	盘	pán	M	乙	二	12
572	旁	páng	N	一/2	二	20
573	胖	pàng	Adj	一/1	二	18
574	跑步	pǎo bù	V//O	一/1	二	8
575	陪	péi	V	一/2	二	17
576	喷嚏	pēntì	N			16
577	朋友	péngyou	N	一/1	一①	7
578	碰到	pèngdào	V		一②	13
579	皮肤	pífū	N	乙	二	10
580	皮儿	pír	N	乙	一③	29
581	啤酒	píjiǔ	N	一/1	二	12

582	篇	piān	M	一/1	一②	15
583	便宜	piányi	Adj	一/1	一②	11
584	片	piàn	M	一/1	一②	11
585	票	piào	N	一/1	一①	29
586	漂亮	piàoliang	Adj	一/1	一②	9
587	拼音	pīnyīn	N			4
588	频道	píndào	N		二	28
589	平	píng	Adj	一/2	一②	30
590	平方	píngfāng	M	乙	二	10
591	平时	píngshí	N	一/2	一②	24
592	苹果	píngguǒ	N	一/1	二	13
593	瓶	píng	M	一/1	一②	12
594	葡萄	pútao	N	丙	二	13
595	普通话	pǔtōnghuà	N	二	一②	10

Q

596	期中	qīzhōng	N			18
597	其实	qíshí	Adv	一/2	一③	27
598	其他	qítā	Pr	一/2	一②	26
599	其中	qízhōng	N	一/2	一②	30
600	奇怪	qíguài	Adj	一/1	一②	26
601	奇迹	qíjì	N	二	二	29
602	骑	qí	V	一/1	一②	13
603	起	qǐ	V	一/1	一①	30
604	起床	qǐ chuáng	V//O	一/1	一②	8
605	气候	qìhòu	N	一/2	一③	17
606	汽车	qìchē	N	一/1	一①	25
607	千	qiān	Nu	一/1	一②	10
608	铅笔	qiānbǐ	N	一/1	二	26
609	签证	qiānzhèng	N	三、四	二	27
610	前	qián	N	一/1	一①	22
611	前天	qiántiān	N	一/2	一②	17
612	钱	qián	N	一/1	一①	13
613	浅	qiǎn	Adj	一/1	二	24
614	青椒	qīngjiāo	N			12

615	轻	qīng	Adj	一/1	一②	18
616	情况	qíngkuàng	N	一/1	一②	18
617	晴	qíng	Adj	一/1	二	20
618	请	qǐng	V	一/1	一①	4
619	请假	qǐng jià	V//O	一/1	一①	16
620	秋天	qiūtiān	N	一/1	一②	17
621	球场	qiúchǎng	N	一/1	一②	28
622	区	qū	N	一/2	一③	22
623	取	qǔ	V	一/2	一②	21
624	去	qù	V	一/1	一①	3
625	全	quán	Adj	一/1	一①	5
626	裙子	qúnzi	N	一/2	三	14
R						
627	让	ràng	V	一/1	一①	15
628	热	rè	Adj	一/1	一①	7
629	热菜	rècài	N			12
630	热带	rèdài	N	丙	三	13
631	热情	rèqíng	Adj	一/1	一②	18
632	人	rén	N	一/1	一①	1
633	人类	rénlèi	N	一/2	一③	29
634	人民币	rénmínbì	N	一/1	一②	21
635	认识	rènshi	V	一/1	一①	18
636	认为	rènwéi	V	一/1	一①	19
637	认真	rènzhēn	Adj	一/1	一①	24
638	仍然	réngrán	Adv	一/2	一③	30
639	日常	rìcháng	Adj	一/2	一③	27
640	日记	rìjì	N	一/2	二	29
641	日语（日文）	Rìyǔ (Rìwén)	N	一/1	二	7
642	容易	róngyì	Adj	一/1	一②	9
643	肉	ròu	N	一/1	一①	11
644	如	rú	V	一/2	二	13
645	如果	rúguǒ	Conj	一/2	一②	22
646	入乡随俗	rù xiāng suí sú				19

S

647	散步	sàn bù	V//O	一/1	二	20
648	嗓子	sǎngzi	N	一/2	三	16
649	沙发	shāfā	N	一/2	一②	23
650	沙拉	shālā	N			11
651	商店	shāngdiàn	N	一/1	一②	8
652	上班	shàng bān	V//O	一/2	一①	19
653	上课	shàng kè	V//O	一/1	一①	3
654	上网	shàng wǎng	V//O	一/1	一①	6
655	上	shang	N	一/1	一①	20
656	勺子	sháozi	N	一/1		22
657	谁	shéi/shuí	Pr	一/1	一①	5
658	申请	shēnqǐng	V	二	二	27
659	身体	shēntǐ	N	一/1	一①	5
660	深	shēn	Adj	一/1	一②	24
661	什么	shénme	Pr	一/1	一①	9
662	生病	shēng bìng	V//O	丙	一②	17
663	生词	shēngcí	N	一/1		4
664	生活	shēnghuó	N	一/1	一①	9
665	生日	shēngrì	N	一/1	一①	24
666	声调	shēngdiào	N	一/1		10
667	声音	shēngyīn	N	一/1	一②	15
668	时候	shíhou	N	一/1	一①	13
669	时间	shíjiān	N	一/1	一①	19
670	食品	shípǐn	N	一/2	一③	24
671	食堂	shítáng	N	一/1	二	8
672	世界	shìjiè	N	一/1	一②	14
673	市	shì	N	一/1	一②	30
674	市场	shìchǎng	N	一/2	一③	13
675	式	shì	Suf	丁	二	23
676	事情	shìqing	N	一/1	一②	18
677	试	shì	V	一/1	一②	14
678	是	shì	V	一/1	一①	1
679	收	shōu	V	一/1	一②	21

243

680	手续	shǒuxù	N	一/2	一③	21
681	首都	shǒudū	N	一/1	二	10
682	寿司	shòusī	N		二	18
683	瘦	shòu	Adj	一/2	二	25
684	书	shū	N	一/1	一①	4
685	书房	shūfáng	N		二	23
686	舒服	shūfu	Adj	一/1	一②	16
687	蔬菜	shūcài	N	一/2	二	11
688	熟悉	shúxi	Adj	一/2	二	18
689	束	shù	M	二	一③	25
690	树	shù	N	一/1	一①	23
691	树叶	shùyè	N		三	18
692	数学	shùxué	N	一/1		22
693	刷卡	shuā kǎ	V//O			21
694	帅	shuài	Adj	丁	二	25
695	双	shuāng	M	一/1	一②	14
696	双方	shuāngfāng	N	一/2	一③	28
697	水	shuǐ	N	一/1	一①	16
698	水果	shuǐguǒ	N	一/1	一①	13
699	水平	shuǐpíng	N	一/1	一②	15
700	睡觉	shuì jiào	V//O	一/1	一①	8
701	说	shuō	V	一/1	一①	7
702	说明	shuōmíng	V	一/1	一②	27
703	丝	sī	N	乙	二	12
704	四合院	sìhéyuàn	N		三	18
705	四周	sìzhōu	N	二	二	20
706	送	sòng	V	一/1	一①	15
707	速度	sùdù	N	一/2	一③	15
708	宿舍	sùshè	N	一/1	二	6
709	虽然……但是……	suīrán……dànshì……		一/1	一②	23
710	岁	suì	M	一/1	一①	7
711	所	suǒ	M	一/2	一③	23
712	所以	suǒyǐ	Conj	一/1	一①	12

		T				
713	T恤衫	T xù shān				14
714	他	tā	Pr	一/1	一①	5
715	他们	tāmen	Pr	一/1	一①	3
716	它	tā	Pr	一/1	一②	18
717	她	tā	Pr	一/1	一①	5
718	台	tái	M	一/2	一③	6
719	太	tài	Adv	一/1	一①	13
720	弹	tán	V	二	二	9
721	汤	tāng	N	一/1	一②	12
722	糖	táng	N	一/1	一②	12
723	趟	tàng	M	一/2	二	27
724	讨论	tǎolùn	V	一/1	一②	18
725	套	tào	M	一/2	一②	15
726	特别	tèbié	Adv	一/1	一②	9
727	特点	tèdiǎn	N	一/2	一②	17
728	疼	téng	Adj	一/1	一②	16
729	踢	tī	V	一/1	二	28
730	提高	tígāo	V	一/1	一②	15
731	提前	tíqián	V	一/2	一③	29
732	体育	tǐyù	N	一/1	一②	17
733	替	tì	Prep	一/2	二	16
734	天	tiān	N	一/1	一①	6
735	天	tiān	N	一/1	一①	20
736	天空	tiānkōng	N	二	一③	18
737	天气	tiānqì	N	一/1	一①	16
738	甜点	tiándiǎn	N			24
739	填	tián	V	一/2	二	27
740	条	tiáo	M	一/1	一②	14
741	条件	tiáojiàn	N	一/1	一②	27
742	跳舞	tiào wǔ	V//O	一/1	一②	25
743	听	tīng	V	一/1	一①	7
744	听	tīng	M			12
745	听力	tīnglì	N		一③	8

746	听说	tīngshuō	V	一/1	一①	21
747	听写	tīngxiě	V	一/1		4
748	挺	tǐng	Adv	一/1	一②	10
749	通知	tōngzhī	V	一/1	一②	26
750	通知	tōngzhī	N	一/1	一②	27
751	同	tóng	Adj	一/2	二	9
752	同班	tóng bān	V//O			9
753	同屋	tóngwū	N	乙		6
754	同学	tóngxué	N	一/1	一①	3
755	同意	tóngyì	V	一/1	一①	27
756	统计	tǒngjì	V	二	二	30
757	偷偷	tōutōu	Adv	一/2	二	17
758	头	tóu	N	一/1	一②	20
759	头发	tóufa	N	一/2	二	10
760	图	tú	N	一/2	一③	22
761	图画	túhuà	N	二	一③	18
762	图书馆	túshūguǎn	N	一/1	一②	8
763	土地	tǔdì	N	一/2	二	10
764	土豆	tǔdòu	N	一/2	二	12

W

765	袜子	wàzi	N	一/1	二	14
766	外币	wàibì	N		二	21
767	外面	wàimian	N	一/2	一①	23
768	外语	wàiyǔ	N	一/1	一①	9
769	玩儿	wánr	V	一/1	一①	6
770	晚饭	wǎnfàn	N	一/1	一①	8
771	晚会	wǎnhuì	N	一/1	一②	25
772	万	wàn	Nu	一/1	一②	10
773	往	wǎng	Prep	一/1	一②	22
774	忘	wàng	V	一/1	一①	16
775	伟大	wěidà	Adj	一/2	一③	29
776	卫生间	wèishēngjiān	N		二	23
777	为什么	wèi shénme		一/1	一①	26
778	位	wèi	M	一/1	一②	3

779	味道	wèidao	N	一/2	一②	12
780	温差	wēnchā	N			16
781	温度	wēndù	N	一/2	一②	16
782	文化	wénhuà	N	一/1	一②	27
783	文明	wénmíng	Adj	一/2	一③	10
784	文学	wénxué	N	一/1	一③	25
785	问	wèn	V	一/1	一①	15
786	问好	wèn hǎo	V//O	一/1		18
787	我	wǒ	Pr	一/1	一①	1
788	卧室	wòshì	N	二	二	23
789	午饭	wǔfàn	N	一/1	一①	8
790	午觉	wǔjiào	N			19

X

791	西	xī	N	一/1	一①	20
792	西班牙语 （西班牙文）	Xībānyáyǔ (Xībānyáwén)	N		二	7
793	西服	xīfú	N	丙		24
794	西瓜	xīguā	N	乙	二	13
795	西红柿	xīhóngshì	N	三、四	二	12
796	西药	xīyào	N			17
797	希望	xīwàng	V	一/1	一②	19
798	习惯	xíguàn	V	一/1	一②	15
799	洗澡	xǐ zǎo	V//O	一/1	一②	8
800	喜欢	xǐhuan	V	一/1	一①	7
801	系	xì	N	一/1	一②	6
802	下	xià	V	一/1	一①	16
803	下半场	xiàbànchǎng	N			28
804	下课	xià kè	V//O	一/1	一①	8
805	下午	xiàwǔ	N	一/1	一①	8
806	夏天	xiàtiān	N	一/1	一②	7
807	先	xiān	Adv	一/1	一①	22
808	鲜花	xiānhuā	N	一/2	二	25
809	显得	xiǎnde	V	一/2	一③	20
810	现场	xiànchǎng	N	二	一③	28

811	现代	xiàndài	N	一/2	一③	9
812	现金	xiànjīn	N	二	一③	21
813	现在	xiànzài	N	一/1	一①	3
814	馅儿	xiànr	N	三、四	三	22
815	相同	xiāngtóng	Adj	一/2	一②	22
816	香蕉	xiāngjiāo	N	一/1	二	13
817	箱子	xiāngzi	N	一/1	二	24
818	详细	xiángxì	Adj	一/2	二	24
819	响亮	xiǎngliàng	Adj	丙	三	30
820	想	xiǎng	V	一/1	一①	5
821	想	xiǎng	OpV	一/1	一①	12
822	向	xiàng	Prep	一/1	一①	22
823	项链	xiàngliàn	N	三、四	三	24
824	像	xiàng	V	一/1	一②	10
825	像……一样	xiàng……yíyàng				25
826	消费	xiāofèi	V	一/2	一③	21
827	小吃	xiǎochī	N		二	29
828	小伙子	xiǎohuǒzi	N	一/2	二	30
829	小姐	xiǎojie	N	一/1	一①	21
830	小区	xiǎoqū	N		三	22
831	小时	xiǎoshí	N	一/1	一①	19
832	小学生	xiǎoxuéshēng	N	一/1	一①	5
833	笑	xiào	V	一/1	一①	24
834	鞋	xié	N	一/1	一②	14
835	写	xiě	V	一/1	一①	10
836	新	xīn	Adj	一/1	一①	14
837	新年	xīnnián	N	一/1	一①	24
838	新闻	xīnwén	N	一/1	一②	6
839	新鲜	xīnxiān	Adj	一/2	二	13
840	信	xìn	N	一/1	一②	18
841	星期	xīngqī	N	一/1	一①	8
842	行动	xíngdòng	N	一/2	一③	29
843	姓	xìng	V	一/1	一②	1
844	休闲	xiūxián	V		二	20

248

845	需要	xūyào	V	一/1	一②	26
846	许多	xǔduō	Nu	一/1	一②	10
847	学期	xuéqī	N	乙	一③	27
848	学生	xuésheng	N	一/1	一①	3
849	学习	xuéxí	V	一/1	一①	3
850	学院	xuéyuàn	N	一/1	一①	7

Y

851	烟	yān	N	丙	一③	23
852	延长	yáncháng	V	一/2	二	27
853	研究生	yánjiūshēng	N	二	二	7
854	眼镜	yǎnjìng	N	一/2	二	25
855	眼睛	yǎnjing	N	一/1	二	25
856	演员	yǎnyuán	N	一/2	一②	9
857	阳台	yángtái	N		二	23
858	样子	yàngzi	N	一/1	一②	18
859	要求	yāoqiú	N	一/1	一②	27
860	药	yào	N	一/1	一②	16
861	要	yào	V	一/1	一①	12
862	要	yào	OpV	一/1	一①	21
863	要……了	yào……le				18
864	椰子	yēzi	N		附	13
865	爷爷	yéye	N	乙	一②	30
866	也	yě	Adv	一/1	一①	2
867	页	yè	M	一/1	一②	4
868	夜晚	yèwǎn	N	一/2	三	16
869	一……就……	yī……jiù……		一/1		29
870	衣服	yīfu	N	一/1	一①	14
871	衣柜	yīguì	N			6
872	医院	yīyuàn	N	一/1	一①	17
873	一定	yídìng	Adv	一/1	一②	18
874	一共	yígòng	Adv	一/1	一②	13
875	一会儿	yíhuìr	Q	一/1	一①	24
876	一块儿	yíkuàir	Adv	一/1	一①	22
877	一样	yíyàng	Adj	一/1	一①	17

878	遗憾	yíhàn	Adj	二	二	19
879	已经	yǐjīng	Adv	一/1	一②	16
880	以后	yǐhòu	N	一/1	一①	8
881	以前	yǐqián	N	一/1	一①	9
882	以为	yǐwéi	V	一/1	一②	27
883	椅子	yǐzi	N	一/1	一②	6
884	一般	yìbān	Adj	一/1	一②	19
885	一边……一边……	yìbiān……yìbiān……		一/1	一①	22
886	一起	yìqǐ	Adv	一/1	一①	7
887	一些	yìxiē	Q	一/1	一①	24
888	一直	yìzhí	Adv	一/1	一②	20
889	亿	yì	Nu	一/2	一②	10
890	意义	yìyì	N	一/2	一②	30
891	因此	yīncǐ	Conj	一/2	一③	26
892	因为	yīnwèi	Conj	一/1	一①	12
893	阴天	yīntiān	N	二	二	29
894	音乐	yīnyuè	N	一/1	一②	5
895	银行	yínháng	N	一/1	一②	21
896	饮料	yǐnliào	N	二	二	11
897	应该	yīnggāi	OpV	一/1	一①	21
898	英语(英文)	Yīngyǔ (Yīngwén)	N	一/1	一②(一③)	6
899	营业	yíngyè	V	一/2	二	21
900	永远	yǒngyuǎn	Adv	一/1	一②	25
901	勇敢	yǒnggǎn	Adj	一/2	二	28
902	用	yòng	V	一/1	一①	4
903	邮局	yóujú	N	一/1	一②	23
904	邮票	yóupiào	N	一/1	一②	24
905	油腻	yóunì	Adj			16
906	游览	yóulǎn	V	一/2	三	7
907	游泳	yóuyǒng	V	一/1	一②	9
908	友好	yǒuhǎo	Adj	一/1	一②	18
909	有	yǒu	V	一/1	一①	2
910	有点儿	yǒudiǎnr	Adv	一/1	一①	14

911	有名	yǒumíng	Adj	一/1	一①	20
912	有时候	yǒushíhou	Adv	一/1	一①	8
913	有效	yǒuxiào	V	一/2	一③	26
914	有意思	yǒu yìsi		一/1	一②	8
915	又	yòu	Adv	一/1	一①	27
916	又……又……	yòu……yòu……				11
917	右	yòu	N	一/1	一②	22
918	愉快	yúkuài	Adj	一/1	二	9
919	雨	yǔ	N	一/1	一②	16
920	语法	yǔfǎ	N	一/1	二	15
921	语言	yǔyán	N	一/1	一②	18
922	玉	yù	N	丁	二	30
923	预习	yùxí	V	一/1		8
924	员	yuán	Suf	一/2	一③	9
925	远	yuǎn	Adj	一/1	一①	23
926	远大	yuǎndà	Adj	三、四		30
927	阅读	yuèdú	V	一/2	二	15
928	越来越	yuè lái yuè		一/2	一②	28
929	云	yún	N	一/1	二	18
930	运动	yùndòng	V	一/1	一②	14
		Z				
931	杂志	zázhì	N	二	一②	24
932	再	zài	Adv	一/1	一①	22
933	再见	zàijiàn	V	一/1	一①	1
934	在	zài	V	一/1	一①	2
935	早晨	zǎochen	N	一/1	一②	16
936	早饭	zǎofàn	N	一/1	一①	8
937	早上	zǎoshang	N	一/1	一①	8
938	造句	zào jù	V//O	一/2		4
939	怎么	zěnme	Pr	一/1	一①	13
940	怎么样	zěnmeyàng	Pr	一/1	一①	18
941	站	zhàn	N	一/1	一①	23
942	张	zhāng	M	一/1	一②	6
943	长辈	zhǎngbèi	N		三	30

944	长大	zhǎngdà	V		一②	23
945	丈夫	zhàngfu	N	一/2	二	30
946	着急	zháojí	Adj	一/1	一②	15
947	照顾	zhàogù	V	一/1	一②	17
948	照片	zhàopiàn	N	一/2	一②	5
949	照相	zhào xiàng	V//O	一/1	一③	13
950	这	zhè	Pr	一/1	一①	5
951	这儿	zhèr	Pr	一/1	一①	11
952	着	zhe	AsPt	一/1	一①	25
953	真	zhēn	Adj	一/1		14
954	真	zhēn	Adv	一/1	一①	20
955	真正	zhēnzhèng	Adj	一/1	一③	19
956	整齐	zhěngqí	Adj	一/1	一②	21
957	正……呢	zhèng……ne		一/1		25
958	正在	zhèngzài	Adv	一/1	一①	25
959	证书	zhèngshū	N	二	二	26
960	政治	zhèngzhì	N	一/1	一③	20
961	之	zhī	StPt	丙	三	29
962	支票	zhīpiào	N	丁	三	21
963	知道	zhīdao	V	一/1	一①	9
964	知识	zhīshi	N	一/1	一②	15
965	直	zhí	Adj	二	一③	29
966	直播	zhíbō	V	三、四	一③	28
967	职员	zhíyuán	N	二	三	5
968	只	zhǐ	Adv	一/1	一②	19
969	只好	zhǐhǎo	Adv	一/1	一③	27
970	只有……才……	zhǐyǒu……cái……		一/2	一②	24
971	纸	zhǐ	N	一/1	一②	24
972	中间	zhōngjiān	N	一/1	一①	20
973	中心	zhōngxīn	N	一/2	一②	20
974	中学	zhōngxué	N	一/1	一①	5
975	中药	zhōngyào	N	一/2	二	17
976	钟头	zhōngtóu	N	一/1	二	19
977	种	zhǒng	M	一/1	一②	9

978	重	zhòng	Adj	一/1	一①	24
979	重要	zhòngyào	Adj	一/1	一①	11
980	周末	zhōumò	N	一/2	二	7
981	猪肉	zhūròu	N			22
982	主食	zhǔshí	N	三、四	三	12
983	主要	zhǔyào	Adj	一/1	一②	15
984	住	zhù	V	一/1	一①	6
985	住宅	zhùzhái	N	二	二	22
986	注意	zhù yì	V//O	一/1	一②	17
987	祝	zhù	V	一/1	一②	18
988	专卖店	zhuānmàidiàn	N		附	14
989	专业	zhuānyè	N	一/2	一②	7
990	准备	zhǔnbèi	V	一/1	一②	4
991	准考证	zhǔnkǎozhèng	N			26
992	桌子	zhuōzi	N	一/1	一①	6
993	自动	zìdòng	Adj	一/2	一③	21
994	自动取款机	zìdòng qǔkuǎnjī				21
995	自己	zìjǐ	Pr	一/1	一②	11
996	自行车	zìxíngchē	N		一②	13
997	自由	zìyóu	Adj	一/2	一②	29
998	总	zǒng	Adv	一/1	一②	19
999	总是	zǒngshì	Adv	一/1	一②	30
1000	足球	zúqiú	N	一/1	一②	28
1001	最	zuì	Adv	一/1	一①	11
1002	最后	zuìhòu	N	一/1	一①	14
1003	最近	zuìjìn	N	一/1	一②	17
1004	昨天	zuótiān	N	一/1		4
1005	左	zuǒ	N	一/1	一②	22
1006	左右	zuǒyòu	N	一/2	一②	22
1007	作文	zuòwén	N	一/2	一②	15
1008	作业	zuòyè	N	一/1	一②	4
1009	坐	zuò	V	一/1	一①	17
1010	座	zuò	M	一/1	一②	22
1011	做	zuò	V	一/1	一①	4
1012	做客	zuò kè	V//O	一/2	二	22

专有名词 Proper Nouns

序号	词语	拼音	课号
	A		
1	阿迪达斯	Ādídásī	14
	B		
2	巴西	Bāxī	28
3	北京	Běijīng	5
4	北京师范大学	Běijīng Shīfàn Dàxué	3
5	必胜客	Bìshèngkè	18
6	兵马俑博物馆	Bīmǎyǎng Bówùguǎn	29
	C		
7	长安	Cháng'ān	29
8	长江	Cháng Jiāng	30
9	陈	Chén	26
	D		
10	德国	Déguó	7
11	东京	Dōngjīng	2
	F		
12	法国	Fǎguó	7
	G		
13	故宫博物院	Gù Gōng Bówùyuàn	20
14	广东	Guǎngdōng	10
15	国家博物馆	Guójiā Bówùguǎn	20
	H		
16	韩国	Hánguó	3
17	汉代	Hàndài	29
18	汉斯	Hànsī	28
19	汉语水平考试	Hànyǔ Shuǐpíng Kǎoshì	26
20	和子	Hézǐ	18
	J		
21	京都	Jīngdū	29

		L	
22	李	Lǐ	4
23	李维斯	Lǐwéisī	14
24	铃木	Língmù	18
25	刘	Liú	15
		M	
26	麦当劳	Màidāngláo	18
27	毛主席纪念堂	Máo Zhǔxí Jìniàntáng	20
28	美国	Měiguó	3
29	《米老鼠和唐老鸭》	《Mǐlǎoshǔ hé Tánglǎoyā》	28
30	明代	Míngdài	20
		N	
31	奈良	Nàiliáng	29
32	耐克	Nàikè	14
33	南希	Nánxī	7
		O	
34	欧阳	Ōuyáng	30
35	欧洲	Ōuzhōu	9
		Q	
36	钱小江	Qián Xiǎojiāng	30
37	乔治	Qiáozhì	4
38	秦代	Qíndài	29
		R	
39	人民大会堂	Rénmín Dàhuìtáng	20
40	人民英雄纪念碑	Rénmín Yīngxióng Jìniànbēi	20
41	日本	Rìběn	1
42	锐步	Ruìbù	14
		S	
43	山下京美	Shānxià Jīngměi	1
44	上海	Shànghǎi	10
45	司马	Sīmǎ	30
46	四川	Sìchuān	12
		T	
47	泰国	Tàiguó	6

48	唐代	Tángdài	29
49	天安门城楼	Tiān'ān Mén Chénglóu	20
50	天安门广场	Tiān'ān Mén Guǎngchǎng	20
W			
51	王	Wáng	15
52	武汉	Wǔhàn	30
X			
53	西安	Xī'ān	29
54	新西兰	Xīnxīlán	13
Y			
55	亚洲	Yàzhōu	10
56	杨歌	Yáng Gē	6
57	意大利	Yìdàlì	18
58	英国	Yīngguó	3
Z			
59	张文心	Zhāng Wénxīn	22
60	珍妮	Zhēnni	4
61	正阳门	Zhèngyáng Mén	20
62	中关村	Zhōngguāncūn	22
63	中关园	Zhōngguānyuán	22
64	中国	Zhōngguó	3
65	中国国际航空公司	Zhōngguó Guójì Hángkōng Gōngsī	29
66	周代	Zhōudài	29

补充词语　Complementary Words

序号	词语	拼音	词性	等级1	等级2	课号
B						
1	八	bā	Nu	—/1	—①	2
2	半	bàn	Nu	—/1	—①	8
3	不	bù	Adv	—/1	—①	1

		D				
4	多少	duōshao	Pr	一/1	一①	3
		E				
5	二	èr	Nu	一/1	一①	2
		F				
6	分	fēn	M	一/1	一①	8
		H				
7	还是	háishi	Conj	一/1	一①	6
		J				
8	九	jiǔ	Nu	一/1	一①	2
		L				
9	两	liǎng	Nu	一/1	一①	2
10	〇/零	líng	Nu	一/1	一①	2
11	六	liù	Nu	一/1	一①	2
		Q				
12	七	qī	Nu	一/1	一①	2
		R				
13	日	rì	Nu	一/1	一①	8
		S				
14	三	sān	N	一/1	一①	2
15	上午	shàngwǔ	Nu	一/1	一①	8
16	十	shí	Nu	一/1	一①	2
17	四	sì	Nu	一/1	一①	2
		W				
18	五	wǔ	Nu	一/1	一①	2
		Y				
19	一	yī	Nu	一/1	一①	2
20	一点儿	yìdiǎnr	Q	一/1	一①	24
21	月	yuè	N	一/1	一①	8

中国文化百题
A Kaleidoscope of Chinese Culture

纵横古今,中华文明历历在目　　享誉中外,东方魅力层层绽放
Unfold the splendid and fascinating Chinese civilization

了解中国的窗口
A window to China

- 大量翔实的高清影视资料，展现中国文化的魅力。既是全面了解中国文化的影视精品，又是汉语教学的文化视听精品教材。

- 涵盖了中国最典型的200个文化点，包括中国的名胜古迹、中国各地、中国的地下宝藏、中国的名山大川、中国的民族、中国的美食、中国的节日、中国的传统美德、中国人的生活、儒家、佛教与道教、中国的风俗、中国的历史、中医中药、中国的文明与艺术、中国的著作、中国的人物、中国的故事等18个方面。

- 简洁易懂的语言，展示了每个文化点的精髓。

- 共四辑，每辑50个文化点，每个文化点3分钟。有四种字幕解说，可灵活选择使用。已出版英语、德语、韩语、日语、俄语五个注释文种，其他文种将陆续出版。

目录 Contents

第一辑 Album 1

第一盘 DVD 1
中国各地之一
Places in China I
- 中国概况　■ 北京　■ 上海　■ 天津　■ 重庆
- 山东省　■ 新疆维吾尔自治区　■ 西藏自治区
- 香港特别行政区　■ 澳门特别行政区

第二盘 DVD 2
中国名胜古迹之一
Scenic Spots and Historical Sites in China I
- 长城　■ 颐和园　■ 避暑山庄　■ 明十三陵　■ 少林寺
- 苏州古典园林　■ 山西平遥古城　■ 丽江古城　■ 桂林漓江
- 河姆渡遗址

第三盘 DVD 3
- 黄河　■ 泰山　■ 故宫　■ 周口店北京猿人遗址　■ 长江
- 龙门石窟　■ 黄山　■ 九寨沟　■ 张家界　■ 庐山

第四盘 DVD 4
- 秦始皇兵马俑　■ 马王堆汉墓　■ 殷墟
- 殷墟的墓葬　■ 殷墟的甲骨文　■ 曾侯乙编钟
- 法门寺地宫　■ 三星堆遗址　■ 古蜀金沙　■ 马踏飞燕

第五盘 DVD 5
中国文明与艺术之一
Chinese Civilization and Art I
- 书法艺术　■ 中国画　■ 年画　■ 剪纸
- 中国丝绸　■ 刺绣　■ 旗袍　■ 瓷器
- 中医的理论基础——阴阳五行　■ 针灸

英文版第一、二、三辑已经出版，第四辑将于2011年出版。
The first three albums of the English edition have been published. The fourth album will be published in 2011.

第二辑 Album 2

中国名胜古迹之二
Scenic Spots and Historical Sites in China II

第一盘 DVD 1
- 天坛 ■ 布达拉宫 ■ 孔庙、孔府、孔林 ■ 敦煌莫高窟 ■ 云冈石窟
- 乐山大佛 ■ 长白山 ■ 华山 ■ 武夷山 ■ 皖南古村落——西递、宏村

中国的民族
Chinese Nationalities

第二盘 DVD 2
- 多民族的国家 ■ 汉族、满族 ■ 瑶族、纳西族 ■ 侗族、朝鲜族
- 苗族、彝族 ■ 蒙古族、壮族 ■ 白族、傣族
- 回族、维吾尔族、哈萨克族 ■ 民族服饰 ■ 民族歌舞

中国文明与艺术之二
Chinese Civilization and Art II

第三盘 DVD 3
- 龙 ■ 中国的城门 ■ 中国的牌楼 ■ 中国的祭坛 ■ 北京的胡同
- 北京四合院 ■ 中国的白酒 ■ 各地小吃 ■ 北京烤鸭 ■ 中国的面食

第四盘 DVD 4
- 神奇的汉字 ■ 茶 ■ 中国功夫 ■ 中国的玉器 ■ 京剧
- 中国民乐 ■ 风筝 ■ 民间面塑 ■ 民间泥塑 ■ 民间皮影

中国的宗教与思想
Chinese Religions and Ideology

第五盘 DVD 5
- 儒家思想 ■ 中国的佛教 ■ 道教与神仙 ■ 宗教建筑
- 孔子和儒家思想 ■ 老子和道家思想
- 佛教名山——峨眉山 ■ 佛教名山——五台山
- 道教名山——武当山 ■ 道教名山——崂山

第四辑即将出版！

第三辑 Album 3

中国各地之二
Places in China II

第一盘 DVD 1
- 黑龙江省 ■ 河北省 ■ 江苏省 ■ 浙江省 ■ 四川省 ■ 安徽省
- 云南省 ■ 福建省 ■ 广东省 ■ 贵州省、海南省 ■ 广西壮族自治区、台湾省

中国各地之三
Places in China III

第二盘 DVD 2
- 吉林省 ■ 辽宁省 ■ 山西省 ■ 陕西省 ■ 甘肃省、宁夏回族自治区
- 青海省 ■ 内蒙古自治区 ■ 湖北省 ■ 湖南省 ■ 河南省 ■ 江西省

中国人物之一
People in China I

第三盘 DVD 3
- 黄帝 ■ 尧舜 ■ 秦始皇 ■ 屈原 ■ 司马迁
- 张仲景 ■ 张衡 ■ 蔡伦 ■ 毕昇 ■ 李时珍

每辑：5张DVD + 5册图书 + 精美书签50枚
定价：￥980.00 / 辑
Each album: 5 DVDs + 5 books + 50 beautiful bookmarks
Price: ￥980.00/album

中国现代建筑大观
Modern Architectures in China

第四盘 DVD 4
- 鸟巢 ■ 青藏铁路 ■ 国家大剧院 ■ 首都机场3号航站楼
- 浦东新高度 ■ 长江三峡工程 ■ 杭州湾跨海大桥 ■ 上海外滩

中国文明与艺术之三
Chinese Civilization and Art III

第五盘 DVD 5
- 中国菜（上） ■ 中国菜（下） ■ 筷子 ■ 扇子 ■ 太极拳
- 杂技 ■ 把脉、推拿、拔火罐、刮痧 ■ 中药 ■ 篆刻 ■《论语》

Embark on your Chinese learning from the website of Beijing Language and Culture University Press

北京语言大学出版社网站: www.blcup.com

从这里开始……

International online orders
TEL: +86-10-82303668
　　　+86-10-82303080
Email: service@blcup.net

这里是对外汉语精品教材的展示平台

汇集2000余种对外汉语教材，检索便捷，每本教材有目录、简介、样课等详尽信息。

It showcases BLCUP's superb textbooks of TCFL (Teaching Chinese as a Foreign Language)

It has a collection of more than 2,000 titles of BLCUP's TCFL textbooks, which are easy to be searched, with details such as table of contents, brief introduction and sample lessons for each textbook.

这里是覆盖全球的电子商务平台

在任何地点，均可通过VISA/MASTER卡在线购买。

It provides an e-commerce platform which covers the whole world.

Online purchase with VISA/MASTER Card can be made in every part of the world.

这里是对外汉语教学／学习资源的服务平台

提供测试题、知识讲解、阅读短文、教案、课件、教学示范、教材配套资料等各类文字、音视频资源。

It provides a services platform for Chinese language learning for foreigners.

All kinds of written and audio-visual teaching resources are available, including tests, explanations on language points, reading passages, teaching plans, courseware, teaching demo and other supplementary teaching materials etc.

这里是数字出版的体验平台

只需在线支付，即刻就可获取质高价优的全新电子图书。

It provides digital publication service.

A top-grade and reasonably-priced brand new e-book can be obtained as soon as you pay for it online.

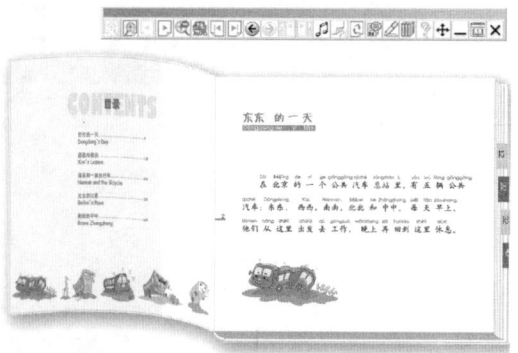

这里是沟通交流的互动平台

汉语教学与学习论坛，使每个参与者都能共享海量信息与资源。

It provides a platform for communication.

This platform for Chinese teaching and learning makes it possible for every participant to share our abundant data and resources.